Social Coordination
and Public Policy

ECONOMY, POLITY, AND SOCIETY

Series Editors

Virgil Storr and Jayme Lemke, Mercatus Center

The foundations of political economy—from Adam Smith to the Austrian school of economics, to contemporary research in public choice and institutional analysis—are sturdy and well established, but far from calcified. On the contrary, the boundaries of the research built on this foundation are ever expanding. One approach to political economy that has gained considerable traction in recent years combines the insights and methods of three distinct but related subfields within economics and political science: the Austrian, Virginia and Bloomington schools of political economy. The vision of this book series is to capitalize on the intellectual gains from the interactions between these approaches in order to both feed the growing interest in this approach and advance social scientists' understanding of economy, polity, and society.

This series seeks to publish works that combine the Austrian school's insights on knowledge, the Virginia school's insights into incentives in non-market contexts, and the Bloomington school's multiple methods, real-world approach to institutional design as a powerful tool for understanding social behavior in a diversity of contexts.

Titles in the Series

Social Coordination and Public Policy

Explorations in Theory and Practice

Edited by Roberta Q. Herzberg,
Gavin Roberts, and
Brianne Wolf

LEXINGTON BOOKS
Lanham • Boulder • New York • London

Published by Lexington Books
An imprint of The Rowman & Littlefield Publishing Group, Inc.
4501 Forbes Boulevard, Suite 200, Lanham, Maryland 20706
www.rowman.com

86-90 Paul Street, London EC2A 4NE

British Library Cataloguing in Publication Information Available

Library of Congress Cataloging-in-Publication Data Available

ISBN 978-1-66691-822-9 (cloth: alk. paper)
ISBN 978-1-66691-824-3 (pbk. : alk. paper)
ISBN 978-1-66691-823-6 (electronic)

Contents

List of Figures and Tables

FIGURES

TABLES

Introduction

Social Coordination and Public Policy: Explorations in Theory and Practice

Roberta Q. Herzberg, Gavin Roberts, and Brianne Wolf

A complete study of the chapters in this volume leaves a reader with a broad appreciation of the respective roles that markets, civil society, and government play in coordinating the social action we observe in that spontaneous order we call "society." Several key factors tie the chapters in this volume together. First, each chapter examines how individuals move from their personal interests to social action across different arenas. Second, the chapters use the theoretical framework of mainline economics to explore these questions about individuals and social action, using the logic of Austrian economics, public choice theory, and institutional analysis to frame their questions. In this tradition, the authors are doing what James M. Buchanan (1999a) argues for in his essay "What Should Economists Do?" For Buchanan, economists and other social scientists should allow the explicit focus on the technical/engineering problem of scarce resource allocation, given full information about ends and means, to fade into the background. Instead, they should let exchange relationships, entrepreneurial discovery, and polycentric governance come to the forefront of social scientific analysis. Finally, the range of methods and disciplinary perspectives used by the authors suggests the benefit of multi-method approaches in examining critical questions in social science.

This volume presents a variety of theoretical and applied work related to the connections between social coordination and public policy using insights from the interrelated and interdependent Virginia, Austrian, and Bloomington Schools. In particular, this volume ranges from Emily-Chamlee Wright's "Essential, Big, Simple, Capable" (EBS-Cap) theoretical framework for the scope of government action in the lead chapter and Alexander Köhler's analysis of social coordination and social justice to Arthur R. Wardle's unromantic scrutiny of compliance markets and Olivia Gonzalez's historical narrative of the Torpedo Factory Art Center in Alexandria, Virginia.

In this brief introductory chapter, we provide some basic foundational knowledge related to these schools of thought and their key insights, while referencing examples of these arguments from chapters in the volume associated with each school.

THE AUSTRIAN SCHOOL

The Austrian School provides insights about entrepreneurs, knowledge, and the market process which facilitate social coordination. Entrepreneurs seek to earn profits by discovering inefficiencies. For example, an entrepreneur might discover a substitute to a monopolized product in a market. These discoveries and the actions they engender benefit society by bringing prices and actions more in line with the reality of scarcity when the discoveries and actions occur in the market process. However, entrepreneurs are also present in political processes, and the discoveries and actions of political entrepreneurs are less likely to align with the public interest. Often, as discussed in some chapters in this volume, political entrepreneurship leads the implementation of public policy to deviate from its original goals in favor of the common good. A primary driver of this deviation is the lack of knowledge available to policymakers, the knowledge problem, which can be taken advantage of by entrepreneurs.

Public policies or policymakers often suffer from what F. A. Hayek referred to as the knowledge problem. The problem is how to allocate resources efficiently given dispersed information among many individuals. In the public policy arena, many problems are treated as though they can be solved through planning because all of the relevant information is known. But Hayek tells us that "knowledge is not given to anyone in its totality" (Hayek 1945, 520). Instead, we ought to rely on individuals' local knowledge of "the particular circumstances of time and place" (Hayek 1945, 522). The market system offers a better solution to the knowledge problem than government planning because it allows each individual to use their own knowledge in pursuit of their goals and coordinate with others who are doing the same through the price system. As Hayek (1945, 526) puts it, "Fundamentally, in a system in which the knowledge of the relevant facts is dispersed among many people, prices can act to coordinate the separate actions of different people in the same way as subjective values help the individual to coordinate the parts of his plan." The chapters in this volume explore ways in which the knowledge problem shows up in various public policy arenas and how the price system offers the most efficient solution to this problem. Hayek emphasizes the ways individuals are able to coordinate at different levels of society, especially individuals and small groups.

M. Nolan Gray's chapter "Entrepreneurial Discovery in Land-Use Planning," explains the respective roles of market and political actors in land use planning in the United States, and how political actors rely on new information discovered by market entrepreneurs. The division of labor between private and public actors in land use planning that Gray describes reinforces Chamlee-Wright's EBS-Cap framework by leaving the dirty work of entrepreneurial discovery to the market and only reserving for the land use regulators that which is essential, big, simple, and within the government's capabilities.

In an especially unique and novel analysis, Olivia Gonzalez explains how civil society can work to solve knowledge problems using the example of an abandoned torpedo factory that has been reinvigorated and reimagined as an art center in Virginia in her chapter, "Destruction to Beauty: The Polycentric Adaptive Reuse of the Torpedo Factory." She explains how similar projects have failed when guided by a far-off central planner without access to local knowledge of ends and means.

The Austrian school of economic thought is older and more established than the Virginian and Bloomington Schools, and some might say the Austrians set the stage for academic entrepreneurs to discover the insights of these latter two schools. James M. Buchanan, one of the founders the Virginia School, regularly provides "shouts out" to the Austrians in his great body of scholarship for providing much of the analysis that led to his discoveries.

THE VIRGINIA SCHOOL

The Virginia School gave rise to public choice theory, or "politics without romance" as wittingly described by James M. Buchanan (1999b). Public choice theory is a broad discipline that characterizes the incentives faced by political actors and analyzes the social outcomes that emerge from the behavior of self-interested political agents under various institutional rules. In short, public choice theory applies the methodology of positive economics to politics. The incentives faced by individuals and groups involved in the political process often interfere with the frequently overoptimistic public-interest view of the political process. Incentive problems are compounded by the knowledge problem faced by even the most publicly interested political actors because it is generally impossible for such individuals or groups to efficiently collect the information necessary to design the policies they imagine. As discussed in the Austrian tradition, the market process, on the other hand, coordinates dispersed information in society efficiently through the price system. In the absence of a price system, other means of social coordination pervade the political process from which public policy emerges. A multiplicity of social-coordination processes from local to global, both planned and spontaneous, have emerged from political processes around the globe and these phenomena led public choice scholars to take a polycentric view of these processes. The chapters in this volume present a range of perspectives related to public choice theory with special focus on political entrepreneurship and polycentrism. These perspectives run from analysis of specific local policies to refinements of overarching theories related to social coordination.

Arthur R. Wardle's chapter, "Compliance Markets without Romance: Lessons from the Renewable Fuel Standard," tackles the discrepancy between the textbook prediction of dramatic efficiency gains resulting from pricing externalities through compliance markets and the messy reality of the Renewable Fuel Standard (RFS) program head on. The textbook theoretical underpinnings of RFS takes the romantic view of the publicly interested government while Wardle explains the mess by stepping back and taking account of the self-interest of the stakeholders. He shows how these self-interested stakeholders discover opportunities to make the best of the RFS opportunities but in seeking these ends, the agents disrupt the efficiency gains predicted by textbook examples.

Julie Thompson-Gomez shows how a relatively small and cohesive group can disrupt the closing of old military bases even though such bases are a clear loss to society as a whole. Profit and loss accounting under a market order would surely have led to such bases being closed. But, these bases lead to concentrated benefits for local constituencies while costs are spread far and wide. A key insight of public choice is that political action is easier among close-knit groups. Thompson-Gomez explains how this insight from public choice plays out on the ground in her chapter, "Local Constituencies, Lobbying, and the Fight to Keep Local Bases Open during the 2005 Round of Base Closure and Realignment."

M. Nolan Gray describes how the incentives of state-actors need not always deviate from economic efficiency concerns. Market entrepreneurship informs political decisions in the context of land use planning and regulation according to his chapter. Regulators in land use planning agencies respond to entrepreneurial actions they observe in markets in part simply to maintain the relevance of their own agencies. Ignoring such signals would lead to such perverse outcomes, like large residential lot sizes in the middle of large cities in the midst of housing and land shortages, that political actors simply must respond to ensure their own political survival.

The unromantic view of political action makes regular appearances across the chapters in this volume and the reader will find many other examples of self-interested action leading to unintended and unpredictable results throughout. Despite the many challenges associated with social coordination, groups and communities often show their ability to tackle these challenges. Elinor and Vincent Ostrom famously discovered ways that relatively small communities found efficient ways to solve the most difficult types of coordination problems such as renewing depleted water reservoirs and achieving economies of scale and scope in policing services. The reader will find more examples of such problems and solutions in this volume. They identified a key mechanism was the decentralization of decision making in social coordination problems, or "polycentrism."

THE BLOOMINGTON SCHOOL

Elinor and Vincent Ostrom's research agenda examines how social coordination occurs, which has inspired numerous contributions to institutional understanding in the mainline tradition (see Aligica and Boettke 2009; Aligica 2013; Aligica 2018; Lemke and Tarko 2021). Specifically, as in many of the studies in this volume, Ostrom's work demonstrates the importance of particular institutional rules for resolving serious social problems (see E. Ostrom 1990; E. Ostrom 2005; V. Ostrom 1992; McGinnis 1999). Mancur Olson (1974) famously argued that collective action for large groups would be unlikely without incentivizing members to coordinate through payment or coercive force. This idea has pervaded scholarship in political science and economics ever since. In some ways, the idea goes back to Hobbes and his theory of the need for a strong state or Leviathan to prevent individuals from pursuing their self-interest at the expense of others in what came to be known as the prisoners' dilemma. In contrast, the Ostroms argued that individuals were capable of designing and sustaining such social institutions, at least under specific conditions.

One of the keys to sustaining these self-governing institutions is the recognition that many governing systems require a polycentric design to maintain the connection between policymakers and citizens. Polycentric governing systems depend on multiple centers of governing authority within a single governing structure. In contrast to unitary governing systems in which policies are made at a single decision level and implemented from above or a decentralized system in which all policies are made (and implemented) in the lowest level of governing closest to the people, polycentric systems have access to both centralized and decentralized levels, as well as many intermediate levels as appropriate to the nature of the good or policy under consideration. These different governing centers permit citizens to access a variety of governing options as they are able to gain interest and involvement. Very localized issues, such as the creation or maintenance of a public park, may be resolved within the community without the need to work out compromises with other communities who value different recreational opportunities. By contrast, the need to address a threat from another nation could logically be addressed at the level of the nation-state, even though it may imply some differences across subunits. The assumption is that the level which incorporates those individuals impacted by the policy change come together to address it and not all policy types are appropriate at any given level. By permitting this differential approach based on the problem under consideration, advocates of polycentricity suggest that policy can better reflect diverse preferences, facilitate coordination, and limit conflict.

Many chapters in this volume analyze a collective action problem but they do not turn to the typical solution for organizing groups—government. Instead, they theorize alternative ways that social dilemmas can be solved by treating collective action as a possibility rather than a problem. Elinor Ostrom (1998, 1) defined social dilemmas as occurring "whenever individuals in interdependent situations face choices in which the maximization of short-term self-interest yields outcomes leaving all participants worse off than feasible alternatives." In the same address, Ostrom (1998, 1) calls for "a behavioral theory of collective action based on models of the individual consistent with empirical evidence about how individuals make decisions in social-dilemma situations." The chapters build on the Ostromian research agenda that showed how communities of private individuals regularly solve local and common-pool resource problems without centralization.

Another unifying theme across chapters in this volume is that social coordination occurs in the context of multiple arenas of decision making. The Bloomington approach recognizes that multiple arenas of social coordination impact the manner in which public policy is carried out in the real world. Textbook treatment of public policy often advises one-size-fits-all solutions to complicated public policy questions but ignores the multitude of incentives faced by the "players of the game" and the subsequent development of diverse forms of social coordination. When faced with these sterile policy prescriptions, communities shape policies to fit their local needs and preferences through social coordination.

As Adam Smith recognized, individuals have their own ideas and incentives and will not live their lives in the ways envisioned by the crafters of public policy. As Smith ([1759] 1982, 233–34) puts it:

> The man of system . . . is apt to be very wise in his own conceit; and is often so enamored with the supposed beauty of his own ideal plan of government, that he cannot suffer the smallest deviation from any part of it. He goes on to establish it completely and in all its parts, without any regard either to the great interests,

or to the strong prejudices which may oppose it. He seems to imagine that he can arrange the different members of a great society with as much ease as the hand arranges the different pieces upon a chess board. He does not consider that the pieces upon the chess board have no other principle of motion besides that which the hand impresses upon them; but that, in the great chess-board of human society, every single piece has a principle of motion of its own altogether different from that which the legislature might cause to impress upon it.

In short, individual human behavior and the possibilities for social coordination are often left out of public policy analysis but are crucial to the success of informal and formal institutional arrangements. The chapters in this volume aim to disentangle these issues of social coordination in public policy in theory and practice.

Below, we have briefly summarized the chapters to follow, especially highlighting how these chapters build on the theme of social coordination and relate to these schools of political economy.

CHAPTER SUMMARIES

Part I: Theories and Methods of Social Coordination

Chapter 1, "Social Coordination in a Complex Society: A Framework for Action" by Emily Chamlee-Wright

In chapter 1, Emily Chamlee-Wright suggests a framework for determining the characteristics of problems that government is best able to address. While almost all social issues can be brought into government, she argues that government is most effective when the problems are essential, big, simple, and where government is most capable, summarizing these characteristics in the short-hand for her framework, EBS-Cap.

Essential problems suggest that the scope for government be constrained to those services or goals that the general consensus determines apply to virtually all within the social setting and that may not be addressed in the absence of government coordination and coercion. Big problems often pose some of the greatest challenges in reaching swift response as they incorporate a degree of protection or redistribution that we value as a whole, but is difficult to achieve in a piecemeal fashion. Simply no other form of coordination may have the capacity to address the scope of the problem. Her argument in favor of government addressing only simple problems is an important reminder of the difficulties posed by limited knowledge in society. If decisions are to be consolidated and coerced by government, it is critical that individuals within a democratic society understand the nature of the problem and the solutions that are posed. When there are complex issues, that understanding is unlikely to be met and support for government action wanes as the realities of its implementation play out. Finally, Chamlee-Wright suggests the importance of humility by policymakers to address only those problems for which it can reasonably expect to improve the outcomes for individuals. Many problems will be suggested to government officials, but if policymakers do not have viable solutions within their institutional capacities to act, it is unlikely the policy can succeed.

Chapter 2, "Rawls, Hayek, Buchanan, and Social Justice: From Rules to Recognition" by Alexander Köhler

In chapter 2, Alexander Köhler examines how F. A. Hayek and James M. Buchanan developed the concept of social justice within their theories of social coordination and contrasts their visions with those held by many modern social justice advocates. He suggests that Hayek and Buchanan each recognized the role of social values within individual preferences over alternative institutions of government, but there are key differences between their approaches and modern analysis.

In order to consider how their work fits into the ongoing discussion of social justice, Kohler carefully analyzes texts across their bodies of work. One of the primary differences between their perspectives and modern conceptions lies in the focus of analysis. For Hayek and Buchanan, the value of any social interaction must be understood from the perspective of the individual, while many modern social justice theorists assume the presence of a pre-existing social preference based on group identity. This difference alters the viable alternatives as the group interests must only improve on average while the individual approach requires that a sufficient number of individuals perceive change as an improvement in their own positions. Köhler suggests that for Hayek, a generality principle operated is the key logic of social justice, while Buchanan argued for equality and involvement of all at the level of constitutional choice.

Chapter 3, "Are RCTs Missing a Point? Local Knowledge and Computer Assisted Learning Interventions" by Carlos Noyola

In chapter 3, Carlos Noyola examines the case of introducing computers into local educational settings in Mexico to evaluate the importance of local knowledge in addressing key policy problems. In particular, he considers whether accessing local input can improve the educational impact of adding computer access outside of the school setting. Such computer access has often been suggested as an answer to improving educational opportunities in under-served communities. However, the degree to which computers are an educational advantage versus a distraction depends on the way in which they will be used and the conditions assumed by analysts. Noyola suggests that in many rural communities these assumptions are not met.

In an effort to consider how understanding local conditions may improve the implementation of computer assisted learning strategies, he uses a focus group approach to solicit knowledge from key constituencies including teachers, administrators, and parents. Following in the tradition of Austrian economics and public choice theory, Noyola implies that a process that incorporates local knowledge and preferences and allows for a greater degree of self-governance will be more effective in improving educational outcomes. Further, he argues that this potential for differences across local settings has implications for research using Randomized Control Trials to establish preferred policies.

Part II: Case Studies in Social Coordination

Chapter 4, "Destruction to Beauty: The Polycentric Adaptive Reuse of the Torpedo Factory" by Olivia Gonzalez

Chapter 4 addresses the following question: what rules, norms, and shared strategies led to the success of the Torpedo Factory Art Center (TFAC) revitalization project? Gonzalez explores TFAC's story as a case study of bottom-up polycentric development. Using Elinor Ostrom's Institutional Analysis and Development (IAD) framework, the chapter systematically assesses what institutions were in place that allowed for the revitalization of the TFAC to successfully take place.

Gonzalez's examination is quite original as the role of institutions is often lacking from discussions of adaptive reuse. Gonzalez focuses on the TFAC's role as a cultural anchor, the community's desire to reinvent the waterfront and the active artistic community, and finally the zoning rules and property rights in historic Alexandria as the key institutions. As such, the chapter argues that the main reasons why the project was successful was because of the bottom-up and polycentric coordination of local artists in the community who, through an entrepreneurial search, discovered a more productive use of the TFAC building. The artists acted as social entrepreneurs who were able to solve the collective action problem of the best use for the building. In her nuanced analytical narrative, Gonzalez focuses not only on the artists' perspective but also other sources like economic assessment reports and news stories, noting that the artists also behaved as an interest group seeking government favoritism. Other cities that take a top-down centralized approach are likely to not be as organically successful, due to the knowledge problems facing public officials. Gonzalez argues that the TFAC project is not as successful as an example of polycentric governance as the project continues. The TFAC transformation is a helpful case study for examining what factors go into a successful adaptive reuse development project—that is finding a productive use for an underutilized building—while also highlighting how poor institutional arrangements can hold it back.

Chapter 5, "Local Constituencies, Lobbying, and the Fight to Keep Local Bases Open during the 2005 Round of Base Closure and Realignment" by Julie Thompson-Gomez

Julie Thompson-Gomez addresses a critical example of an institutional response to an ongoing political dilemma, the case of military base closings under the Base Realignment and Closure (BRAC) policy. By examining the history of BRAC closures, she suggests a changing pattern in recent years to make the binding nature of the original BRAC design seemingly less effective in achieving efficiencies in reorganizing base utilization and funding. Using the logic of public choice theory regarding rent-seeking and public good provision, she suggests reasons for the breakdown of more recent agreements. Beyond this general analysis, Thompson-Gomez examines a specific case in which local citizens and leaders challenged the BRAC recommendations to save Cannon Air Force Base.

Her analysis suggests the ingredients necessary for the local community to overcome the collective action problem and fight back against the national interests as represented in the proposed closure. As with many collective action problems, a small core of interested leadership became a key factor in the successful coordination of local response and action. As with many issues in the governing arena, this case outlines the challenges of evaluating policies within a polycentric order. What may be good from the national level, may be fought by those most impacted by the policy itself. The question to be answered is whether the policy is best addressed at the given level under consideration. The example here may simply reflect the standard common pool dilemma in which individual communities seek to draw faster from the common budget pool than they are willing to contribute, a strategy that resulted in the creation of BRAC in the first place. How do the institutional arrangements, coupled with the differing impact of the policy under consideration, impact the ability of government to act effectively? Thompson-Gomez considers whether BRAC provides a solution to a serious social dilemma or simply creates an obstacle to finding the right level to balance contending interests in a polycentric system.

Chapter 6, "Social Media and Social Movements: How Technology Has Aided Coordination" by Ellen Hamlett

This chapter explores how the internet has helped to reduce transaction costs and solve the knowledge problem of social coordination. Hamlett asserts that the knowledge problem causes a type of transaction cost that hinders the political exchange process. Using Hayek's analysis of the knowledge problem, Coase's explanation of the transaction costs that result from exchange, Buchanan's theory of politics as exchange, public choice theories of collective action, and following Don Lavoie's analysis regarding technology and the facilitation of market exchange, Hamlett builds upon the social movements organizations literature, arguing that technology helps facilitate and improve political exchange. Specifically, Hamlett shows that internet is helping solve the knowledge problem through streamlining the exchange of information and thereby reducing the transaction costs of discovering and gathering information.

Using the Black Lives Matter (BLM) movement as a case study, Hamlett shows how the knowledge problem that Hayek outlines as the idea that knowledge is dispersed among individuals which makes it difficult for people to coordinate, can be ameliorated through the use of the internet. She finds that BLM has been successful because it has utilized decentralized decision-making facilitated by social media that empowers local leaders. Social media creates a unique opportunity for activists to engage with each other in a meaningful way, creating unique communities that are not limited to physical locations. Hamlett also notes potential dangers coming from the ease of sharing information in the digital era, focusing on "slactivism" and the proliferation of "fake news," though she finds the gains for social coordination and change from the internet outweigh potential costs.

Chapter 7, "Stakeholder Primacy as a New Institutional Framework for Entrepreneurial Market Process?" by Mikołaj Firlej

Mikołaj Firlej investigates the emerging institution of stakeholder primacy in his thought-provoking chapter by comparing and contrasting the evolution of legal rules and court decisions in Canada and the United States. Firlej argues that despite different rules regarding the purpose of corporation, court decisions tend to support the institution of shareholder primacy in these countries. Firlej then argues that the institution of stakeholder primacy cannot be expected to emerge from and be enforced by a spontaneous market process. This is because shareholder primacy is not a single rule, but a legal principle that is operationalized by many specific rules. Thus, the potential non-adherence to this principle by an individual entrepreneurial action would likely result in excessive costs because one would challenge the key tenant of the institutional framework governing the behavior of market participants. One common criticism of shareholder primacy is that shareholders over-value short term gains at the expense of long-term investments. However, Firlej explains that U.S. courts have not supported such short-termism in case law, and it is unlikely that such behavioral inefficiency could last as some shareholders would see that larger gains were available by reallocating towards longer term investments, and they would take advantage of such an arbitrage for exactly the reason that stakeholder advocates are skeptical, that is, profit seeking.

Part III: Challenging Social Problems: Environmental and Natural Resource Applications

Chapter 8, "Compliance Markets Without Romance: Lessons from the Renewable Fuel Standard" by Arthur R. Wardle

Arthur R. Wardle provides a pragmatic analysis of compliance markets like cap-and-trade policies in his chapter. Wardle questions the romantic view that market imperfections like externalities can be easily corrected through the political process as the incentives of political entrepreneurs and politicians interfere with the efficiency gains imagined in the design of such policies. The chapter provides a succinct summary of the economic efficiency-enhancing benefits of compliance markets derived in economics textbooks, and explains these benefits are clear if such policies are properly designed, implemented, and enforced. But, do the designers, implementers, and enforcers of such policies really face incentives consistent with the "proper" administration of such policies in terms of the efficiency-enhancing goals? And even if they do face the right incentives, do they have the necessary knowledge?

Wardle argues the theoretical answers to these questions are a likely "no," and provides empirical evidence to support that claim using the recent history of the Renewable Fuel Standard (RFS) policy and the associated market for Renewable Identification Numbers (RINs). Wardle carefully walks the reader through several examples of how policymakers have deviated from the textbook model in the implementation of RFS. These examples highlight both lack of key knowledge and pervasive incentive incompatibility among planners. For example, the textbook requires a policymaker to choose a specific good that will be the object of the compliance market, and even at that seemingly simple yet necessary juncture, Wardle explains how a lack of key knowledge interferes. Further, political actors face incentives to provide exemptions at the planning, implementation, and enforcement stages of the

RFS process. Wardle concedes that compliance markets are "probably the best governing institution yet conceived" for a certain class of environmental problems, but his chapter forces us to think more critically about their implementation and applicability.

Chapter 9, "A Calculus of Communication: Deliberation, Knowledge, and Public Choice in the Context of Water Management" by Emil Panzaru

This chapter re-examines the utility of deliberative democracy, defined as a form of social coordination based on the use of language to persuade others to arrive at a common decision. Though democratic deliberation, as opposed to the market, is argued to be the superior mode of social coordination because it is reflexive and provides a way to learn about the perspective of others through conversation, Panzaru argues that deliberation is a form of planning, in that it is dedicated to a form of social production that is both democratically arranged and rationally executed (as opposed to the spontaneous order of the market or the often-hierarchical nature of tradition). Further, Panzaru critiques the purported epistemic advantage of deliberation over exchange by appealing to the Hayekian knowledge problem.

The chapter applies this analysis of social coordination to policy through a case study of indigenous groups acting on ecological matters, especially the indigenous water management system referred to as the "ekwar" in Kenya. The chapter finds that the market can provide a better means of communication between individuals because the market allows for individualized, decentralized responses and does not rely on altruism to reach a unified decision. The market and price mechanism allow for better management of water because prices both communicate information about the use of the resource to individuals and incentivize individuals who own private property—local herdsmen and women of riverbank areas—to bring their knowledge into the public sphere.

Chapter 10, "Entrepreneurial Discovery in Land-Use Planning" by M. Nolan Gray

M. Nolan Gray explains how the *dirigisme* system of public land-use planning in the United States evolves in efficiency-enhancing directions to the extent that it incorporates new knowledge created through entrepreneurial discovery. In his chapter, Gray presents an enigma: how does a land-use planning system wrought with inefficient zoning and subdivision regulations survive in an economic order based on the efficient distribution of tacit knowledge and entrepreneurial alertness? The chapter systematically deciphers this riddle using examples of how state-led public land-use planning has survived via its willingness and ability to incorporate entrepreneurial discovery through regulatory relief. Of course, public land-use planners' incorporation of entrepreneurial discovery is imperfect and varies from location to location.

Gray explains how the city of Houston decreased the minimum lot size by a factor of more than three in response to private entrepreneurs seeking relief from the larger minimum size. Unfortunately, this example likely reflects an exception rather than a rule. This willingness of land-use planners to respond to relief requests via permanent regulatory reflects one mechanism through which land-use planners incorporate entrepreneurial discovery and the knowledge that discovery generates. One concern of this *dirigisme* system and the incorporation of entrepreneurial discovery it allows are the rent-seeking opportunities such a system is likely to engender. Is land-use planning "law" applied equally? This seems unlikely given the detailed and enlightening narrative presented in M. Nolan Gray's chapter and would be a fruitful avenue for future research.

REFERENCES

Aligica, Paul Dragos. 2013. *Institutional Diversity and Political Economy.* Oxford, UK: Oxford University Press.

———. 2018. *Public Entrepreneurship, Citizenship, and Self-Governance.* Cambridge, UK: Cambridge University Press.

Aligica, Paul Dragos, and Peter J. Boettke. 2009. *Challenging Institutional Analysis and Development: The Bloomington School.* New York City, NY: Routledge.

Buchanan, James M. 1999a. "What Should Economists Do?" In *The Logical Foundations of Constitutional Liberty, Volume 1,* 28–42. Indianapolis, IN: Liberty Fund.

———. 1999b. "Politics without Romance: A Sketch of Positive Public Choice Theory and Its Normative Implications." In *The Logical Foundations of Constitutional Liberty, Volume 1,* 45–59. Indianapolis, IN: Liberty Fund.

Hayek, Friedrich A. 1945. "The Use of Knowledge in Society." *American Economic Review* 35 (4): 519–30.

Lemke, Jayme, and Vlad Tarko, editors. 2021. *Elinor Ostrom and the Bloomington School: Building a New Approach to Policy and the Social Sciences.* Montreal and Kingston, Canada: McGill-Queen's University Press.

Michael McGinnis, editor. 1999. *Polycentricity and Local Public Economies: Readings from the Workshop in Political Theory and Policy Analysis.* Ann Arbor, MI: University of Michigan Press.

Olson, Mancur. 1974. *The Logic of Collective Action.* Cambridge, MA: Harvard University Press.

Ostrom, Elinor. 1990. *Governing the Commons: The Evolution of Institutions for Collective Action.* Cambridge, UK: Cambridge University Press.

————. 1998. "A Behavioral Approach to the Rational Choice Theory of Collective Action: Presidential Address." *American Political Science Review* 92 (1): 1–22.

————. 2005. *Understanding Institutional Diversity*. Princeton, NJ: Princeton University Press.

Ostrom, Vincent. 1992. *The Meaning of Democracy and the Vulnerability of Democracies*. Ann Arbor, MI: Michigan University Press.

Smith, Adam. [1759] 1982. *The Theory of Moral Sentiments*, edited by D. D. Raphael and A. L. Macfie. Indianapolis, IN: Liberty Fund.

PART I

Theories and Methods of Social Coordination

Chapter 1

Social Coordination in a Complex Society

A Framework for Action

Emily Chamlee-Wright

The legitimate object of government is to do for a community of people whatever they need to have done, but cannot do at all, or cannot so well do, for themselves in their separate and individual capacities. In all that the people can individually do as well for themselves, government ought not to interfere. [. . .] From this it appears that if all men were just, there still would be some, *though not so* much, *need of government.*

—Abraham Lincoln, Fragment on Government

July 1, 1854

The central question of this volume is, "How should a complex society govern itself to get things done?" How should we solve vexing social problems like intergenerational poverty and climate change, for example, or respond to crises such as natural disasters or global pandemics? Among the forms of social coordination available to us, which gives us the most effective route to a workable solution without creating significant problems in its wake?

The "how should we get things done" question is both big and small. The question is small in the sense that, in the course of our daily lives, we regularly encounter some version of it. CEOs of private companies continuously ask whether it is better to "make or buy," i.e., to coordinate the value chain through rational design within the firm or to rely on the undesigned market at work outside the firm. A neighbor needs transportation to and from her chemo treatments. Does it make more sense to assemble a group of neighborhood volunteers, i.e., rely on a civil society solution, or use a ridesharing service, i.e., turn to the market? These are the micro-challenges we encounter in market and civil society settings on a daily basis.

The big version of the question has occupied the minds of the great thinkers for millennia. Consider, for example, discussions of political order by the ancient philosophers. Adam Smith and Karl Marx are relatively recent in the lineup of great thinkers who have plumbed the depths of this question, with radically different visions for how a complex society best achieves social coordination.

But it's the space between the small and big versions of the question where I will focus my attention. I will take it as given that the big questions are more or less settled, that we are operating within a (largely) liberal democratic society that relies on the market to coordinate the production and distribution of most goods and services. In such a society, government is expected to perform the basic administrative functions of the state and has a responsibility to get additional things done under specific circumstances. Further, in such a society, people enjoy broad freedoms of association and can therefore coordinate with their fellow citizens to get things done in ways that do not rely on either market or government coordination.

I'll also take it as given that the small questions related to "make vs. buy" and "market-provision vs. volunteer-provision" are well-handled, or at least handled well-enough, by private actors, and as such, are not typically the subject of public policy debate.

It's in the meso level—the in-between space—where public policy resides, where it's not obvious whether Problem X should be solved through the market mechanism, government administration, or left to the voluntary sector within civil society. It's in this meso level that the social coordination problems are the trickiest in the sense that incentives may not align toward an obvious or ideal solution.

In what follows, I will discuss what makes some of these meso-level social coordination problems so tricky. I will offer a framework for thinking through the question of what kinds of projects lend themselves to government action and which are better left to markets and/or private civil society.

I ground this discussion in contexts related to post-disaster recovery and crisis management. In addition to being important areas of public policy, extreme environments like these are analytically useful. In a post-disaster setting, the coordinating mechanisms on which members of the public ordinarily rely are often wiped out or stressed beyond their limits. Such disruption wipes away existing patterns, allowing us to raise anew the question of which coordinating mechanism is best suited to fill the void. Similarly, extreme environments like the emergence of a global pandemic present novel, large-scale, serious problems that need to be solved rapidly. In such environments, solutions are seldom obvious, real tradeoffs exist, and the human response to any given intervention may be highly unpredictable. It's in such environments that a general guide to action is most valuable.

MARKET FAILURE, GOVERNMENT FAILURE, AND GOVERNMENT CAPACITY

Most arguments favoring government action follow some variant of the market failure problem—that left on their own, markets generate cases of significant externalities (e.g., global climate change), fail to provide important public goods (e.g., public safety and public health), or fail to solve collective action problems (e.g., coordination of community recovery in the aftermath of catastrophic disaster).

Critiques of the market failure literature point to the fact that government remedies can also fail. For example, administrative costs associated with regulation can be greater than the inefficiencies the regulations were designed to correct. Rent-seeking behavior often ensures that the interests of public actors and regulatory agencies align with the regulated industry rather than the public they were supposed to protect. And government agencies tasked with providing critical resources to the public often do not have access to the local knowledge required to get support where it is needed most urgently (Haeffele and Storr 2020; Haeffele and Hobson 2019).

The second problem with the market failure critique is that what may seem obviously impossible to achieve through the market or civil society is, in fact, often possible. This is not just a problem of "not giving credit where credit is due," there is real positive harm in this error. By failing to see possible alternatives to government action, we undercut the mechanisms that strengthen market responses, the art of association, and social capital. After crowding out other mechanisms that do similar work, government leaves citizens more dependent upon government, making the necessity of government action a self-fulfilling prophesy. This leads to a vicious cycle in which government grows larger and broader, becoming an even greater target for rent-seeking and political influence (Aligica and Tarko 2014; Choi and Storr 2019; Lofthouse 2019).

Critiques of market failure arguments aside, students of public policy must take, as our starting point, the world as it is, and in that world, government exists. In the face of vexing social and economic problems, citizens will demand that government act. To justify their existence or to amass resources and authority, government actors and agencies have a strong incentive to respond to this demand. Government, in other words, will do *something*.

It's reasonable for policy researchers—even those armed with public choice critiques of government failure and arguments favoring free-market solutions—to ask, "What *should* government do?" Sometimes the answer will be "Nothing." Do nothing and the solution will emerge in the market and civil society sectors." But if this is our answer at every turn, we take ourselves out of most policy conversations. In the world as it is, citizens want a state that has the capacity to get things done. It is the policy advisor's job to identify appropriate directions toward which that capacity should be aimed (Cowen 2020).

To that end, what follows is a framework for thinking through an appropriate "division of labor" between government, markets, and civil society.

ESSENTIAL, BIG, SIMPLE, CAPABLE (EBS-CAP): A DECISION FRAMEWORK FOR GOVERNMENT ACTION

Any accounting of the relative strengths among markets, civil society, and government should begin with the most obvious attributes. Markets are good at getting people to do the necessary thing when they otherwise wouldn't know that the need in question was a need, and when they would not otherwise have a strong interest in addressing the need. In the aftermath of disaster, for example, distant suppliers of portable generators may not know that generators are needed in the affected region. And even if they do, absent market signals, they have little incentive to take on the costs of delivering generators to where the need is greatest. A higher-than-ordinary price for portable generators solves both these problems.

Of course, markets do not address every need, which is where civil society often steps in. Civil society responses work well in contexts where there is an intrinsic (non-market) interest in providing what is needed and when local knowledge of the particular circumstances is robust. A local church, for example, may provide shelter and provisions for disaster victims as part of its religious mission to serve its members and surrounding neighborhood. However, civil society organizations often (though, not always) lack the resources needed to scale their response to meet large-scale challenges.

Government response comes with the benefit of greater capacity to mobilize significant resources. Further, activities carried out by government have the force of legal authority, such as the mandates issued under the Defense Production Act. That said, government action tends be slower to respond to feedback and less adept at adjusting to local conditions. As such, the stakes are high when defaulting to government action as it is harder to correct mistakes and the effects of miscalibrations and bad decisions are felt system wide.

Even after accounting for these obvious differences, it is still not always clear which coordination mechanism has the comparative advantage in solving complex problems. As noted earlier, the fact that a collective action problem exists does not necessarily mean that markets and civil society cannot address the problem. And in cases where market failure is a legitimate concern, we need to consider whether government failure may be worse than the market failure it is intended to address. What follows is a description of a filtering device I call the EBS-Cap Framework[1] to sort instances in which government action may be appropriate from those that should be left to the private market and civil society sectors.

EBS-Cap is an abbreviation for goods and services—what I will call "projects"—that are considered *essential*, *big*, and *simple*, and for which government is comparatively *capable*. Among the most important words in the previous sentence is the word "and." If for any given project, or task within a project, one of these criteria is not met, government should not attempt to undertake.

As I discuss below, each filter operates at a relatively high level of abstraction. Good judgment will always require assessment of particular circumstances. But taken together, the EBS-Cap Framework narrows the field of prospective projects for which government action may be appropriate. With a narrower field of prospects, it becomes easier to exercise that judgment.

Essential: A necessary (but not sufficient) condition for considering government action is that the proposed project is critical to the social order.

Admittedly, "essential" is an abstract standard. What counts as essential shifts in the face of exogenous shocks. It changes over time as tastes, technology, and affluence influence citizens' expectations. For example, indoor plumbing, considered essential in the industrialized world, remains an uncommon luxury for more than half the world's population. That said, as a standard, "essential" is not *hopelessly* abstract. We can eliminate a good many prospective projects from consideration because they do not pass the "straight-face test" of qualifying as such. And while we may be skeptical of many claims that this or that project is essential, some will rise to the top as reasonable contenders. In the wake of catastrophic disaster, search and rescue operations are typically and appropriately considered essential. In a pandemic, the development and wide distribution of a vaccine is likely to be considered essential. Note that I have not said anything about whether government must be the entity to do the searching, the rescuing, the developing or the distributing. I'm making the far more modest claim that in the face of challenges like these, the population will see such things as essential.

It may be objected that the essential standard is too obvious to include in the framework. Why would government, one might ask, ever consider pursuing a project that was not essential? A quick scan of publicly-supported programs and projects, however, is enough to suggest that government finds it tempting to pursue the non-essential (see, for example, Kennedy 2021; Perticone 2017). World history is rife with examples of vanity infrastructure projects for authoritarian regimes. Boondoggles that serve the interests of a particular industry but are not essential to the social order would not make the cut if we applied the "essential" filter. Though it may seem obvious, one of the most important roles a policy advisor plays is to remind government to refrain from doing the unimportant.

When government fails to heed this counsel, its capacity to respond effectively to legitimate and pressing priorities is diminished.

Big: In contexts where government action is being considered, and we've narrowed the set to essential projects, we then want to sort between the big projects and the small.

Here again, what counts as big can change as the context changes, but in general, *big* simply means those projects that are beyond the capability of individuals, households, and communities. Again, not all projects that are both essential and big require government provision. In fact, most do not. Insurance risk pools, large-scale manufacturing, and transcontinental shipping are just a few of the big things that markets provide. That said, when combined with the essential criterion, the big criterion helpfully narrows the field of prospects further.

In contexts where multiple overlapping problems need solving, such as in crisis situations and post-disaster settings, the most valuable interventions are those big and essential things that tap capacity of private citizens intent upon rebuilding their homes, neighborhoods, and broader communities. In 2005, Hurricane Katrina flooded 80% of the City of New Orleans. Before anyone could return and begin the process of rebuilding, the water had to pumped out of the low-lying city. Before gutting, mold remediation, and repairs could commence in earnest, electrical services needed to be restored and basic infrastructure needed to be repaired. This is the big stuff that is beyond the capacity of individuals, households, and neighborhood organizations. The critical point is that once these big and essential things were addressed, individuals, households, and neighborhood communities were able to tap their capacity to drive the recovery process (Chamlee-Wright and Storr 2009).

It's important to note that big does not necessarily mean expensive. For many months following Katrina, yachts and downed trees still blocked thoroughfares and access points to neighborhoods, frustrating the efforts of individuals and community groups intent upon rebuilding their neighborhoods. Once barriers like these were removed, individuals and civil society groups were able to make progress on the projects that *were* within their grasp e.g., setting up coordination sites for volunteers, gutting homes, beginning repairs, and returning local enterprise to the neighborhood. Ironically, it's the aggregate of these private solutions to such significant but smaller-scale problems that actually drive the recovery. Government can play a positive role by removing the barriers that get in the way of such bottom-up solutions.

More generally, by filtering out small projects from the prospective pool of projects government might provide, we leave greater scope for market and civil society to take up such projects. It's here that a process of social learning takes hold. Market and social entrepreneurs experiment and test out ideas. In such an environment, bad ideas are quickly abandoned; good ideas are replicated and scaled, and more of the things we need to get done get done.

Simple: Once we've narrowed the field to the essential and the big, we then want to narrow further by sorting the simple from the complex. At first blush, it may seem appropriate to assign to government those projects that are essential, big, and complicated. On the contrary, government is better suited to take on the essential, big, and simple.

William Easterly makes this point when diagnosing why it is that decades of international development aid have failed to end global poverty (Easterly 2007). Easterly's answer is that we've been asking development assistance to take on something far too complex. Development aid, Easterly observes, is like a cow. Cows can do many useful things. Cows can provide a poor family with milk, butter, cheese, and more cows. But, he cautions, we shouldn't expect the cow to win the Kentucky Derby. If we ask foreign aid to put cash in the hands of expectant and new mothers, it can do that. Premature births and infant mortality will fall. But as soon as we ask foreign aid to do something complicated like end global poverty, we're asking it to do the wrong thing.

Easterly's point can be generalized to all projects that we might ask government to take on. The more elaborate, the more complex, the more complicated the project, the less likely it will be that government is well-situated to achieve success. We certainly see this in the aftermath of catastrophic disaster. In the wake of Hurricane Katrina, the first impulse was to create a government commission and charge it with the task of redeveloping the City of New Orleans so that it would be rebuilt better than it ever was before the storm. What emerged instead was a thicket of bureaucratic roadblocks, delays in relief assistance, and uncertainty about the rules and regulations that would govern the recovery process. All of this left displaced residents, business owners, and social service providers on the sidelines, exacerbating the crisis (Chamlee-Wright and Rothschild 2007).

Crisis management is prone to a similar impulse. When the first COVID-19 vaccines were made available, the impulse was to ensure that the rationing scheme was designed to get the vaccine into the arms of those at greatest risk. This approach tracked with the best advice coming from the public health community. But it proved far more complicated in practice, which left valuable vaccines on the shelves unused for weeks at the height of the pandemic.

In hindsight, it would have been much more effective to ration according to a single simple criterion, such as age, that can be verified quickly and easily (Joslin 2020; McDaniel and Freund 2020).

The central reason why government tends to fail when it takes on complicated projects is that the complex social processes it intends to rebuild, direct, or influence are rarely (if ever) designed from the top-down. Such processes tend to emerge from the bottom-up, without the benefit of the social engineer's guiding hand. As such, the knowledge that is needed to coordinate a complex social process is fundamentally dispersed. As soon as you ask government to take on anything as complex as social coordination among vast numbers of dispersed individuals, we are asking the cow to win the Kentucky Derby. We're setting it up to fail (Coyne and Hall 2019; Haeffele 2019).

Most importantly, when we filter out complicated and grandiose projects from the pool of prospective government action, we avoid the worst cases of what F.A. Hayek called the "fatal conceit," the conceit that leads us to believe that we are capable of redesigning the social order from the top-down.

Capable (government well-positioned to provide): Now that we've narrowed the field of projects that may be considered appropriate for government action to those that are essential, big, and simple, we now need to ask Easterly's question. What projects is government most capable of taking on? In cases where the problem to be solved is complex, which tasks within the project is government capable of taking on?

The foregoing discussion offers some relevant examples: getting flood waters pumped out of a submerged city, coordinating first responders and utilities providers to get basic services restored, and removal of major debris from thoroughfares and neighborhood access points.

Another task that government is well-positioned to take on in moments of crisis and post-disaster recovery is to get cash out the door quickly to individuals and service providers. This capability is admittedly blunt. A cash transfer does not guarantee that individuals and households will use the cash wisely. After the fact, the public will no doubt hear of individuals who should not have received taxpayer funds at all. Some social service organizations will do a better or worse job of administering the funds. But in a moment of crisis, the myriad needs vary widely across individuals and from one day to the next. The fungibility of cash enables individuals impacted by the crisis to address those needs swiftly and in ways that relate to their particular circumstances. With cash on hand, organizations are better able to exercise discretion, adapting their strategy as conditions on the ground change.

Contrast this approach with one-size-fits-all forms of relief, such as FEMA trailers for hurricane or tornado victims displaced from their homes. FEMA trailers are costly to store, difficult to transport, and cumbersome to administer. These obstacles often lead to high-cost delays in getting the resource to disaster victims. For the $65,000 spent on every trailer, displaced residents could relocate and secure permanent housing elsewhere, or pay for repairs on their damaged home. Given the wide variety of problems an extreme environment presents, the cash-out-the-door capability is a better default than government provision of specific goods and services that, by design, can only serve a narrow set of needs.

Operations that require the mobilization of trained personnel to enter hazardous conditions, such as in search and rescue operations, is another area where government may be particularly capable. Government authority gives local, state and federal officials the ability to deploy first responders and National Guard troops, for example. It should be noted, however, that civil society also has capacity in this regard. In the throes of a crisis, people rely on family, friends and neighbors for such services. About a half dozen disaster relief organizations that play off the "Cajun Navy" moniker grew out of southwestern Louisiana residents using their own boats to rescue neighbors in the aftermath of Hurricane Katrina. Ideally, when government steps in, it leaves room for private citizens to complement their efforts.

Government also has the capability of adjusting its own regulatory requirements to adapt to changed circumstances. Regulations that may make sense in ordinary times can be prohibitively onerous in extreme environments. Strict requirements for caregiver/child ratios for daycare businesses, for example, inhibit the provision of this essential service in the aftermath of a disaster, right when parents need childcare most urgently as they attend to the various challenges a post-disaster environment presents. Myriad other regulations that shape the environment in which small businesses struggle to bring services back online could also be scaled back. Preferably, such adjustments are worked out in advance so that they can go into effect the moment an emergency has been declared (Chamlee-Wright and Rothschild 2007).

This treatment of government capability is certainly not exhaustive. The main point is that no matter what the context, we improve our policy advice if we begin our analysis by asking the question, "what does government do well?" rather than setting the ideal outcome we desire as the goal of government action. Modern government can get very useful things done. By focusing on government's comparative capabilities rather than grandiose plans of what we desire, we rein in expectations of what good governance looks like and we avoid the perilous mistake of letting the perfect be the enemy of the good.

CONCLUSION

Above I lay out a framework for thinking through what kinds of projects government has a comparative advantage in taking on. I'll close by turning our attention back to the market and civil society. By recognizing that EBS-Cap projects are the best contenders for government action, we see more clearly that markets and civil society are better positioned to take on all the other projects that fall outside the EBS-Cap framework. This does not merely include non-essential, small, and complex projects, but all the other permutations as well, e.g., essential and small, big and complex, essential and complex, non-essential and big, and so on. This underscores the tremendous capacity that rests within the private market and civil society sectors to get things done.

REFERENCES

Aligica, Paul Dragos and Vlad Tarko. 2014. "Crony Capitalism: Rent Seeking, Institutions and Ideology." *Kyklos* 67 (2): 156–76.

Chamlee-Wright, Emily and Daniel Rothschild. 2007. "Disastrous Uncertainty: How Government Disaster Policy Undermines Community Rebound." Mercatus Policy Series, Policy Comment No. 9. The Mercatus Center at George Mason University.

Chamlee-Wright, Emily and Virgil Storr. 2009. "Filling the Civil Society Vacuum: Post-Disaster Policy and Community Response," Mercatus Policy Series, Policy Comment No. 22. The Mercatus Center at George Mason University.

Choi, Seung Ginny and Virgil Henry Storr. 2019. "A Culture of Rent Seeking." *Public Choice* 181 (1): 101–26.

Cowen, Tyler. 2020. "What libertarianism has become and will become—State Capacity Libertarianism." *Marginal Revolution.* January 1. https://marginalrevolution.com/marginalrevolution/2020/01/what-libertarianism-has-become-and-will-become-state-capacity-libertarianism.html (Accessed July 14, 2022).

Coyne, Christopher J. and Abigail R. Hall. 2019. "State-Provided Defense as Noncomprehensive Planning." *The Journal of Private Enterprise* 34 (1): 75–85.

Easterly, William. 2007. *White Man's Burden: Why the West's Efforts to Aid the Rest Have Done So Much Ill and So Little Good.* Oxford, UK: Oxford University Press.

Haeffele, Stefanie (Ed.). 2019. *Knowledge and Incentives in Policy: Using Public Choice and Market Process Theory to Analyze Public Policy Issues.* Lanham, MD: Rowman & Littlefield International.

Haeffele, Stefanie and Virgil Henry Storr (Eds.). 2020. *Bottom-up Responses to Crisis.* London, UK: Palgrave Macmillan.

Haeffele, Stefanie and Anne Hobson (Eds.). 2019. *The Need for Humility in Policymaking: Lessons from Regulatory Policy.* Lanham, MD: Rowman & Littlefield International.

Joslin, Courtney M. 2020. "COVID-19 Vaccine Administration and Pharmacist Scope of Practice Reform." *COVID-19 Response Policy Brief.* The Mercatus Center at George Mason University.

Kennedy, Sean. (2021). "2021 Congressional Pig Book Summary." Citizens Against Government Waste. https://www.cagw.org/sites/default/files/pdf/2021PigBook .pdf.

Lofthouse, Jordan K. (2019) "Institutions and Economic Development on Native American Lands." *The Independent Review* 24 (2): 227–48.

McDaniel, Christine and Caroline Freund. 2020. "Three Steps to Facilitate Global Distribution of a COVID-19 Vaccine." In *Revitalizing Multilateralism: Pragmatic ideas for the new WTO Director-General*, edited by Simon J. Evenett and Richard Baldwin, 155–63. London, UK: Centre for Economics Policy Research Press.

Perticone, Joe. (2017). "The most ridiculous projects the government funded in 2017." *Insider*. November 28. https://www.businessinsider.com/james-lankford -federal-fumbles-report-of-government-waste-2017–11 (accessed July 14, 2022).

NOTES

1. Unfortunately, I am not known for my ability to conjure up sticky shorthand descriptors.

Chapter 2

Rawls, Hayek, Buchanan, and Social Justice

From Rules to Recognition

Alexander Köhler

John Rawls, James M. Buchanan, F.A. Hayek: indubitably three of the most important economists and philosophers of the twentieth century. Contemporary theoretical frameworks rarely exist in a vacuum; popular academic discourse between scholars very much depends on the exchange of ideas and the engagement with the material of their peers of past and present. Rawls, Buchanan, and Hayek are the peers informing today's conversations, and in many ways they laid the cornerstone for how we understand justice and individual liberty today. What can we learn from Rawls, Buchanan, and Hayek regarding social justice, and how does their understanding differ from modern social justice? How is this linked to their idea of individual liberty, and how does this liberty relate to the age of identity politics? If modern social justice is understood as a combination of redistribution and recognition, twentieth-century liberal writing and its focus on the former offer important insights to understand today's duality of redistribution *and* recognition.

Rawls, one could argue, aimed to find a way to marry liberalism and equality. His impact on social justice, both then and now, is remarkable. F. A. Hayek, however, opposed the term "social justice" as a whole. Yet Hayek was not completely opposed to Rawls and his writings; instead, he thought highly of him and even claimed that the differences between them were "more verbal than substantial" (Hayek 1982, xiii). Rawls, on the other hand, cites Buchanan often in *A Theory of Justice*. The interlinks between three heavyweights of classical liberalism, economics, and twentieth-century philosophy are worthy of being explored regardless, much more so considering the renewed relevancy of their concepts for contemporary discourse around social justice, especially in individualistic societies.

Much of the Western world today consists of liberal democracies with, to different degrees, limited market economies, many of which have seen a rise in so-called identity politics and the mainstreaming and increased desirability of some form of social justice. Comparing the three thinkers and their ideas on liberty and justice with modern interpretations of the concepts may provide an idea on how to marry, at first sight, conflicting understandings of a modern free society.

SOCIAL COORDINATION AND SOCIAL JUSTICE

Social coordination, that is, "the mechanism that transforms the uncoordinated behavior of individuals in society into coherent systemic outcomes" (Dutt and Veneziani 2020, 1), aims at solving social problems through the coordination of interactions of different actors (Beetham 1996). Don Lavoie (1985) draws on tradition, market, and planning to be the main drivers of social coordination; for Beetham it is the market and hierarchies. While they differ in terminology, their ideas are largely interchangeable. An element of liberty, the market, is juxtaposed to or combined with a form of morality, more precisely *what ought to be*: "Markets are arrangements which coordinate the actions of large numbers of people automatically, and on a lateral basis, [. . .] without infringing their freedom or requiring inequalities of the status. Hierarchies, by contrast, coordinate action vertically, via a structure of consciously exercised authority and compulsion, in which people's status is 'by definition unequal'" (Beetham 1996, 20–21). Thus, hierarchies arrange society in a desirable way, one that is *good* in its subjective, moral sense.

Yet the desired outcome of social coordination is not as clearly defined, but dependent on the motives and goals of those shaping the processes and tools of social coordination. It is neither inherently good nor bad, but a concept contingent on the values of those who enact it. Traditionally, within a modern liberal society, the desired outcome was assumed to be a discrimination-free society where individual liberties are respected. Yet as we have seen a shift from individual to group rights, from negative liberties to justice as recognition, this may no longer suffice.

The past years have marked a shift in popular discourse. From LGBTQIA+ rights, women's rights, the cause of indigenous people, the fight against ableism, racism, anti-Asian hate or xenophobia, the struggle for minority rights and against discrimination is at the forefront of discussions in our private lives and on the political stage, on Twitter and TikTok, during street protests and emerging mediums like podcasts: "Learn to do good; seek justice, correct oppression; bring justice to the fatherless, plead the widow's cause" (Isaiah 1:17 ESV).

Of course, the idea of social justice and the fight for it was not invented in the twenty-first century. When exactly the term became institutionalized and comprehended the way we do today is unclear, many scholars refer to the industrial revolution of the nineteenth century and the emergence of unions, the increased access to communication, and through that a general increase in class consciousness, as a starting point for a consolidated idea of social justice and the quest for it. Whilst differences in status, wealth, living standards, and opportunities in general always existed, it is through the realization that there are others in one's position, regardless of what position that might be, and the increased broadcasting through media, communication, and travel that many do now perceive social injustices on a larger scale and found their voice to call for rectification.

While many may rally behind a call for a socially just world, what constitutes such is highly contested. As many as there are interest groups and ethnic, sexual, or religious minorities, there are a similarly wide range of ideas on what such a socially just world should look like. Social justice is often perceived as a zero-sum game, gains of one group must result in losses for another. Advancements in women's rights happen at the expense of black people, gay rights overshadow the plight and struggles of trans people. Many advocates of social justice however proclaim that the opposite is true, that true social justice necessarily is based on multiple truths existing at the same time. The theoretical framework to understand and analyze this notion was coined intersectionality.

Intersectionality is the idea that discrimination and marginalization can happen along multiple fault lines: One can be both a woman and queer and the lived experience changes as these identities and the discrimination that comes with them intersect. Kimberlé Crenshaw first laid out the concept in her 1989 essay "Demarginalizing the Intersection of Race and Sex": the idea that systems of discrimination and oppression overlap and that to analyze and improve the status quo of marginalized groups, different spheres of domination must be taken into account. Crenshaw originally applied the concept to black women, acknowledging that depicting women as a unified category allowed for their exclusion and the prioritizing of the most privileged (Crenshaw 2011). It is through intersectionality, she argues, that unconditional social justice can be achieved, as we account for individual identities within the broader picture, exiting the logic of a zero-sum game.

Intersectionality is therefore a tool to understand how individual characteristics and identities result in injustices. From describing and analyzing these biases follows the need to rectify them, to create a *socially just* environment. Social justice is usually understood as an outcome, a point in time after the fact, where all possible (in-)justices are accounted for and benefits, as well as disadvantages, have been redistributed in a way that is generally seen to be just. Understood through an intersectional lens this must include all dimensions of oppression, women in general and black women more specifically, queer people and working-class queer people equally. Redistribution is not per definitionem necessary to reach social justice; however, this is rather due to the lack of a unified definition than to unpopularity amongst advocates of social justice. In fact, throughout recent history, redistribution has been the go-to solution of governments to feed their populace's desire for a more just society. This might not necessarily be due to an ideological conviction that redistribution is the best way to achieve social justice, but more so because it is highly visible, easy to implement and, at least in the short-term, effective. More substantial reforms in the league of Rawlsian theoretical frameworks often prove too complex for short lived election cycles and limited public attention spans.

One example is the taxation of inheritance: In this case truly unearned wealth, meaning that of parents or other benefactors, is passed on. While there is no law that explicitly addresses such inheritance as unjust, the heavy taxation of it and the resulting redistribution of wealth, is in essence an act of achieving social justice: The unjust fact of unearned wealth is rectified by taking part of this wealth and communalizing it.

The way social justice is understood today, however, has shifted from purely economic terms toward a more holistic approach, combining redistribution with recognition in a general political and societal climate governed by identity politics. This shift will be dissected further at a later point in this paper.

SOCIAL JUSTICE AND LIBERALISM

Reverting to social justice as it has been understood for the past 150 years, the main theme was redistribution. Where, however, does the money go? Where does it need to be redistributed to achieve social justice? Who makes this decision? Whilst many will support the call for a just society, few will claim to have the recipe to achieve a perfectly socially just world—and those who do shall not be believed. No single human or central authority may have the necessary knowledge of all occurring injustices, and the lived experiences they produce, to truly determine what social justice should look like.

Hayek's knowledge problem, the fact that the information required for rational economic planning is spread out amongst actors and not held by one individual or authority, may be adapted to the quest for a socially just society:

The peculiar character of the problem of a rational economic order is determined precisely by the fact that the knowledge of the circumstances of which we must make use never exists in concentrated or integrated form but solely as the dispersed bits of incomplete and frequently contradictory knowledge which all the separate individuals possess. (Hayek 1945, 519)

Replacing "rational economic order" with social justice, the similarities become evident. No single individual can claim to be able to consider all dimensions of oppression, marginalization, and disadvantage, much less to know how to rectify them. Beyond no one having the complete required information, no one has the power to transform a society into a socially just one. Simultaneously, truth and its perception are subjective and multiple concepts of what is "true" oppression may exist, rendering a single person being able to oversee and understand oppression in its entirety less likely. The same holds for a centralized authority or government. It should be added that existing injustices often serve those in power, so current systems that produce and reproduce unequal outcomes are unlikely to reform themselves.

If social justice cannot be achieved by fabricating an outcome through redistribution that accounts for every possible dimension and form of injustice, is there a way to interfere with the market, with opportunity, with the starting points of our lives that could render our society more socially just? Yes, John Rawls would say. An ideal society, with its rules designed behind the famous veil of ignorance, would be socially just. Although Rawls cites James M. Buchanan often in *A Theory of Justice*, Buchanan's approach is much less invasive, but perhaps more realistic: In true contractarian fashion, he emphasizes the importance of informed consent, not the maximation of benefits. Hayek, himself an admirer of Rawls and his work, is known as a strong critic of social justice, yet a defender of the universal provision of basic services.

Instead of focusing on the outcomes, Hayek, Rawls, and Buchanan respectively argue for the necessity to ensure that the underlying rules of human relations are socially just: The institutions and regulations that frame our societies, that govern our interactions and our markets, that pave our way toward (or away from) a degree and influence our life expectancy, need to be designed in a way that is socially just. Such would be, contractarian theorists believe, the way to truly achieve justice: to establish socially just rules to the game that everybody consents to and allow real life to unfold therein. In reality this could manifest as a societal consensus or social contract, which like any other democratic political project survives only as long as the electorate supports it.

Hayek, Rawls, and Buchanan are outstanding thinkers of (classical) liberalism and not necessarily scholars one would imagine at the forefront of a fight for social justice. However, it has been argued that this is a misconception of the overlapping, yet different, understandings of liberalism of the aforementioned scholars.

In the following, the merits of Rawlsian, Hayekian, and Buchanan's writings on social justice will be discussed as well as juxtaposed and compared to the way social justice is understood today. The consequences on social coordination of the claim that justice is not dependent on outcome but on due process will be investigated as well as the validity of this as social justice shifts toward justice as recognition.

JOHN RAWLS

John Rawls is seminal to twentieth-century philosophy and political theory. His 1971 publication *A Theory of Justice* is widely regarded as the rebirth of normative political philosophy. Rawls was a theorist of the contract tradition; among his peers are the likes of Thomas Hobbes, John Locke, and Jean-Jacques Rousseau. They are united by the idea that society and its rules of justice and morality are best to be understood as a treaty amongst members regarding the adoption of principles and institutions which maximize benefit. The contracting parties, individual members of society, forfeit certain objectives and desires to achieve the greater benefit of functional cooperation with others.

A fictional "natural state" is the starting point of the theoretical constructs applied by Rawls and his colleagues: How would a society without said rules and institutions operate? What would then compel us to enter the contract, what are potential gains, and what compromise could individuals reach?

Rawls derived his idea of social justice by imagining an original position in which people are placed behind a "veil of ignorance": Individuals are ignorant of their positionality in society, their abilities, and talents, and are unaware of their personal conception of the good and religious sentiments. They do not have access to information about themselves or others which might cloud their impartiality toward creating what ought to be a just society. The rationale behind this is as simple as it is brilliant: People will not be in a position to tailor the rules and principles that govern society to suit themselves (Rawls 1971).

> No one knows his place in society, his class position or social status; nor does he know his fortune in the distribution of natural assets and abilities, his intelligence and strength, and the like . . . the parties do not know their conceptions of the good . . . This ensures that no one is advantaged or disadvantaged by the outcome of natural chance or the contingency of social circumstances. Since

all are similarly situated and no one is able to design principles to favor his particular condition, the principles of justice are the result of a fair agreement. (Rawls 1971, 11)

Therefore, parties are required to make their choice on a just society based on the understanding that they could be virtually in any place in said society: Perhaps best off, possibly worst off, members of a religious minority or the political majority and vice versa. The aim is to construct a setting in which everyone's positionality is to be taken into account as principles are chosen.

Under the veil of ignorance, Rawls argues, people will make the rational choice to promote primary goods: liberty, opportunity, income and wealth, and self-respect (Rawls 1971, 54). He then derives two principles:

1. Each person is to have an equal right to the most extensive total system of equal basic liberties compatible with a similar system of liberty for all.
2. Social and economic inequalities are to be arranged so that they are both:
   a. To the greatest benefit of the least advantaged ("difference principle")
   b. Attached to offices and positions open to all under conditions of fair equality of opportunity.

Basic liberties, according to Rawls, include political and civil liberties such as freedom of thought and belief, of speech, assembly, and association as well as the freedom from torture and arbitrary arrest, and the right to own property. These freedoms may clash—however, they always take precedence over the economic justice aspects articulated in the second principle, thus it can never be rational to trade in the right to vote for economic benefit.

Rawls supposes natural risk-aversity of people under the veil of ignorance, which would lead them to choose principles that maximize the benefit of the least well-off. His theory is egalitarian in that it requires special justification for departures from equality, consequently in a just society, inequalities must be warranted. Herein lies the rationale for the "difference principle": Inequalities are justified if they benefit the least well-off. He does not advocate for particular policies of wealth redistribution but believes that by giving incentives for effort and the development of talent, everyone, including those who are least advantaged, will be better off—the reminiscence of trickle-down economics is not coincidental. Rawls's conception of a socially just society includes a state which is neutral about differences in the ways subjects lead their lives under the pretext that economic policy benefits those at the bottom.

Rawls's *A Theory of Justice* was a turning point in twentieth-century political philosophy, and as such inspired an academic discourse on justice that continues until today. One popular critique of Rawls's framework is that it fails to mention racial injustice, arguably *the* topic of contemporary conversations on social justice. Similar to most U.S.-American liberal thought of the twentieth century, it is alleged that his understanding of social justice is limited to a white, middle-class scenario. It is his focus on ideal theory that limits the applicability to real-life societies, according to Charles W. Mills. It erases the lived experience of racialized individuals and the political history of colonialism and postcolonialism: Rawls's failure is attempting to work out the ideal society first, and then address the society we have (Mills 2017).

As a contractarian, it is evident that Rawls is not concerned with just outcomes but focuses on a level-playing field and just rules to begin with.

F. A. HAYEK

Friedrich August von Hayek, commonly referred to as F. A. Hayek, was an Austrian-born economist and defender of classical liberalism in the twentieth century. At the onset of World War II, he was naturalized as a British citizen and went on to teach at the London School of Economics, UK, the University of Chicago, USA, and lastly the University of Freiburg, Germany. In 1974 he was awarded the Nobel Prize in Economic Sciences together with Gunnar Myrdal for their "penetrating analysis of the interdependence of economic, social and institutional phenomena (Nobel Foundation 1974)."

Hayek disapproved of the concept of social justice. He famously believed it to be "an empty phrase with no determinable content" (1982, 133). He considered it to be a "hollow incantation [. . .] which today makes fine sentiments the instruments for the destruction of all values of a free civilization" (1982, xvi).

In "The Constitution of Liberty," however, Hayek acknowledges that "in the Western world some provision for those threatened by the extremes of indigence or starvation due to circumstances beyond their control has long been accepted as a duty of the community" (1960, 285). This "old poor law" has since been adapted into modern universal health care and unemployment assistance in much of the global North.

Yet Hayek did not believe it to be necessary that this is provided by a strong government, but rather he suggested the provision of communal duties and services by private companies (Wapshott 2012) which are enforced by the state but ran by "quasi-commercial corporations competing for citizens" (Hayek 1982, 146).

Hayek states that social justice "described from the beginning the aspirations which were at the heart of socialism" (1982, 65). From just conduct of the individual under classical liberal order, the world has moved toward a world of "authorities with power to command people what to do" (1982, 66) under the guise of social justice. He appears to fear that any effort to institutionalize redistribution to achieve social justice is a slippery slope toward creating a socialist society.

To understand Hayek's stance on social justice one has to consider his writings on spontaneous order and the free price system. He believed the latter to be a result of the former, instead of being a conscious invention. Accordingly, societal relations in a market economy are self-generating in nature, as opposed to a conscious order, which means that in an organization and within a spontaneous order respectively, "two different kinds of rules or laws [. . .] prevail" (1982, 2). Therefore "what today is generally regarded as 'social' or distributive justice has meaning only within [. . .] the organization; but that it is meaningless in [. . .] spontaneous order."

Hayek believes that an organized society that is constructed in a way that is considered just is impossible as it would require a "conscious account of all the particular facts which enter into the order of society" (1982, 13). As there are necessary limitations to our conscience and knowledge, so exist limitations to how we can account for inequalities, thus one cannot, he states, comprehend them in their entirety.

Such a spontaneous unorganized society is bound together by one "true" common interest, which is the possibility for citizens to pursue their individual goals and life paths. Hayek references Lyndon B. Johnson's domestic policy coined the "Great Society" in 1964, aimed at eradicating racial injustice and poverty in the United States. Hayek's liberalism is one in which negative liberty trumps positive liberty, such that rules may "consist solely in prohibitions from infringing the protected domain of each individual (Hayek 1984, 368)." He, therefore, rejects not just the term social justice, but the concept of shaping society to enable individuals or social groups which would, in Rawlsian terms, be the least well-off.

A market-based society appears to be wholly incompatible with the concept and aims of social justice, according to Hayek. A central authority with the power to enforce redistribution according to group-based needs is diametrically opposed to a market order.

Rawls's thought experiment, of a society consciously designed after certain principles to the ends of achieving social justice, is deemed futile by Hayek (although it should be noted that Hayek published *The Mirage of Social Justice* without taking full account of John Rawls's *A Theory of Justice*):

> In a free society in which the position of the different individuals and groups is not the result of anybody's design—or could, within such a society, be altered in accordance with a generally applicable principle—the differences in reward simply cannot meaningfully be described as just or unjust. (Hayek 1982, 83)

JAMES M. BUCHANAN

James M. Buchanan was an American economist most famous for his work on utility maximization and self-interest in the twentieth century. He received the Nobel Prize in Economic Sciences in 1986 for his work on public choice theory. His stations as a scholar included the University of Virginia, USA, and George Mason University, USA, where he was teaching until he retired.

Public choice theory is the idea that the same principles used to interpret people's decisions in a market setting are applied to political interactions. The end to which individuals take these decisions is their self-interest. Therefore, just as one makes a rational decision in a market transaction, weighing different options and choosing the one which is presumed to be to one's greatest benefit, public choice theory states that one makes utility-maximizing choices. The cost and benefits each individual weighs in their decision remain highly subjective and psychological in nature (Buchanan 1969).

In Buchanan's hypothetical construct, citizens share a similar risk-aversity as described by Rawls, however, he articulated this risk-aversity in terms of trade-offs. David Reisman (1990, 22) describes Buchanan's theory as a form of "constitutional contracting to end the state of nature at the cost of some personal liberty, voting rules and compensation tests to ensure that the rights of minorities on particular issues are properly respected, and constitutional reform to protect the vast bulk of the citizenry from the violence and depredation of politicians and bureaucrats."

Buchanan, as a contractarian constitutionalist, shares many assumptions with John Rawls. Yet, he draws a different conclusion. While Buchanan appreciates Rawls's arrival at the difference principle, Buchanan fears that Rawls is too definitive in assuming that the principle will emerge from the original position and veil of ignorance. Instead, he concludes that people may arrive at other principles to govern their socially just world. For this fallacy, Rawls's "book deserves to gather dust on the idealist bookshelf" (Reisman 1990, 62). As Brennan and Buchanan (1999, 108) argue, "Justice takes its meaning from the rules of the social order [. . .] To appeal to considerations of justice is to appeal to relevant rules. Talk of justice without reference to those rules is meaningless."

Buchanan was strongly influenced by Knut Wicksell, a Swedish economist who laid the foundation for what was to become public choice theory. Wicksell's (1896, 89) stance on justice and fairness excluded redistribution: "It would seem to be a blatant injustice if someone should be forced to contribute toward the costs of some activity which does not further his interest or may even be diametrically opposed to them."

The idea of self-interest and utility maximization as the driving force behind human action and decision-making carries over from Buchanan's thoughts on individual and group behavior in political processes to his view on justice and social justice specifically.

Buchanan believes justice to be dependent on rules, not outcomes, he highlights his understanding of justice as one based on agreement or consent: "The provision of consent on a voluntary basis amounts to offering a promise to abide by the rules. Just conduct is conduct in accord with promises given" (Brennan and Buchanan 1999, 111). Justice is not determined by an outcome, it does not depend on whether a situation is just: what matters is whether the onset, the rules, and the entrance into the interaction or transaction were just. Were the rules of the game clear? Are the procedures of entering and participation just? Were participants coerced into partaking?

The definition of justice as consent and justice as just conduct that Buchanan favors has its own limitations: Can one truly have all the necessary knowledge to give consent and enter a just contract or interaction? What about freely chosen harm?

RAWLS, BUCHANAN, AND HAYEK: A COMPARISON

The underlying ideological conviction that unites Rawls, Hayek, and Buchanan is a strong belief in individual liberty and freedom, as they are ultimately all scholars of liberalism. Recalling Rawls's principles developed in the original position, the individualistic dimension of his understanding of social justice becomes apparent: "Each person is to have an equal right to the most extensive total system of equal basic liberties compatible with a similar system of liberty for all" (Rawls 1971, 54). Put differently, there should be no interference with personal liberty as long as this liberty does not infringe on the liberty of others, one of the baselines of classical-liberal thought. Buchanan would agree with this, as he believes that given the opportunity, individuals would choose personal freedom and autonomy over top-down enforcement of what is believed to be just rules and redistribution (Reisman 1990).

Rawls and Buchanan agree on key aspects in their conceptualization of a just society, yet differences remain. As noted previously, both Rawls and Buchanan deny that justice is about achieving just outcomes, but believe it is about just conduct: A set of rules, consented to by all parties, that ensure a fair and equal "game" (Reisman 1990). Results, whether they reflect popular understandings of justice or are perceived to be highly unequal, cannot be the basis of an analysis of justice because, amongst other things, there is no universal truth and understanding of what is just: "A just social system defines the scope within which individuals must develop their aims, and it provides a framework of rights and opportunities within and by the use of which these ends may be equitably pursued" (Rawls 1971, 31).

One of the underlying assumptions of Rawls's hypothetical original position and veil of ignorance is the presumed risk-aversity of humans. As they are not aware of their own position in the society of which they are designing the rules, Rawls (1971, 134) believes they will construct a society that maximized benefits for the least well-off, as the individuals behind the veil of ignorance could potentially end up in said group: "It is not worthwhile for him to take a chance for the sake of a further advantage, especially when it may turn out that he loses much that is important to him."

Buchanan and Hayek in their understanding of a society guided by liberal principles seem to arrive at similar yet different conclusions. The negative liberties so prominent in Hayek's writing do resonate with Rawls's first principle of justice. Yet Rawls's second principle, the arranging of social and economic inequalities, appears incompatible with Hayek's general caution toward positive liberty. The spontaneous order, a key to Hayek's theory and his understanding of the way a society works, seems to be irreconcilable with Rawls's maximin principle: If society is ordered unconsciously, and that is believed to be the only natural way, any arrangement forbids itself. It should be mentioned however that Hayek, too, acknowledges that there might be instances of deviant spontaneous order that require legal instruments of correction.

SOCIAL JUSTICE IN THE TWENTY-FIRST CENTURY

Thought experiments and theoretical frameworks are important to arrive at an understanding of what *ought to be*, yet rectifying social injustices requires real-life action. A popular tool to do so is affirmative action. Societies plagued by tremendous historical, often racial, injustices have used affirmative action as a "quick" relief. The Oxford Dictionary (2022) defines it as "the practice or policy of favoring individuals belonging to groups regarded as disadvantaged or suffering from discrimination." By the time segregation, which was legally mandated under Jim Crow laws in some instances, was abolished in the United States in the 1960s, the facts and persistence of racial discrimination were obvious and various measures were adopted to counteract this, including affirmative action in state employment, student recruitment, and racial districting under Lyndon B. Johnson's Great Society doctrine. In South Africa, too, apartheid gave way to various forms of affirmative action. Until today, under the policy of "broad-based black economic empowerment (BEE)," firms are evaluated according to their inclusivity and diversity in categories such as ownership and skills development. Brazil has made use of affirmative action as well, adopting quotas for Afro-Brazilians for universities, albeit only in the early 2000s, long after it had abolished its formalized racial discrimination in the form of slavery. Affirmative action is an active tool of redistribution, but also one that offers *recognition* of past injustices and ways to alleviate them.

Hayek was born at the end of the nineteenth century, John Rawls and James M. Buchanan were both born at the beginning of the twentieth century. A lot has changed in the discourse around social justice since their active time as academics. It is impossible to grasp modern ideas of social justice without considering the movements that have emerged in the last decade: From the Occupy Movement to Fridays for Future, MeToo and Black Lives Matter: modern interpretations of what constitutes social justice appear to go much further than Rawls's, Buchanan's, and Hayek's notions, which are mainly concerned with redistributive aspects of justice and largely based on negative freedoms.

Identity politics is at the center of popular discourse, and with it come questions of social justice, redistribution, and recognition. To some, it is the new gold standard, the only way of addressing inequalities that have plagued our societies since the beginning of time. To others, it has become a term to project distaste for progressive politics and politicians onto. The aim of this paper is not to discuss identity politics as such—one might argue that all politics is identity politics—yet social justice and identity politics in the twenty-first century go hand in hand.

More important than the extension beyond economic questions of justice is the overarching aim of social justice as recognition, which emerged in the new millennium. Proponents of modern social justice work toward a "difference-friendly world, where assimilation to the majority or dominant cultural norms is no longer the price of equal respect" (Fraser 2009, 72). According to Fraser, traditional notions of social justice were substantially informed by the economic debates of the nineteenth and twentieth centuries: Following Marxism, "the last thing the proletariat needs is recognition of its difference" (Fraser 2009, 75), but rather redistribution of wealth and the means of production. Individual and group-based experiences of injustice and oppression were to be sacrificed toward the greater good of universal economic liberation. Yet as the Cold War ended and market economy became the default economic order of most nations, the binary of owners versus workers and the attached ideas of justice as redistribution lost their appeal and did not provide the answers those who faced social injustice were looking for.

Social justice today includes economic justice and gender equality, women's rights, climate justice, and racial justice. It is not the mere absence of obstacles to fulfill one's mostly economic potential that constitutes modern social justice, it is rather about rectifying past and ongoing injustices in a multitude of dimensions. Negating or sacrificing other experiences of social injustice to achieve a common but narrow economic goal has lost its appeal today.

Most current crises can be tied to a social justice issue: Healthcare and the opioid crisis, different crises of refugee management in different parts of the world, gun violence, food insecurity, and the list goes on. People increasingly understand and acknowledge the intricacies of an interconnected world, especially the gap between the global South and the global North. A food shortage due to a drought in East Africa does not remain a local humanitarian crisis but is understood as a result of climate change and man-made carbon emissions from the global North. Food security becomes an issue of climate justice which in turn is an issue of social justice. Economics as a lens is insufficient to analyze these issues.

Rawls, Buchanan, and Hayek understood—and largely opposed—social justice in an egalitarian redistributive sense. While this was true for their time, and had been since the second industrial revolution and the mainstreaming of an understanding of class relations between owners and workers, today we "encounter a second type of social justice claim in the 'politics of recognition'" (Fraser 2009, 72). Hence, it is not just the scope of what we understand as social justice today that has increased, it is also the goal that has changed. A socially just world today for many is one where differences are recognized without discriminatory ranking of us vs. them, majority vs. minority. This is attributed to the rise of identity politics, that is "politics founded in the shared experiences of injustice of members of certain social groups" (Heyes 2002). However, one could argue that we have never known anything else but identity politics, except that it used to be socially conservative, majority-based identity politics—centered around the stereotypical "old white man"—and what has actually risen is the voice of *other* identities besides traditional hegemonic voices.

The overarching commonality between Rawls, Buchanan, and Hayek is that their level of analysis is the individual. They understand justice in general and social justice more specifically as a matter of personal freedom. Rawls describes it in the original position, where individuals construct a world based on fear for their *own* positionality. Buchanan believed it to be unjust for someone to have to contribute to a cause that does not concern them, and Hayek believed group control over individual action to achieve social justice to be a nightmarish socialist dystopia.

Modern social justice shifts this focus from the individual level to the group level. The advent of identity politics as it is understood today meant a new consciousness for common injustice and discrimination experienced by members of the same group. While individual compensation may still play a role, efforts are often centered around in-group support, the recognition of adversities faced by the respective group, and a new form of celebration or appreciation of the group characteristics that have led to their discrimination in the first place. Here too, justice as rules and just conduct is elementary to rectify what is deemed unjust, but they fall short of answering the questions of those who seek social justice today.

What, then, is the value of Rawls's, Buchanan's, and Hayek's thoughts on social justice in today's world? Some aspects of their writing can be extrapolated from the individualistic level to a group and community-based understanding of social justice. Other thoughts remain the basis of discussions around social justice today, both for those who favor progressive understandings of justice as well as more traditional and conservative factions. Siding with Nancy Fraser and her understanding of modern social justice as a combination of redistribution and recognition, twentieth-century liberal writing and its focus on the former offers important insights to understand today's duality of redistribution *and* recognition.

JOHN RAWLS AND MODERN SOCIAL JUSTICE

As a contractarian, it becomes evident that Rawls is not concerned with just outcomes but with just rules. Criticism of Rawls's *A Theory of Justice* has, as mentioned earlier, always been based on the fact that his understanding of what injustice is and in what contexts it can be experienced is limited. Imagine a queer person facing homophobic discrimination in the job market: Rawls's concept might lead to a more egalitarian recruitment process, yet the person might still face discrimination at the actual workplace. Social justice as recognition however would mean that sexual identity is approached in a "difference-friendly" way: Firstly, being openly homosexual is not an obstacle to getting hired, but beyond that one may find a queer network at the workplace and procedures and guidelines to file complaints and report cases of discrimination based on one's sexual orientation. Or Black students not being forced to wear certain hairstyles, Muslim employees taking work off on Eid in majority Christian societies, and so forth. Exercising redistributive justice, or even affirmative action, to achieve Rawls's ideal society are only the first step toward what social justice is today. With redistribution must come recognition.

JAMES M. BUCHANAN AND
MODERN SOCIAL JUSTICE

Buchanan focused on just rules and just conduct. Comparing this to what social justice in its contemporary interpretation means, Buchanan's approach appears somewhat short-sighted. Much like Rawls's theory, there is an appeal in the way he imagines and constructs an ideal society, where a just rule base governs a just society. Although he differs in the conclusions he draws, the limitations of Buchanan's "original position" remain. Today, ideal theory is perceived rather as the starting point of useful analysis and reform. It precedes the effort to fix a status quo in which rules are not universally respected and enforcement is limited, and more importantly, a reality in which a set of rules cannot encompass all aspects of social injustice.

It is common practice for contracts, codes of conduct, and terms and conditions to include or adhere to some form of non-discriminatory standards. Yet social justice as we understand it today is about more: Recognition of difference and the benefits of these differences, recognition of past and present achievements of minorities or disadvantaged groups. A revision of the way we understand and teach history and the biases that have been perpetuating toward a holistic understanding of world history and the contributions made by the global South, the atrocities committed by the global North, and vice versa. Just conduct as favored by Buchanan falls short of addressing most of these issues. His sole focus on just conduct falls short regarding the lived experiences of many disenfranchised people because conduct and compliance with set rules depends on power dynamics—a middle class person may be able to employ the law and higher authorities, a marginalized person has distinctly less avenues of recourse.

F. A. HAYEK AND MODERN SOCIAL JUSTICE

From just conduct of the individual under classical liberal order, we have moved toward a world of "authorities with power to command people what to do" (Hayek 1982, 66) under the guise of social justice. Revisiting the analysis of Hayek's thoughts on social justice, one notices uncanny similarities to popular, or more fittingly *populist* responses to social justice and identity politics today. It is reminiscent of discussions around cancel culture, "snowflakes," and the perceived censoring through enforcement of inclusive and non-discriminatory language. Following the principle of charity, one may not assume that this is what F. A. Hayek meant, yet it is important to acknowledge the links, however distant they might be, between liberal thought and reactionary populism. Freedom of speech and discrimination-free speech should not be mutually exclusive but seen as two sides of the same coin. The concept of paternalistic and authoritarian modern social justice "warriors" is often instrumentalized by conservative hardliners, a straw man fallacy par excellence.

Between Buchanan's justice as conduct and modern social justice as recognition, Hayek takes an interesting position: The impossibility of accounting for all conceivable forms of oppression and injustice and therefore the futility of trying to construct an all-encompassing system of just rules appears to counter Buchanan. At the same time, however, he signals support for one of the main assumptions of justice as recognition: Following Nancy Fraser's as well as Kimberlé Crenshaw's intersectionality, social injustice is not a clear-cut, linear phenomenon but rather a highly individual and multi-dimensional issue. Hayek's analysis supports this, yet he falls short of drawing the conclusion Fraser and Crenshaw do. Instead of plainly dismissing any effort of achieving social justice due to the aforementioned reasons, they propose solutions that go beyond establishing a set of rules: The differentiated appreciation and recognition of injustices and inequality with, as Fraser writes, "the best of the politics of redistribution with the best of the politics of recognition" (2009, 77).

Hayek deserves to be read and understood charitably, and by doing that, his exhaustive considerations on the knowledge-problem become the basis of a flexible approach toward the recognition of similarities and dissimilarities in people, not exercised by a central authority or government but constantly negotiated as privileges shift and new categories emerge.

SOCIAL JUSTICE, COORDINATION, AND MODERNITY

Maintaining the assumption that the aim of social coordination, and in fact, the inherent goal of any modern liberal society, is to provide and enforce social justice or a regulatory and institutional framework that does such, then the true quest of normative political philosophy of studying social coordination and deriving public policy therefrom, must be to find ways to achieve such a state.

John Rawls himself defined his theory as ideal theory, a fully just society based on idealized assumptions. It was his firm belief that ideal theory is a necessary step before developing non-ideal theory (Robeyns 2008). Herein lies the value of his teachings for social coordination: Social coordination is done with a socially desirable outcome in mind. What ought to be and what are the mechanisms and tools that can lead us there? Imagining an ideal society in which benefits for the least well-off are maximized offers a goal to work toward, one to bring us closer to social justice.

Hayek's Knowledge Problem, on the other hand, the impossibility of one individual or institution acquiring all facts necessary to achieve a desired economic or social outcome, illustrates why the distinction between ideal and non-ideal theory is paramount when discussing social coordination and social justice. One has to understand that what is imagined cannot be achieved simply through social coordination, as neither the knowledge nor the power to enforce is concentrated in a way that would allow such. Even if this was possible, a society where differences in individual endowments are due to some greater design, is not *free*.

Buchanan's understanding of justice as consent offers a link between the ideal outcome imagined and reality. To avoid perceived and real injustices of redistribution and a path toward Hayek's nightmare of socialist authoritarianism, social justice must be found within rules, because "justice takes its meaning from the rules of the social order" (Brennan and Buchanan 1986, 108). Herein lies the starting point of justice as recognition, for it must be established what ought to be to recognize the mistakes of the past.

This essay aimed to offer an understanding and a comparison between Rawlsian, Hayekian, Buchananian, and the modern idea of social justice. It is the shift from justice as redistribution to justice as recognition, from the individual to a group-based approach. Yet this shift is not absolute, modern social justice demands a combination of both redistribution and recognition, as Fraser highlights. Such an outcome may hardly be achieved solely through intervention after the fact. It is described in the terminus "social coordination" itself, that it includes a framework, rules, and institutions that coordinate behavior and interactions of citizens.

REFERENCES

Crenshaw, Kimberlé. 1989. "Demarginalizing the Intersection of Race and Sex: A Black Feminist Critique of Antidiscrimination Doctrine, Feminist Theory and Antiracist Politics." *University of Chicago Legal Forum* 1989 (1): Article 8. http://chicagounbound.uchicago.edu/uclf/vol1989/iss1/8.

———. 2011. "Demarginalising the Intersection of Race and Sex: A Black Feminist Critique of Anti-discrimination Doctrine, Feminist Theory, and Anti-racist Politics." In *Framing Intersectionality: Debates on a Multi-Faceted Concept in Gender Studies*, edited by Helma Lutz, Maria Teresa Herrera Vivar, and Linda Supik, 25–42. Farnham, UK: Ashgate Publishing Company.

Beetham, David. 1996. *Bureaucracy*, 2nd ed. Buckingham, UK: Open University Press.

Dutt, Amitava Krishna and Roberto Veneziani. 2020. "Social Coordination." *Review of Social Economy* 78 (1): 1–3.

Brennan, Geoffrey and James M. Buchanan. 1999. "The Reason of Rules: Constitutional Political Economy." In *The Collected Works of James M. Buchanan, Vol. 10*. Indianapolis, IN: Liberty Fund.

Buchanan, James M. 1969. *Cost and Choice*. Chicago, IL: Markham Publishing.

Fraser, Nancy. 2009. "Social Justice in the Age of Identity Politics: Redistribution, Recognition and Participation." In *Geographic Thought,* edited by George L. Henderson and Marvin Waterstone, 72–91. London, UK: Routledge.

Hayek, Friedrich A. 1945. "The Use of Knowledge in Society." *American Economic Review* 35 (4): 519–30.

———. 1960. *The Constitution of Liberty*. Chicago, IL: The University of Chicago Press.

———. 1982. *Law, Legislation and Liberty*. London, UK: Routledge.

———. 1984. "The Principles of a Liberal Social Order." In *The Essence of Hayek,* edited by Chiaki Nishiyama and Kurt R Leube, 363–82. Stanford, CA: Stanford University Press.

Heyes, Cressida. 2002. "Identity Politics." *The Stanford Encyclopedia of Philosophy* (Fall 2020), edited by Edward N. Zalta. https://plato.stanford.edu/archives/fall2020/entries/identity-politics/.

Lavoie, Don. [1985] 2016. *National Economic Planning: What is Left?* Arlington: Mercatus Center.

Mills, Charles W. 2017. *Black Rights/White Wrongs*. New York: Oxford University Press.

Nobel Foundation. [1974] 2021. "Prize in Economic Sciences 1974: Press Release." https://www.nobelprize.org/prizes/economic-sciences/1974/press-release/.

Oxford Dictionaries. 2022. "Affirmative Action." Oxford University Press. https://www.lexico.com/definition/affirmative_action.

Rawls, John. [1971] 1999. *A Theory of Justice*. Cambridge, MA: Harvard University Press.

Reisman, David. 1990. *The Political Economy of James Buchanan*. London, UK: Palgrave Macmillan.

Robeyns, Ingrid. 2008. "Social Justice: Ideal Theory, Nonideal Circumstances." *Social Theory and Practice* 34 (3): 341–62.

Wapshott, Nicholas. 2012. *Keynes Hayek: The Clash that Defined Modern Economics*. New York: W.W. Norton.

Wicksell, Knut. [1869] 1958. "A New Principle of Just Taxation." In *Finanztheoretische Untersuchungen,* tr. by James M. Buchanan, in R.A. Musgrave and A.T. Peacock, eds., *Classics in the Theory of Public Finance*. London, UK: Macmillan.

Chapter 3

Are RCTs Missing a Point?

Local Knowledge and Computer Assisted Learning Interventions

Carlos Noyola

Education is important for economic growth (Hanushek and Woessmann 2011). In fact, more broadly, it is important for the well-being of a society. More educated individuals enjoy higher levels of earnings, but also live longer, suffer less from teen pregnancy, present lower divorce rates and in general report higher levels of life satisfaction (Burgess 2016). Therefore, it is not surprising that economists have turned a lot of their attention to understand the ways in which education can be expanded or improved.

Particularly, economists have focused, in recent years, on the effect of different school inputs on learning outcomes. Given the proliferation of the use of computers worldwide, high quality studies (usually deemed to be RCTs) have focused on the effect of computers on learning (Glewwe, et.al 2013). However, they largely ignore the incentives faced by those who participate, which is to say, they ignore local knowledge and simply implement what researchers think is best.

Although previous research has shown that local participation in the decision-making process of public policy can be detrimental when technical decisions are involved (Khwaja, 2004), it has also shown that local knowledge can be very helpful when it comes to non-technical decisions (Khwaja 2004; Davis and Ostrom 1991). After conducting focus groups with teachers and parents from a Primary school in Mexico, I show that local knowledge is important for the research design of interventions with computers, I argue that coproduction of the intervention design could solve the problem, and, based on my findings, I propose a way to conduct an RCT to evaluate whether the incorporation of local knowledge changes the results.

A SIMPLE FRAMEWORK FOR ANALYZING
PREVIOUS RESEARCH

Trying to understand institutions, Ostrom focused on what she called "a referent for the term institutions" (Ostrom 1986, 5), and developed a framework—Institutional Analysis and Development (IAD)—for better understanding their roles in the situations usually studied by economists (and social scientists, in general) as well as to develop a better research design. Central to the IAD framework is the action-situation, defined as a situation "where individuals interact, exchange goods and services, solve problems, dominate one another, or fight" (Ostrom 2011, 11). Ostrom describes the variables that should be specified to understand it, including the participants, the positions they take, the outcomes they can influence, the information possessed by them and the ways in which they process the information to decide their course of action to produce outcomes.

Two ideas were key to her framework: 1) rules cannot be studied in isolation and 2) they affect the action-situation in which events take place, and this requires analysts model the way in which that precise situation is affected by the rules in order to proceed with any analysis. Ostrom thus defined the rule-structured situation as the situation where individuals decide their course of action weighing their incentives against the rules in place (Ostrom 1986). By rules, here Ostrom meant "linguistic entities that refer to prescriptions commonly known and used by a set of participants" (Ostrom 1986, 5).

I build on Ostrom's ideas to develop a framework for analyzing the assumptions of the researchers when conducting randomized experiments aimed at improving learning outcomes through some form of computer assisted learning program. I also draw on Andrew Schotter's idea of rules (Schotter 1981). According to Andrew Schotter (1981), there are "conventions of behavior" in any given game described by its rules, either implicit or explicit. It is to this "conventions of behavior" that I refer to as the determinants of the possibilities that any person has when faced with an intervention, and particularly, with an intervention that involves some kind of computer assisted learning program. For example, even if there is no rule saying that participants cannot sell the computer they were given, participants understand they should not do so; but if they are provided with a computer, and no one is watching, there is no need for them to use it, and even if they are asked to use it, there is no infringement in browsing the web instead of looking at the applications installed in the device. I do not want to look at the intentions of the intervention, but at what can be called equilibrium properties, i.e., the outcome resulting from what agents actually do with the design of the game, not the design per se. In this sense, the following analysis of previous interventions is close to Schotter.

Combining Schotter's idea of "conventions of behavior" and Ostrom's definition of a rule-structured situation, I define a *structured-situation*, in the context of persons facing an intervention by researchers, as one in which agents decide their course of action selecting from the set of possible actions defined by the conventions of behavior that the intervention created.

This implies that in order to analyze a structured-situation we cannot look at every piece of it (i.e., the intervention and those who receive the intervention) as a separate phenomenon; neither can we assume that everything else will remain unchanged. Instead, we must look at the whole situation and consider the interactions of agents with the intervention. That is, recognize the configurational character of the structured-situation.

The problem arises when researchers are trying to predict behavior directly from specifying the design of the experiment, instead of looking at the intervention as a variable in itself that defines the structured-situation. Here, those who receive the intervention are static participants who merely receive information and act mechanically to deliver an outcome, so that no local agency is recognized for them. Applying a political economy approach, we can think of this as a centralized solution to the problem, in which only the regular producer (i.e., researchers) is the only producer of the service (i.e., the experiment) (Davis and Ostrom 1991). In the spirit of Ostrom, we can say that a centralized RCT regime creates potential for perverse consequences.

Since behavior is difficult to change, we have to understand how agents behave, what they value (i.e., their preferences), and how they process information to make decisions, in order to know how the intervention might lead to better outcomes. This means we are moving toward a framework like the one represented in figure 3.1, where participants of the experiment are viewed as crucial agents in the process, with local agency, and whose interaction with the intervention is what ultimately determines the final outcome.

Similar to Ostrom (1986), I view interventions here not as directly influencing behavior, but rather changing the structure of the situation from which agents choose their decisions. In this sense, interventions take, in this case, as domain, the set of possible school inputs, or more specifically, computer assisted learning inputs, and as range the variables of the specific situation under analysis (i.e., the preferences of the agents, their decision-making process, etcetera). This seems to point toward what Ostrom termed coproduction. If the outcome is determined not only by the research design of economists, those other individuals whose actions are crucial could also provide inputs for the intervention (Ostrom 1996). In the following section I will show how

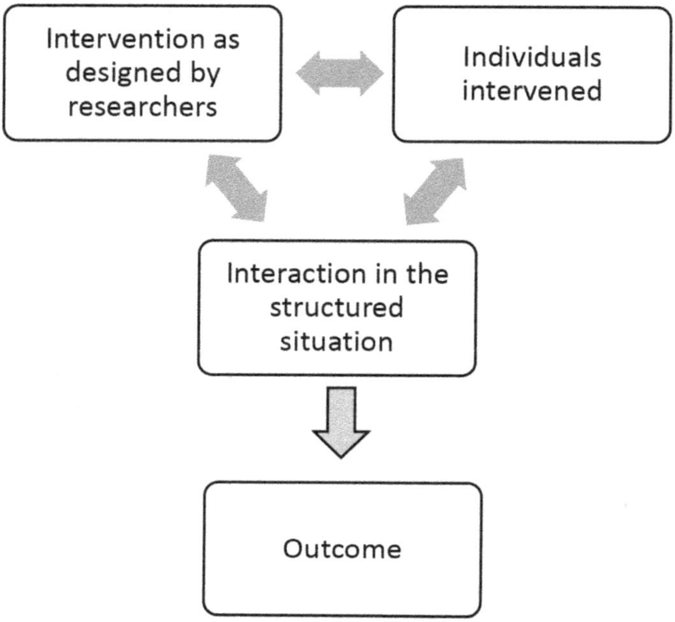

Figure 3.1. RCT Framework that Considers Participants of the Experiment as Crucial Agents.
Source: Carlos Noyola.

outstanding RCTs looking at the effect of computers on education have failed to coproduce the intervention.

THE LACK OF UNDERSTANDING OF THE STRUCTURED-SITUATION IN PREVIOUS HIGH-QUALITY RESEARCH

After developing the framework, I turn to study five randomized controlled trials that implemented some type of Computer Assisted Learning (CAL) program to try to improve academic achievement of students in different settings. To select the randomized experiments, I looked for papers that had been previously analyzed by other economists and deemed of enough quality (where quality studies mean RCT's). Thus, I focused on two important reviews of literature on the effects of different school inputs on learning outcomes: Glewwe etal. (2013) with his review of 79 papers on the effects of different types of investment in academic achievement, and the survey of 77 randomized experiments on interventions on learning made by McEwan (2015). In the case of the former, Glewwe and his colleagues include a subsection of analysis in which they only include the studies they consider to be of high quality, all of which are randomized controlled trials. I restricted my attention to high-quality studies. Finally, I specifically looked for papers using computers for teaching and/or self-learning among students, which means I excluded from my analysis studies looking at the impact of videogames on learning.

Three main arguments justify the use of case studies in such an analysis. The first is that particular studies can call into question the plausibility of general claims. In this case, the general claim called into question is that randomized controlled trials are of high quality per se, simply because they randomize, without any need for further understanding. Second, particular studies guide us on what to look for in other research. Here, the framework used to analyze the interventions can be used to evaluate other randomized experiments. And finally, the ways in which particular studies were conducted can teach us how general mechanisms operate. It is hard to grasp the importance of assumptions about the relevance of local knowledge in the intervention unless its consequences are shown in a specific setting.

One of the first experiments trying to identify the effects of computers on learning was conducted by recent Nobel Prize winners Abhijit Banerjee, Esther Duflo, and their colleagues (2007). The RCT focused on improving learning outcomes of mathematics in India. They benefitted from a government program that in the early 2000's provided all 100 public primary schools in the city of Vadodara with four computers each.

Students of grade 4 solved mathematics questions using a computer two hours a week. Importantly, questions were tailored to the students' level of ability. One hour was delivered during class time (substitute) and the other was either immediately after or before school day. As it is clear, no input from the school community (i.e., parents, teachers and students) was taken into account for the intervention design.

Although at the end of the intervention they found treated students to perform 0.47 standard deviations better than their counterparts in the control group, the impact faded quickly one year after the program was over. Students assigned into the control group were allowed to use computers as they pleased, but the authors maintain that "in practice, we never found them being used for instructional purposes" (Banjeree et al. 2007, 1241), which shows that computers *can be* used for learning purposes, but that does not mean they *will be* used in such a way, and suggests that simply installing learning software into a device is unlikely to yield results. The conventions of behavior still allow participants to use computers for other purposes in the structured-situation. This is important because it provides evidence that students can opt for not using a learning software installed in the device.

Although the authors do not explicitly make the point, they seem to recognize students as key agents making decisions regarding the intervention and having an impact on the outcome. They assert that "many interventions which increase school participation do not improve test scores for the average student" (Banjeree et al. 2007, 1236), and maintain it is at least in part due to the fact that "neither the pedagogy nor the curriculum has been adapted to take into account the influx of children and their characteristics" (Banjeree et al. 2007, 1236). Therefore, in their study, the questions asked to any pair of students are specifically chosen to match the students' level of ability, and the teacher is trained not only to solve technical problems of the computer, but to help students understand mathematics problems whenever needed, even though no general instruction of mathematics as in a traditional lesson was given.

The structured-situation, however, is not fully comprehended, because the ways in which the school community can affect the intervention are not fully understood before the experiment, and it is merely a result from the intervention that the experimenters recognize the uselessness of the treatment when not complemented by appropriate teacher supervision and support.

Barrera-Osorio and Linden (2009) carried out a randomized experiment to find out the effect of providing computers to schools on learning outcomes. Provision of computers was accompanied by two training phases. The first one focused on technical issues of the computers, while the second one on training teachers to make the best of the new equipment in the learning environment. Importantly, the aim is to train teachers on how to incorporate technology for teaching Spanish.

Barrera-Osorio and Linden (2009) found no effect, either on Spanish test scores, nor on any specific component of Spanish (i.e., grammar, pragmatics, paraphrase). The results were the same when they looked at achievement in mathematics. Comparing the results of the baseline survey they found computers were not only not used for teaching Spanish, but, overall, the use of computers for in-class activities did not increase. Given the fact that, in total, instructors in schools treated were trained for 20 months, it is worrying that such a costly program did not yield any significant result in terms of student outcomes.

Colombian teachers can decide whether to use computers or not, and for what purposes, since computers have many functions besides being helpful in Spanish lessons. In the design of the intervention, researchers do not consider that while teachers understand, for example, that taking computers to their houses for their own use is incorrect (in fact, it would probably be illegal), there is nothing forcing them to use computers as the training session suggested or to change the delivery of their classes.

The framework proposed establishes that interventions are not independent of those who receive the intervention. One cannot be studied without the other. However, Barrera-Osorio and Linden illustrate how, even when they seem to be aware of the interdependency, some scholars do not incorporate it into their analysis. For instance, Barrera-Osorio and Linden (2009, 4–5) assert that "positive outcomes of the use of computers in schooling are linked to changes in the pedagogy, and introducing technology alone will not change the teaching and learning process." Nonetheless, after they find that there was a modest increase overall in the use of computers, but none of it due to more usage for teaching, they conclude, without any support from the data, that teachers "have been using the computer for preparatory activities rather than for in class activities" (Barrera-Osorio and Linden 2009, 23). They do not consider that, for example, instructors could be using computers for purposes bearing no relation to their jobs, such as communicating with family members or using social media. This reflects the fact that researchers are analyzing the situation implicitly assuming a framework in which everything depends on the input they provide, and the only possible change derives from it.

In a more recent study, Julian P. Cristia and his colleagues (2017) looked at the effect of a large program aimed at improving learning outcomes by providing children with laptops for use both at school and at home. The program significantly increased computer access, with 1.18 computers per student in treated schools, compared with only 0.18 computers per student in schools in the control group. They used data from 319 schools in rural areas in Peru to evaluate the effect of computer access on mathematics and language test scores 15 months after the implementation of the treatment.

In contrast with the previous studies analyzed, their experiment involved not only increased access to technology at the school, but also at home. Although teachers are responsible for the use of laptops during school time, they are unable to control what students do with the equipment once school is over. This introduces students as relevant decision-makers in the structured-situation, and increases the relevance of parents. Finally, it is important that when analyzing the data, researchers benefit from computer logs to better understand how the technology provided was used.

Increased computer access did not change students' academic performance in mathematics nor in language. Even though achievement did not improve, computer usage did increase substantially. 82 percent of students in treated schools reported using a computer at school in the previous week, compared with only 26 percent in the control group. Moreover, the average length of a session was 40 minutes. This immediately suggests that the use of computers did not involve activities to enhance the learning process.

After analyzing the data, Cristia and his colleagues explain that the program did not change reading habits. Interestingly, they assert that "this is perhaps surprising, given that the program substantially increased the availability of books to students" (Cristia et al. 2017, 297). They look at users as static members, and do not consider the incentives created by the intervention and the structured-situation resulting from it, as if they had no local agency. While there is evidence, for example, of the importance of the number of books available at home when predicting learning outcomes (Glewwe et al. 2013), books are merely a signal of other things, rather than the cause itself. Having a book without reading it will not lead to more knowledge.

Moreover, the study of Banerjee and his colleagues (year) shows the dangers of not considering students' preferences. Availability of computers increased, and it led to an increase in their use, but not to an increase in the quality of instruction. Using data from computer logs, they found that at least 40 percent of the time was invested in games, music and video recording, while less than 50 percent of time focused on basic applications expected to be helpful for school activities, such as a calculator or word processor. This suggests that the intervention could even be damaging students, by wasting as much as 40 percent of the time they are allowed to spend on laptops. Without a description of the context of the participants and how they can affect the outcomes, there is no understanding of the structured situation.

In another randomized control trial, Fang Lai and his colleagues studied the effect of Computer Assisted Learning (CAL) on student achievement (2015). They focus on the effect on disadvantaged students, and carry out their experiment in schools for migrants in Beijing. To improve academic outcomes, they implement a computer assisted learning tutoring program specifically designed to help students with mathematics.

The increase in mathematics test scores of students assigned to treated schools was only 0.15 standard deviations, not even making it to the threshold of 0.2 standard deviations, widely accepted in empirical economics research to be a small effect. The program had no spillover effects, that is to say, test scores in language did not increase.

Lai and his colleagues trained a teacher to supervise the tutoring session, which took place either immediately after classes or during lunch time. The fact that they do not see that the success of the intervention also depends on the actions of those upon which the intervention is imposed means that they are missing a central point in the formulation of the structured-situation. If, for example, students just want to play during their break, or feel hungry after finishing school (and there are reasons to think that is the case, since breaks at school are designed for students to enjoy leisure time, and students usually go home for a meal after school) then they will not be motivated to learn and may even be unwilling to follow the instructions of the tutor. There is evidence that even court decisions are influenced by extraneous factors, such as mental depletion caused by lack of food (Glöckner 2016). This reflects a common mistake of researchers, who believe the intervention design to be able to predict one and only one action, rather than considering the local agency of those who receive the intervention.

Furthermore, the teacher in charge of supervising the tutoring session was neither a mathematics teacher nor the home-room teacher of the students. This could seriously affect the intervention if, for instance, students have a problem with something during the use of the software and nobody is able to answer their questions because the teacher is not trained in that subject.

Mo et al. (2013) studied the effect of a program very similar to that studied by Cristia and his colleagues in Peru, but they did it in China. Similar to the study conducted by Fang Lai, et al. (2015), Di Mo and her colleagues focused exclusively on disadvantageous students, and to that purpose they conducted their experiment at schools for migrants in Beijing, China.

After distributing the laptops, the intervention included one training session, which lasted for two hours. Six months after the intervention, when they evaluated the students, they found, in line with the findings of Cristia et al. (2017), that students' computer skills benefitted significantly from the program, but that was not the case either with Mathematics or Language. In the case of the former, the effect is so small to be considered of economic relevance (less than 0.2 standard deviations) and in the latter it is not significant at all.

Similar to Fang Lai, et al. (2015), they do not study the particularities of the migrant schools they are using for their randomized experiment, and the only information given is that they serve students from disadvantaged backgrounds. In contrast with the study of Fang Lai, et al. (2015), Mo et al. (2013) at least make explicit some of their expectations regarding how students will act when provided with the computers. Since the idea of their project is based on the OLPC project designed at MIT, they highlight their project emphasizes self-learning more than the original project does. This means they expect children to find out how to use the material, in this case, laptops, by themselves. However, their assumption that children also will open one of the incorporated software packages by themselves (consistent with official school curriculum) simply ignores the preferences of children, who are here important decision makers in the intervention. This is, once again, consistent with a centralized framework where students are simply expected to react mechanically, without attempting to delve deeper into their role in the process of crafting the final outcome.

The set of actions the participants can take is also not explained. Thus, there is no specification of the variables of the structured-situation. Mo et al. (2013, 15) explain that the "laptops were all capable of accessing the internet," but it seems that for them this has no relevant implication. They either believe or assume that simply by including software for learning and lengthy user manuals for every application, students, after undergoing a two-hour training session, will decide to use the learning packages systematically, without any attention to their preferences (e.g., if they like watching videos or recording audio).

FURTHER DISCUSSION

The previous study of randomized controlled trials looks at the effect of incorporating technology in the learning process and shows that, for the most part, researchers fail to specify how the structured-situation is configured. Furthermore, none of the studies allowed for the intervention design to be coproduced by researchers and the school community. Even when researchers seem to be aware of the meaningful ways in which the intervention can be affected by the local agency of the school community, studies fail to incorporate that into the analysis.

This failure can substantially affect key results of their studies. The interdependency of the elements involved should be recognized and studied before implementing an intervention. Particularly, individuals taking part in the intervention, either students or teachers, cannot be assumed to be static, and allowing them to craft their own institutions would improve the educational system by increasing the coexistence of multiple schemes of intervention (Ostrom and Davis 1991). For instance, baseline surveys investigating the preferences and constraints of students, teachers and parents may be a good start, but only if they serve to construct a model of the individuals and how will they process the intervention better. Another, perhaps better possibility, is to give participants a voice in designing the intervention.

Asim Khwaja (2004) developed a model for understanding the effects of local participation in outcomes of development projects. The model is based on the idea that those whose effort is more important for the decision should be given ownership over the decision. According to his model, increasing community participation for projects requiring technical decisions has a negative impact on project maintenance, but in the case of nontechnical decisions local participation improves project maintenance. Khwaja tested the model prediction using data from 132 infrastructural projects in northern Pakistan. For that, he first constructed a measure of project maintenance with data provided by specialists in infrastructure. Following that, he interviewed local residents to know whether they had participated in the project, and divided the questions into technical and nontechnical decisions. He found a significant negative impact on project maintenance from participation in technical decisions, but a significant positive one when the participation is in areas that require no technical knowledge. His results provide evidence that local participation is important when investments from the community are crucial for the development project. In other words, coproduction, that is, the process through which inputs for local projects are provided not only by an external organism (e.g., the government or researchers) but also by the students/families themselves, is very important in areas with no requirement of technical knowledge.

The interventions studied in this paper may include some technical decisions (such as the type of computer to be installed), but for the most part the intervention requires a lot of community investment. If teachers or students do not collaborate (e.g., supervising for what purposes are computers being used by students), as has been shown, the interventions have no effects. Coproduction of RCTs using parents' and teachers' knowledge could prove very helpful when it comes to deciding what applications to include in the computer, when to deliver the tutoring sessions and how to organize them. Furthermore, the knowledge of the community may not only be helpful, but essential for lasting effects.

To understand different levels of stickiness among institutions Boettke and his colleagues (2008) developed a framework that distinguishes three types of institutions: foreign-introduced exogenous institutions (those completely coming from abroad, such as imposed by development agencies), indigenously introduced exogenous institutions (those introduced by local authorities, but not spontaneous), and indigenously introduced endogenous institutions (spontaneous orders). They concluded that programs purely exogenous aimed at promoting development are unlikely to work, since they lack the social memory required for workability. According to them, "any path to progress with a reasonable probability of success must ultimately be rooted in indigenous institutional order" (Boettke et al. 2008, 354). Coproducing the design of the experiment, as Ostrom suggested in general for educational institutions in our society (1991), could serve as a bridge connecting the exogenous order of the intervention with the social memory and history of the community. A more self-conscious study of the multiple levels of analysis required, that recognizes the contributions of those who receive the interventions, could yield better results[1].

FOCUS GROUPS

Following the results of Khwaja (2004) and Ostrom (1991), it is important that participants have a say in the design of the intervention, that is, to coproduce the intervention, in those nontechnical issues in which they possess knowledge which researchers lack. Based on the previous analysis of interventions, I identified four key areas in which local knowledge could be helpful: 1) when the best moment of the day for the intervention is, 2) how often should students be using the material, 3) whether computers should be used as complements or substitutes and 4) whether the material should be standardized. By local knowledge, I mean the knowledge of teacher and parents together, since they constitute the school community (the studies previously analyzed focus on primary schools, and it does not seem sound to consider students' opinion as to what is best for them at that age, albeit their preferences should be taken into account).

To better understand local knowledge in those areas, I carried out focus groups. As well as the previous studies (and to increase comparability), I did my research in a primary school. Similarly, I conducted focus groups with parents and instructors of a community with a high level of poverty, on the one hand because it is what the previous studies did, but also because one of the primary concerns of economics is to understand how to improve the living conditions of those at the bottom. Focus groups do not provide us conclusive results at a large scale, but they possess the same benefits of the case studies mentioned earlier. First, they serve to call into question the validity of the ways in which RCTs are conducted. Second, they can guide us on what to look for in other experiments, and finally, they can teach us how research-ers' assumptions operate and a way in which they may be affecting research itself. Besides, compared with other large-scale methodologies, focus groups are relatively cheap. A drawback, however, remains, which also applies to the RCTs studied: the results from one community are not easily generalizable for other communities. The basis for comparison is that these are all margin-alized communities located in underdeveloped countries.

The school Escuela Primaria Federal Liberación is located in the suburbs of Tehuacán, a municipality with a high level of poverty according to the index of poverty elaborated by the National Council of Population (CONAPO), despite being located in the suburbs of the second most important city of the state of Puebla. For the academic year 2020–2021 it had 492 students regis-tered for all six grades offered. There are 17 instructors working full time and 6 working half time, the latter mostly teaching the least important subjects of the curriculum, such as a painting workshop that every classroom takes once a week. According to government data there are only two computers at the school, which makes it a good candidate for a CAL intervention.

Two other reasons were important in choosing that school. First, although it is located in a highly marginalized community, it is close enough to a large urban center so that both parents and students are constantly exposed to the use to computers and other types of electronic devices, and appreciate that they may be useful in their lives. Parents from schools located in rural, isolated communities may see no point in using computers when all the activities in their daily life are related to physical work with no electronic device required. Second, due to the lockdown imposed after the outbreak of COVID-19, I was unable to talk in-person to the principal of any potential school to be included in the study, and therefore I had to rely on previous research for contact information.

I first contacted the school principal to explain the purpose of the research and how it would work, assuring him complete confidentiality. The principal agreed, emphasizing that he would neither encourage nor discourage participation in focus groups, but only provide me with emails of both parents and professors to contact them, so that participation would be completely voluntary. I was not allowed to conduct interviews with students, due to privacy concerns and the fact that interviews had to be conducted online. Also, the principal asked me not to record any of the focus groups or to disclose any names. I was only allowed to take notes and refer to the role played (i.e., instructor or parent) and gender (i.e., male or female).

Out of 492 students, 451 had an email account for the parents registered. I sent an email to the 451 parents and the 23 teachers, explaining the research project and the purpose of the focus group. I clearly stated that I have no connection with the government in any form, that their identities would be totally confidential, that they would not be recorded and that participation was completely voluntary. Only 41 parents and 10 instructors answered the first email, out of which all the instructors were full time. I then proceeded to propose three different days and times at which to participate. Only 6 teachers (including the school principal) and 9 parents answered back to schedule their participation. Thus, I divided the groups evenly in three, so that 2 instructors and 3 parents participated in each. In the end, however, only 5 instructors (including the school principal) and 7 parents participated. One teacher apologized a few minutes before the focus group for not being able to participate, and two parents did not show up in the last focus group. This, nonetheless, is the number of participants required to achieve what has been termed "theoretical saturation" (Breen 2006, 466).

Following Krueger (2008) on how the interview should be organized and the different types of questions that ought to be included to make a smooth transition from the opening to the topics that the researcher is most interested in, table 3.1 presents the questions posed. Before the start of every focus group I emphasized the importance of not only giving their opinion but the reason why they thought it was the case.

All three of the focus groups lasted for 40 minutes, the maximum amount allowed by Zoom, which also had the benefit of avoiding asking too much time of the participants (Daniels, et. al. 2019). It was necessary in all three focus groups to ask the last four questions, because in none of them did the participants specify the hour of the day, the number of sessions per week or month, whether computers should be used as substitutes or complements and whether the content should be personalized when the general question of guidelines was asked.[2]

Table 3.1. Focus Group Questions. *Source:* **Carlos Alejandro Noyola Contreras, follow-ing Krueger, Richard A., and Mary Anne Casey. 2008.** *Focus Groups: A Practical Guide for Applied Research.* **New York City, NY: Sage**

Krueger's categories	*Questions*
Opening question	What experiences have you had with the use of computers for learning inside the classroom?
Introductory question	In what ways have the computers been introduced?
Transition question	If computers were to be introduced for learning in the school, what guidelines and /or restrictions would you establish so that students benefit the most?
Key questions	Should computers be used at any particular hour of the day (e.g., in the afternoon, during lunch time, in the morning)?
	How many times per week should computers be used? (number of sessions)
	Should computers be used for exercises (complements of teachers), for learning new topics (substitutes of teachers), or both?
	Should the material presented in the computer be tailored to each student's needs or standardized?
Ending question	Finally, is there anything related to computer-based learning methods which has not been discussed and you would like to add?

PATTERNS IN FOCUS GROUPS

Focus groups suggest that local knowledge often is in sharp contrast with conclusions from previous studies. The conflict between the design of the economists and local knowledge points toward the importance of local inputs for designing the experiment. Coproduction is one way to solve this conflict. There are at least three patterns that emerged from the focus groups in which this is clear and deserves attention. First, there is a consensus among parents and teachers that classes with computers should be conducted in the morning. However, no study established that classes should be in the morning, and some included classes in the afternoon and even during lunch. The explanation, in most cases, that students' performance becomes worse in the evening, but is better after a night of sleep, is in line with evidence that even court decisions are influenced by external factors, such as mental depletion caused by lack of food, which means that cases scheduled for the first hours of the day receive more attention than those scheduled closer to lunch time (Glöckner 2016). This is in sharp contrast with two of the studies previously analyzed (Banerjee, et al. 2007; Fang Lai, et al. 2015), where computer assisted sessions often took place after school day. This shows the importance of studying carefully the structured-situation defined before, in this case the incentives faced by students: no one is willing to pay attention to a class when the body is asking for food.

Second, there is a clear pattern pointing toward the importance of time for computer usage (i.e., students cannot use them as they please) and a broad consensus that there should be one session per day of computer assisted learning. In the case of the former, the reasons varied from concerns of distractions on the web or other applications unrelated to the class to concerns about students mistaking computers for the goal or the way to solve everything, instead of understanding that they are simply a medium, a useful tool, but only one among many others. This clearly opposes to the guidelines of most of the studies analyzed (Barrera-Osorio and Linden 2009; Cristia, et al. 2017; Mo, et al. 2013), where either teachers were to decide how to use the computers or students were given a laptop and allowed to take it home after school to use as they please, in both cases without any time limit. In the case of the latter (one session per day of computer assisted learning), the reasoning was, on the one hand, that for students to use the technology proficiently they have to practice constantly; while on the other hand it is important to remind them that it is one tool of many available, reason why one teacher even argued in favor of having one day without using computers at school. Almost all of the RCTs left the number of sessions unspecified, and in the study in which the number of sessions was specified (Banerjee, et al. 2007) students used computers only during two sessions per week, not once a day, as local knowledge here suggests.

The last point in which local knowledge does not match the research design implemented in the RCTs is the consensus that the material presented in the computer should be tailored to each student's needs. However, only one study did so (Banerjee, et al., 2007). Nonetheless, here it is important to recognize the possible challenges that personalized material implies in terms of time and effort. Although it was pointed out by one teacher that the whole aim of the educational system is to be personalized, due to the different needs of each student, it was also emphasized (in the last focus group) that there are real limitations toward achieving this goal, such as the lack of resources in schools in poor communities (as the one studied here) and the often prohibitively large number of students per instructor that overwhelms their workload.

The other key point to highlight from the focus groups is that the understanding of the local community need not match, and in fact is in some cases very different, from what researchers assume. Boltanski and Thévenot (1999) address this problem when examining disputes without violence, and how can they be solved. The first step, they explain, is that participants have to reach common ground to understand each other. In their words, what is needed is "a common definition which allows to connect this situation with other ones identified as similar" (Boltanski and Thévenot 1999, 361). This is to what they refer to as "the establishment of equivalence" (Boltanski and Thévenot 1999, 361), when two or more parties (usually drawing on similar experiences) agree on the meaning of concepts that allow them to interact, discuss and reach agreements. In ordinary life, however, establishing equivalencies is usually not subject to deliberate reflection, as they explain, and that is why, if we are to understand the "the critical operations performed by actors" it is crucial, they maintain, "to recognize the normative principles which underlie the critical activity of ordinary persons" (Boltanski and Thévenot 1999, 364). Here is where the focus groups come in, by allowing us to understand the motives of ordinary members of the school community.

Economists value education because it builds human capital and there is evidence that human capital translates into better living conditions (Burgess, 2016). Furthermore, researchers, by designing interventions that involve activities for students after school hours, implicitly assume that their only occupation is to study, as is normally the case in developed countries. Reality, however, is sometimes quite different, as the results from these focus groups show. Almost a third of those parents who participated in the research explained that their children perform important duties immediately after school and for the rest of the day, either helping with the family business or taking care of the farm animals they possess (pigs, turkeys, etcetera). For them, school is not the only duty of their children, and perhaps not even the most important, since working in the family store or feeding the animals is crucial for family income. Thus, in light of the argument proposed by Boltanski and Thévenot (1999), there is a lack of equivalence in the relationship between the researchers and those who receive the intervention. When they think of education researchers and parents from poor communities in underdeveloped countries may not be understanding the same thing. While researchers conceive children fully dedicated to school, at least for a significant part of the students here school is simply one among other activities. Given that four out of the five interventions required involvement of students after school hours, it is clear that the little success of the interventions is, at least in part, probably due to a lack of understanding on the part of the researchers of the local conditions. However, this lack of understanding could be solved by allowing the school community to provide inputs (i.e., knowledge about the specific situation of the school, teachers and students) for the intervention design.

However, the results should not be overstated. First, although here parents and teachers generally agreed on the ways in which the intervention should be carried out, this need not be the case. In fact, it could be that parents and teachers have different preferences and therefore conflicting views on how to implement an intervention. In that case further research would be needed in order to analyze the ways in which they differ and the possible impact of those differences in the design of the RCT. On the other hand, even though the number of participants is such that theoretical saturation is reached (Breen 2006), the group is not representative, and there is a possibility that focus groups suffer from selection bias. A new study conducted in person, once the health situation improves, would make it possible to include a greater proportion of the school community to better understand the patterns in local knowledge. Nonetheless, these results call into question the centralized approach adopted by economists conducting RCTs while suggesting that a public economy approach in which interventions are coproduced by researchers and the school community could be a way for researchers to overcome their lack of knowledge about the particularities of the school they are dealing with.

EVALUATING THE IMPACT OF LOCAL KNOWLEDGE

The previous analysis reveals the salient importance of local participation when designing interventions to evaluate the effect of computers, but this is not conclusive of whether computers have a positive or negative effect on learning outcomes. For that, it is necessary to evaluate interventions including local participation against groups with an intervention without local participation. This analysis extends easily to evaluate results of a design that involves local participation against a group where no intervention was conducted.

In this case, there are three groups of participants: teachers, parents, and students. Although the intervention aims to improve the outcome of the latter, its success critically depends on the actions of both teachers and parents, especially when the students are in primary school, as is the case in the interventions previously studied. Second, it is difficult to argue that primary school students can be trusted when it comes to what is best to improve their learning outcomes. Moreover, as I explained before, I was not allowed to interview students due to privacy concerns. Thus, local participation focuses on teachers and parents.

If an intervention is to consider local participation, interviews and/or focus groups, such as the ones I implemented here, should be the first step, so that the results can be incorporated into it. According to the results of the three focus groups that I carried out, there is consensus regarding what to do in four important aspects of the intervention: computer assisted learning sessions should be scheduled in the morning (not after school or during lunch time); one session per day should be provided; the material should be tailored to each student's needs and time limits should be established for computer usage. The latter, however, is implicitly guaranteed if either classes are only scheduled during the morning or there is only one session per day, or both. Thus, we are left with three important variables to include in the analysis.

A simple randomized control trial looking at whether the inclusion of local knowledge on interventions on education works would have the control group get the intervention according to the design made by the researchers without any input from the participants, and the treatment group receive the intervention according to a research design that includes one class per day with computers, only in the morning, and with material tailored to each student's needs. Since coproduction in this case would imply that teachers and parents play an active role in the intervention, and here they shape the intervention design and play an active role in the implementation (teachers deliver classes using computers and parents bring children to school and help them with homework), we could think of teachers and parents coproducing the intervention (Ostrom 1996). The equation for evaluating the intervention would look like this:

$$Y_i = B_i \beta + X_i^T \delta + \epsilon_i$$

One option is to randomize at the school level, in which case Y_i is the outcome variable for school i. Another option, however, is to randomize at the community level (Y_i is the outcome variable for municipality i, for instance), although this could be significantly more costly in practice, both because more equipment is needed and more people have to be interviewed. Of course, whatever the level, the randomization should take place among schools or communities that are as similar as possible. One selection criterion, for example, could be to focus only on schools of marginalized areas of certain regions, as previous studies have done. B_i is a dummy variable indicating whether the school was treated or not, and X_i^T is a vector of controls, which includes factors likely to explain some of the unexplained variance in the outcome variable, such as the average income for a household within the municipality where the school is located, the average length of parents' schooling in the community, the crime rate (for every 100 people), a dummy indicating whether the mayor of the municipality belongs to the party of the state's governor, and the percentage of high achievers that the school had prior to the experiment. If it is still believed that the intervention that does not take into account the opinion of participants may have an effect, the analysis can be easily extended, as I said before, to including a third group, where no school receives an intervention, and B_i would simply take three values, allowing to compare the results of the schools receiving both types of the intervention between themselves and with those in the new control group.

As objective measures of learning outcomes, results of standardized tests, the most widely used measure when it comes to education, are useful as indicators of impacts in the short or medium-term. Although more complicated and costly, measures of impacts in the long-run could include probability of attending college and, once they enter the labor market, earnings. An objective measure of motivation both for students and teachers is absenteeism, because enthusiastic teachers and students who enjoy their classes will try to attend school as much as possible. Another measure, if we think that an intervention could motivate students enough so that they encourage other children to attend school, is enrollment. This is especially true if the intervention is carried out in poor communities, where it could have spillover effects in the form of more parents sending their children to school.

Subjective measures of achievement and motivation can come from well-designed interviews after the intervention is over. It cannot be assumed that participants will have incentives to tell the truth when the intervention involves providing them with costly technology. The risk of collecting information that is not accurate cannot be eliminated, but it can be lessened to some extent. For instance, it is crucial to let participants know that the computers provided are not conditioned to obtaining positive results, and that they will keep them regardless of the results of the experiment and their responses to the questionnaires. Once teachers and students know that computers will remain theirs, it is more probable they will be willing to report any negative outcome or drawback of the intervention.

Even though it is not very believable that some schools decide not to participate in the experiment, it could be, as the study conducted by Barrera-Osorio and Linden (2009) suggests, that the equipment provided in the intervention is not used for learning purposes. Therefore, schools should be monitored carefully. One option is to benefit from computer logs, like Julian P. Cristia et al. (2017) did, to supervise the use of computers constantly. Another option is to install software in the equipment that blocks any application not authorized by the researchers (i.e., only applications of mathematics and analytical reading can be used).

Perhaps it could be argued it is not ethical to simply divide schools that are very similar in their level of poverty and allow some to benefit from new technology for instruction but not the rest. Following the scheme of other highly successful government programs (e.g., Progresa in Mexico) the program could well evaluate learning outcomes of students after 18 months (or another fixed period determined by researchers as sufficient to detect any meaningful effect) and, if the results are found to be significant and positive, all schools considered eligible according to the selection criteria could be given the same technology, subject to the same rules.

CONCLUSION

I have shown that previous studies looking at the effect of using computers on learning outcomes, considered of high quality by other researchers, have not paid attention to local knowledge when designing their interventions. This, I showed, implies they lack a full understanding of the configurational character of the situation in which their interventions work (a thing I have called the structured-situation): interventions change the environment, the incentives faced by participants, and thus it is important to study how the intervention will affect them before the implementation.

Based on the results of Khwaja (2004) and Ostrom (1991), supporting the idea that local participation in nontechnical decisions significantly contributes toward the success of an intervention, and following the emphasis of the studies analyzed, I conducted three focus groups with parents and teachers (the school community) of a primary school located in a poor municipality of the state of Puebla, Mexico. Questions were designed based on the important nontechnical aspects of the interventions studied in this article: best time of the day to conduct computer assisted classes, number of sessions per week, whether computers should work as complements or substitutes of teachers and whether material presented in computers should be tailored to each student's needs or standardized.

While there was debate regarding the use of technology as complement or substitute, teachers and parents mostly reached consensus in the other three aspects: classes should be conducted in the morning, one session should be conducted per day and the material should be personalized. Another point constantly emphasized both by parents and instructors was the importance of time limits for the use of computers. This is in sharp contrast with the high quality studies analyzed, in which classes were often delivered during lunch time or after school hours, sessions were for the most part unspecified, left for the school to decide or, in the case of interventions involving the delivery of a laptop to every child, with no time limits to computer usage; in the case of standardized or personalized material, only one study had the material tailored to each student's needs.

The success of interventions could be affected by the fact that different needs of the community have been overlooked. Researchers assume primary students devote their time only to school, or at least to be their primary duty, whereas for many children in poor communities school is one duty among many, and perhaps not the most important. Some parents explained that their children, for example, are in charge of feeding farm animals or helping in the family store, both important for household income. Such students, therefore, cannot take part in activities after school hours, such as extra classes, tutoring programs or using laptops for learning new topics in the afternoon, as was expected in the interventions studied here.

These results have important policy implications. Since a key goal of public policy, and economics in general, is to improve the well-being of society, and there is evidence that education is an important aspect of it, governments are interested in ways to improve the learning outcomes of students. From the results presented here, we can conclude that local knowledge can be a missing piece for designing a school curriculum that allows students to benefit the most from new technologies. This is the first step, and it makes clear that we cannot simply conclude from past research that computers are useless for learning across all settings. A new intervention that includes the three aspects identified by the local community studied here may provide the basis for better and more effective computer assisted learning.

REFERENCES

Banerjee, Abhijit V., Shawn Cole, Esther Duflo, and Leigh Linden. 2007. "Remedying Education: Evidence from Two Randomized Experiments in India." *Quarterly Journal of Economics* 122 (3): 1235–64.

Barrera-Osorio, Felipe, and Leigh L. Linden. 2009. "The Use and Misuse of Computers in Education: Evidence From a Randomized Controlled Trial of a Language Arts Program." *World Bank Policy Research Working Paper* 4836.

Boettke, Peter J., Cristopher J. Coyne, and Peter T. Leeson. 2008. "Institutional Stickiness and the New Development Economics." *American Journal of Economics and Sociology* 67 (2): 331–58.

Boltanski, Luc, and Laurent Thévenot. 1999. "The Sociology of Critical Capacity." *European Journal of Social Theory* 2 (3): 359–77.

Breen, Rosanna L. 2006. "A Practical Guide to Focus-Group Research." *Journal of Geography in Higher Education* 30 (3): 463–75.

Burgess, Simon. 2016. "Human Capital and Education: The State of the Art in the Economics of Education." *IZA Discussion Paper No.* 9885.

Cristia, Julian, Pablo Ibarrarán, Santiago Cueto, Ana Santiago, and Eugenio Severín. 2017. "Technology and Child Development: Evidence from the One Laptop per Child Program." *American Economic Journal: Applied Economics* 9 (3): 295–320.

Daniels, Nicola, Patricia Gillen, Karen Casson, and Iseult Wilson. 2019. "STEER: Factors to Consider When Designing Online Focus Groups Using Audiovisual Technology in Health Research." *International Journal of Qualitative Methods* 18: 1–11.

Davis, Gina, and Elinor Ostrom. 1991. "A Public Economy Approach to Education: Choice and Co-Production." *International Political Science Review* 12 (4): 313–35.

Glewwe, Paul W., Eric A. Hanushek, Sarah D. Humpage, and Renato Ravina. 2013. "School Resources and Educational Outcomes in Developing Countries: A Review of the Literature from 1990 to 2010." In *Education Policy in Developing Countries*, Edited by Paul W. Glewwe, 13–64. Chicago, IL: University of Chicago Press.

Glöckner, Andreas. 2016. "The Irrational Hungry Judge Effect Revisited: Simulations Reveal that the Magnitude of the Effect is Overestimated." *Judgement and Decision Making* 11 (6): 601–10.

Hanushek, Eric A., and Ludger Woessmann. 2011. "The Economics of International Differences in Educational Achievement." In *Handbook of the Economics of Education* 3, Edited by Eric A. Hanushek, Stephen J. Machin, Ludger Woessmann, 89–200. Amsterdam, Netherlands: North Holland.

Ijaz Khwaja, Asim. 2004. "Is Increasing Community Participation Always a Good Thing?" *Journal of the European Economic Association* 2 (2–3): 427–36.

Krueger, Richard A., and Mary Anne Casey. 2008. *Focus Groups: A Practical Guide for Applied Research.* New York City, NY: Sage.

Lai, Fang, Renfu Luo, Linxiu Zhang, Xinzhe Huang, and Scott Rozelle. 2015. "Does Computer-Assisted Learning Improve Learning Outcomes? Evidence from a Randomized Experiment in Migrant Schools in Beijing." *Economics of Education Review* 47: 34–48.

McEwan, Patrick, J. 2015. "Improving Learning in Primary Schools of Developing Countries: A Meta-Analysis of Randomized Experiments." *Review of Educational Research* 85 (3): 353–94.

Mo, Di, Johan Swinnen, Linxiu Zhang, Hongmei Yi, Qinghe Qu, Matthew Boswell, and Scott Rozelle. 2013. "Can One-to-One Computing Narrow the Digital Divide and the Educational Gap in China? The Case of Beijing Migrant Schools." *World Development* 46: 14–29.

Ostrom, Elinor. 1986. "An Agenda For the Study of Institutions." *Public Choice* 48: 3–25.

———. 1996. "Crossing the Great Divide: Coproduction, Synergy, and Development." *World Development* 24 (6): 1073–87.

———. 2011. "Background on the Institutional Analysis and Development Framework." *Policy Studies Journal* 39 (1): 7–27.

Schotter, Andrew. 1981. *The Economic Theory of Social Institutions.* Cambridge, UK: Cambridge University Press.

Wynne, Brian. 1989. "Sheepfarming after Chernobyl: A Case Study in Communicating Scientific Information." *Environment: Science and Policy for Sustainable Development* 31 (2): 10–39.

NOTES

1. Neglecting the first-hand knowledge of teachers would be similar to those politicians who, without knowledge of the particular situation and any consideration for those involved, gave orders to farmers that did not match with reality in Wales, after the region was affected by radiation in the 1980s, thus causing further damage to their business (Wynne 1989). In 1986, the Chernobyl accident took place. In the following months, clouds carrying radioactive material spread the particles around Europe.

Particularly, the heavy rain in northern England caused a substantial portion of radio-active particles to fall in the region of Cumbria and North Wales. This prompted the government to intervene in order to prevent sheep exposed to the particles to be consumed by the public. But the way in which government officials responded, because they ignored the specific context, was highly inefficient.

2. For a detailed description of the focus groups, please contact the author.

PART II

Case Studies in Social Coordination

Chapter 4

Destruction to Beauty

The Polycentric Adaptive Reuse of the Torpedo Factory

Olivia Gonzalez

When walking into the Torpedo Factory Art Center (TFAC), visitors face a minimalistic aesthetic—glazed concrete floors, white walls, and high ceilings with industrial lighting and piping.[1] Stairways, railings, and studio doors are painted red and blue accent colors to brighten up the space. Some walls exhibit artwork or flyers about upcoming exhibits. The designers took great effort to represent the thriving art community that now populates it, without obscuring the building's past. In fact, still, on display on the building's main floor today lies a 3,000-pound Mark 14 torpedo case—21 feet long and painted green.

This same torpedo case was manufactured in the building 77 years ago (Lewis 1983). The TFAC was originally known as the U.S. Naval Torpedo Station and was built by the federal government in 1918 to act as a naval munitions factory in Alexandria, Virginia. After its decommission following WWII, the facility changed ownership and was eventually transformed into the community art center we see today.

The revitalized art center provides a glimpse into the city's industrial past. Although this region is currently recognized as a cultural highlight of the Washington-DC area, it was previously just one of many industrial buildings that formed the city's identity as a center for national defense during the mid-twentieth century. Following WWII, the torpedo factory became less relevant, and the building became a storage facility for government records. In 1969, Alexandria bought this complex from the federal government for $1.6 million (Torpedo Factory Art Center 2022).

Although there was a shared sentiment among city officials that some of the industrial buildings would be torn down to provide more green space and access to the waterfront, they did not have a definitive plan. Concurrently, the community's Art League—an organization providing studios for local artists—was looking for a new space. Artists from the Art League, led by Marian Van Landingham, identified the old torpedo factory complex as a prime area to relocate.

Marian Van Landingham drew up a proposal for city officials that painted the picture of an adaptive reuse experiment. She proposed using the complex as a space for art studios where visitors could come to watch painters, sculptors, and printmakers, among others, while they immersed themselves in their work. She envisioned the space as a center for artists to work and for the public to learn.

The transformation of the torpedo factory building presents a unique case study of bottom-up polycentric development. Many stakeholders in the community were involved, ranging from artists and architects to planners, developers, and engineers. The interactions among these local groups, metropolitan leaders, and federal leaders demonstrate a polycentricity success story. The artists in this case study acted as the entrepreneurial drivers of change.

This was a success story to the extent the artists acted as social entrepreneurs to help solve the collective action problem associated with identifying a productive use for the torpedo factory building (Chamlee-Wright and Storr 2010). However, the artists also acted as an interest group that benefited from government favoritism. They had unique access to the torpedo factory building under a subsidized public-partnership arrangement. This creates a unique set of additional problems where the incentives facing artists do not lead them to manage public resources most efficiently.

This chapter explores what factors contributed to the success of the transformation of the torpedo factory building and highlights the areas where it fell short. The project may be a national model for adaptive reuse, but it was not perfect. The TFAC transformation is a helpful case study for examining what factors go into a successful adaptive reuse development project, while also highlighting how poor institutional arrangements can hold it back.

I define success as the identification of a productive use for an underutilized building. The TFAC complex could have been completely demolished to allow for more green space along the Alexandria waterfront area, or it could have been repurposed entirely for housing or commercial uses. It is difficult to identify the "objectively" best use when such a decision involves incorporating the many preferences of everyone in the community. The TFAC project can be assessed with regard to the social coordination that resulted in solving the knowledge problem facing governmental officials.

For this chapter, I use the Institutional Analysis and Development (IAD) framework to analyze the TFAC transformation as a case study in polycentric development aimed at solving the collective action problem; the problem I will define more explicitly in the next section.

I study the transformation through an institutional lens using an analytical narrative. I rely heavily on Marian Van Landingham's book for representing the artists' perspective of the TFAC project (Van Landingham 1999). To provide a more balanced understanding of what happened, I also rely on economic assessment reports, news stories, and original language of rules and regulations influencing the project. Using this approach, I hope to shed light on why the revitalization of this military building succeeded, while attempts in other cities have not.

THE COLLECTIVE ACTION PROBLEM

Adaptive reuse is a process by which a building is repurposed, often with the goal of maintaining its historic features (Austin et al. 1988; Mohamed et al. 2017). The main problem we are analyzing, however, is not an adaptive reuse problem alone. Due to the involvement of many different actors in the community and the public resources at stake, the torpedo factory project is also a collective action problem.

A collective action problem arises when a group of individuals in society would be better off if they were to cooperate to accomplish something that would benefit all of them, but they fail to do so (Brown, McLean, and McMillan 2018). This is usually due to poor incentives or conflicting interests between these individuals. Although every member in the community could potentially benefit from cooperating to find a use for the torpedo factory, the cost of coordinating with everyone would be quite high. Therefore, it is usually easier for smaller groups of people to coordinate to solve problems, and that is why interest groups often step in to do so (Olson 1965). These interest groups are often motivated to act because of the concentrated benefits they would receive (obtaining a subsidy or the approval to utilize a government building, for example) and their ability to diffuse costs over the entire population (taxes to fund the subsidy or the maintenance of the building). Many public policy problems are collective action problems.

In chapter 1 of this volume, Emily Chamlee-Wright introduced a conceptual device that is useful here. The EBS-Cap framework she introduces helps filter through potential projects the government could take on to help solve collective action problems in many different contexts. As a quick refresher, it advocates that the government take on projects that are "essential," "big," "simple," and for which the government itself is "capable" to take on. In the

TFAC's case, I define the collective action problem at play as the following: Finding a productive use for the derelict torpedo factory and corresponding waterfront area along the Potomac River in Alexandria, Virginia. Using the EBS-Cap framework, it quickly becomes clear this problem is not uniquely suited for the government to solve alone.

Adaptive Reuse is Not Essential, Big, or Simple

The project of revitalizing the torpedo factory and the corresponding water-front was only essential in the sense that doing so would bring about more economic activity for the community. It was not, however, essential in the same way as expediently responding to 911 calls or providing high quality and inclusive educational options to disadvantaged youth in the community. It was not an essential problem for the Alexandria City government to solve relative to its other commitments and priorities.

It also certainly was not a big problem, on a national or local scale. More efficiently organizing Alexandria's economic activity was not a problem for residents in Denver or Miami, nor should it be a big problem for Alexandria itself. Although it probably at times felt like a big problem to city planners considering the years it took to solve, I would not define it as big in the sense that it was a project that was beyond the capabilities of the individuals, households, and community of Alexandria, as Chamlee-Wright defines big projects in her framework in chapter 1 of this volume.

I would define the problem as complex, however. Identifying a use for the torpedo factory was no simple task. It might appear simple because of the way we make decisions about the use of our own resources every day. On an individual level, we are all deciding what to do with resources all the time. I do so when I pick out a home to buy. A company does so when it decides what buildings to rent out as office space. This calculus becomes more complex the more you scale it. The nature of the complexity is not solely a function of scale, however.

The Knowledge Problem Facing Alexandria

The decision of what house I should buy or how an office building should be utilized are both decisions made in market contexts. Prices of homes can tell me a lot about the market. I may not know precisely all the reasons why houses in an area are relatively expensive, but they will certainly influence when I can buy. Or if they consistently stay high, I may need to look further from my job's location. In extremely dense areas like New York City and San Francisco, home prices are famously high due to the combination of high demand and insufficient supply of housing. This is certainly the case in the Washington-DC area surrounding the torpedo factory as well.

Prices help solve a knowledge problem for homeowners and renters who are on the search to decide what job market to locate near. On the micro-scale, prices influence everyone's behavior and help us to respond to the ebbs and flows of resource scarcity. In the aggregate, this amounts to more efficiently managed resources, but not due to the control of any one individual or organization.

The collective action problem of finding a use for the torpedo factory is ultimately a knowledge problem. The relevant information needed to most efficiently find a productive use for the torpedo factory was, and still is, distributed among the minds of many individuals in Alexandria. As economist F. A. Hayek (1945) has famously written, this knowledge problem is most effectively solved by the price system. Prices help to coordinate individuals in a dynamic process that tends toward the efficient management of resources. This dynamic process is what helps tap into the many different minds of the relevant individuals affected by a decision.

Another key lesson from Hayek's work is that there are qualitative characteristics of knowledge making it impossible to aggregate to any one place or person, especially for tacit knowledge. This is why the problem we are facing here is not a simple one; one that cannot be delegated to a local planner to solve.

The main role for the government in this context is to improve its policies and rules in such a way that leaves more room for efficient bottom-up responses. This gets at the last criteria for judging whether a project should be taken on by the government: is the government capable? Is it well-positioned to provide a solution to the problem? In the case of the torpedo factory, the government was definitely capable of using the building, but not necessarily capable of finding the *most productive use* for its use. This distinction is key, and the reason is because of the knowledge problem.

The importance of adequately utilizing the appropriate knowledge is also highlighted in adaptive reuse literature (Alauddin, Ishak, and Shuib 2016). Adaptive reuse projects often raise complexity in the design and construction process, especially when compared to conventional new building projects. Adaptive reuse projects can suffer when there is incomplete and inaccurate design information (Shipley, Utz, and Parsons 2006; Karim et al. 2007) and a dearth of capable professional expertise (Ball 1999; Kurul 2007). Availability of historical information of the building is also key (Shehata et al. 2015). Alauddin, Ishak, and Shuib (2016) highlight the role of leveraging knowledge from project to project over time.

Similar to Hayek, Alauddin, Ishak, and Shuib (2016) corroborate the importance of understanding the difference between tacit and explicit knowledge. Explicit knowledge, when depicted in drawings, reports, or historical information, is easier to aggregate to inform decision-making. Tacit knowledge, on the other hand, is related to an individual's mental maps, beliefs, and paradigms. Often, it is embedded in our social and organizational relationships through shared norms.

These aspects make strategies for transferring knowledge between projects particularly important. Knowledge is often dispersed amongst architects, surveyors, engineers, project managers, city planners, and contractors. This literature emphasizes the nature of knowledge and how it contributes to managing the intellectual capital of project team members as being one of the greatest challenges in adaptive reuse projects (Kululanga and McCaffer 2001). I would like to connect this body of research with Hayek's work on the economic knowledge problem. They are related in that they both imply tacit knowledge makes it particularly difficult, if not impossible, for knowledge to be aggregated to a central location for planning purposes. Hayek would likely respond to this research by adding that knowledge is similarly dispersed in the initial identification of a building's promise as a site for adaptive reuse, not only in the transferring of knowledge between already identified projects.

THE INSTITUTIONAL ANALYSIS AND DEVELOPMENT FRAMEWORK

What makes TFAC's cooperative venture work where others around the country have failed? The combination of individuals seems to be an important factor. Everyone pulls his or own weight. There are engineers, creative thinkers, and those like Pat Monk, who was a physicist and is now a full-time sculptor. And there is Kathleen Kelly, a fine printmaker, who is one of the rocks of the TFAC as it stands today. Kelly is steady and undaunted when problems arise. She copes extremely well and is a great problem solver. Each person serves a particular role in making the TFAC work. (Goldman 1989, 72)

This is an excerpt of TFAC artist Betsy Schein Goldman's writing who tries to get at the root of TFAC's success. Individual ingenuity was no doubt a key factor in the TFAC's success. What is left out of Goldman and others' accounts is the role institutions played. The TFAC artists had to navigate a variety of rules and regulations when trying to secure space for themselves. Exploring the role institutions play does not have to shortchange the resourcefulness of the TFAC artists. Instead, it opens up dialogue for what factors may be unduly inhibiting just as creative and capable individuals in other localities.

By institutions I mean the rules, norms, and shared strategies constraining the behavior of all individuals involved in the TFAC transformation. Institutions can be formal—like the official policies and rules of the city about what buildings can be developed in certain areas. Or they can be informal—the norms and culture in a community can be more or less encouraging of the type of coordination the initial artist community employed to get the TFAC project started. Together, these institutions create the "rules of the game" facing individuals as they interact with each other in society (North 1990; North 1991).

To say the TFAC's transformation was because of the people alone would imply that locals in other cities that have attempted but have so far failed to get community art centers off the ground, are simply lacking ambition. What often stands between an individual and the successful completion of a revitalization project is the institutional environment that they face.

Although entrepreneurship is a characteristic that is accessible to any person, entrepreneurial *opportunities* can vary by institutional context. Economists Peter Boettke and Christopher Coyne (2009) describe how entrepreneurial energies can manifest in different institutional environments. Institutions have this effect because they influence the payoffs individuals face when making decisions. Social entrepreneurs, like the artists involved with forming the TFAC, do not face the same payoffs as conventional entrepreneurs that create for-profit businesses in the completely private sphere. This is because the artists did so under the umbrella of a nonprofit organization.

Although they did not operate under a strict profit motive, they were still incredibly motivated and entrepreneurial; the artists just had to respond to unique incentives and feedback mechanisms that came with the institutional landscape they found themselves in. Boettke and Coyne highlight how incentives change for individuals for these types of entrepreneurs across different spheres—public and private—in society, but they can also vary geographically. Social entrepreneurs in Alexandria, Virginia, face different incentives than social entrepreneurs in Allentown, Pennsylvania.

Characteristics researchers have identified as important in adaptive reuse projects include, but are not limited to: environmental impacts (Sanchez, Esfahani, and Haas 2019), the era the original building was constructed in and the price of construction materials at the time of the conversion (Parpas and Savvides 2020), and cultural setting and local attitudes (Shen and Langston 2010; Rezaei, Rasouli and Azhdari 2018; Mehr and Wilkinson 2020).

Researchers have also highlighted the value that adapting commercial buildings provides to communities (Bullen 2007; Jones and Franck 2019). Through redevelopment, adaptive reuse projects can help manage resources more efficiently and revitalize areas economically (Vardopoulos et al. 2020).

Last but not least, adaptive reuse for the purpose of responding to manufacturing decline or abandoned industrial complexes, like in the case of the torpedo factory, is fairly common as well (Bottero, D'Alpaos and Oppio 2019; Louw 2016; Vecchio and Arku 2020). In this volume, chapter 5 by Julie Thomson-Gomez explores the political economy of military base closures that resulted from the Base Realignment and Closure (BRAC) commission. Communities unsure of what to do following a BRAC base closure in their area can also look to adaptive reuse as a potential way forward (Schliemann et al. 2017; Günçe and Misirlisoy 2014).

The role of institutions, on the other hand, has been understudied in the adaptive reuse literature. It has not been entirely neglected, but it has not been wholistically studied. Irdinal Afief and Harifuddin Thahir (2020) take into consideration land use planning and design for adaptive reuse projects, with a particular mindfulness about the role of zoning regulations. Bullen and Love (2011) identify building regulations and planning restrictions as common barriers to projects. Zoning regulations create constraints "within which adaptive reuse architects and developers must design their projects" (Nasta 2019, 130). In this volume, chapter 10 by M. Nolan Gray explores how these constraints are themselves the result of entrepreneurial discovery.

In order to understand the unique institutional landscape facing the TFAC artists, this chapter uses the Institutional Analysis and Development (IAD) framework. The IAD framework, originally developed by Elinor Ostrom (2005), is helpful for conceptually mapping out how institutions influence different situations. It starts with the "action situation," which is composed of participants that interact given a fabric of exogenous, or pre-existing contextual, variables. An action situation is the situation we are trying to understand.

Here I examine the transformation of the TFAC building as "an action situation." The contextual variables that paved the way for the TFAC's transformation all fit in one of the following three categories: (1) biophysical/material conditions, (2) attributes of the community, and (3) rules.

It is important to take stock of all contextual variables. Doing so helps provide a common language for understanding what took place and can further be applied for comparison to other situations.

Given these variables, I can examine how participants in the community interacted to revitalize the TFAC. The contextual variables are what is taken as given by the participants in an action situation. The participants are the local artists, city officials, developers, art associations, as well as the residents surrounding the TFAC who were initially apprehensive about the development. Next, I summarize the contextual variables of the TFAC revitalization action situation, which can all be seen in table 4.1.

Table 4.1. Contextual Variables of the TFAC Revitalization Action Situation. *Source:* Olivia Gonzalez

Variable	Category
Location of the TFAC building	Biophysical/material conditions
Rundown nature of the TFAC building and surrounding waterfront area	Biophysical/material conditions
Extreme durability of the TFAC building	Biophysical/material conditions
General dissatisfaction with the underuse of the torpedo plant buildings and waterfront area	Attributes of the community
Growing artist community looking for studio space	Attributes of the community
Rising rents for studio space in the waterfront area	Attributes of the community
The TFAC is located in the Old and Historic Alexandria District (OAHG), subject to Article 10–100 of the Zoning Ordinance.	Rules
All building alterations must go through the Board of Architectural Review (BAR), as outlined in the Zoning Ordinance.	Rules
Land along the waterfront under unclear property rights until 1981	Rules
The Economic Recovery Tax Act of 1981	Rules

Biophysical/Material Conditions

The Torpedo Factory Art Center building was not always the "central cultural anchor" it is today (Alexandria Archaeology 2010). It was at the heart of the industrial and commercial hub of Alexandria, Virginia, throughout the nineteenth and twentieth centuries. Alexandria's port along the waterfront area had always served as a critical resource, but its main purposes significantly evolved over this timeframe. It contributed to Alexandria's city growth following its inception and then became a critical resource throughout many wars. It was not until later in the twentieth century, when the need for the area as a national defense hub had declined, that the waterfront area had appreciated potential for cultural and recreational activities. By the 1970s, when artists in the community were looking for a new space, the torpedo plant buildings had depreciated in quality and value (Alexandria Archaeology 2010).

The extreme durability of the wartime buildings—which were built to withstand explosions—played a large role in the torpedo plant's fate. When city officials were debating what to do with the TFAC building, Deputy City Manager Rusch estimated total demolition plus cleanup would cost somewhere between $1 and $1.5 million (Van Landingham 1999, 64). Rusch's calculations showed that destroying the industrial buildings would cause the city

to lose money, whereas minimizing demolition and allowing private development of at least some buildings held promise for a return on investment. The
reality of the torpedo plant buildings' durability made the demolition of the
entire complex financially unlikely from the start.

Attributes of the Community

There was a general dissatisfaction with the underuse of the waterfront area,
held by city officials and local community members. Additionally, there was a
growing artist community looking for space to coordinate and interact within.
Many of the initial artists were military wives looking to combine their desire
for a creative outlet with their need to support their families (Goldman 1989).
The artist community was growing and studio rents had been rising.

Rules

The TFAC building is in the Old and Historic Alexandria District (OAHD),
a zoning district established by the City Council in 1946 (City of Alexandria,
Virginia). It was only the third designated historic district in the United States,
following the examples set by Charleston and New Orleans (Wadland 2018).
Alexandria's historic district was created with the goal "to protect community
health and safety, to promote the education, prosperity and general welfare of
the public through the identification, preservation, and enhancement of buildings, structures, landscapes, settings, neighborhoods, places, and features
with special historical, cultural, artistic, and architectural significance" ("The
Zoning Ordinance of the City of Alexandria, Virginia," Article X, Section
10–100). The City Council also created a Board of Architectural Review
(BAR). Every proposed plan for the torpedo plant buildings had to go through
the BAR as well as the City Council.

The OAHD is subject to regulations outlined in Article 10–100 in the
Zoning Ordinance. Buildings in this district are eligible for federal financial
incentives when they are placed on the National Register of Historic Places.

The zoning rules created a more onerous process for the TFAC artists than
if they were to propose such a project for development in non-historic city
districts. Demolition and renovations both have to be reviewed by the BAR,
in addition to more minor architectural elements like accessibility structures,
sheds, storm doors, gutters, and signs. For all of these issues, individuals
are subject to a strict appeals process if they wish to contest rejected permit
applications.

The BAR processes all applications according to standards set out in
the city's zoning ordinance. These standards are written for preserving and
protecting the historic district. They also work to make sure buildings are

harmonious with the "historic aspect of the George Washington Memorial Parkway" ("The Zoning Ordinance of the City of Alexandria, Virginia," Article X, Section 10–105).

The BAR was part of the many discussions between city officials, artists, and developers outlined in this chapter. When the request for proposals was issued to help draft a plan for the redevelopment of the whole waterfront area, developers' proposals were sent to the BAR in 1978 before being forwarded to the City's Planning Commission that would in turn provide advice to the City Council.

Beyond the zoning rules the artists and developers had to navigate, there was a significant change in property rights that influenced the attractiveness of the waterfront area. In October of 1981, the federal government and the City of Alexandria reached an agreement settling an eight-year-old suit over who owned the land along the Potomac River (Van Landingham 1999, 123). The federal government's lawsuit over the Alexandria City waterfront property was filed in 1973, but the federal government's claim to it went back to 1846 when Alexandria was retroceded to Virginia in one of the compromises that originated before the Civil War. The 1981 agreement clarified ownership, primarily by giving Alexandria City and private landowners clear titles to most of the disputed land (Battiata 1981).

This clarification of property rights significantly impacted the attractiveness of developing the waterfront area. David J. Chitlik, a city real estate assessor at the time is quoted in a Washington Post article as saying the land "literally went from no value to . . . one of the most desirable sites for development in the Washington area" (Murphy 1984).

This implies that between 1973 and 1983, the ownership of the waterfront area was uncertain (Battiata 1981). It is not surprising that it had not attracted a lot of attention from developers initially. There were not a lot of incentives to propose ideas. When property rights are insecure, entrepreneurs have less motivation to innovate because they cannot know for sure if what they contribute will be theirs to reap the rewards from.

This institutional change is especially important in light of Nobel Laureate Ronald Coase's theorem on property rights and transaction costs. His famous theorem states that in a world of zero transaction costs, any dispute over property rights can still result in an economically optimal solution, regardless of the initial distribution of the rights (Coase 1960). However, the real world rarely has zero transaction costs; therefore, the implication is that the initial distribution of property rights is essential in determining whether an optimal economic solution is reached. Coase has argued that the next best solution is to compare those institutional arrangements that can obtain a solution closest to that which would be derived by a world of zero transaction costs. This adds more context to the artists' decision to propose they occupy the torpedo plant buildings in 1974.

If the land surrounding the torpedo factory buildings was unattractive to developers, then the artists would have been facing less competition for the torpedo plant buildings. This is because the absence of secure property rights increased transaction costs for potential developers and artists alike. There was no clear competitive bidding process for the initial securing of the torpedo factory project. These aspects deterred developers while making the artists go through more hoops to get political attention when they initially presented their idea. Transaction costs included the time and effort Van Landingham and the other artists spent convincing politicians, planners, and members of the community to back their project.

It is not surprising a final decision on the redevelopment project was not made until 1982, after the clarification of property rights. Following the city's requests for proposals, developers would submit their ideas for redevelopment in 1978 long before the suit was settled, but this is likely because they were aware of the settlement in progress and they took a gamble hoping their proposals would be accepted by the time everything was settled; knowing that if they could get the contract just before property values would rise, they would be securing a huge opportunity. The growing expenses of the lawsuit and the costs it created for delaying development motivated the government to push for settlement in 1981 (Battiata 1981).

The city even made steps to prime the waterfront area for development in the years leading up to the lawsuit settlement. It updated its zoning plan for the waterfront area by setting height limits and rezoning much of the area. City officials desired redevelopment but also wanted to be cautious about preventing high-rise residential and industrial buildings from being constructed (Murphy 1984). It also gave the city veto power when federal officials would propose an elevated highway along the waterfront.

Another rules-based contextual variable, the Economic Recovery Tax Act of 1981, played a large role in influencing the leasing structure of the TFAC building. This 1981 act is well known for its sweeping tax cuts, but what is less known is how it created a tax loophole for local governments.

The TFAC renovations in the early 1980s cost the city $3.1 million in bond money. Deputy City Manager Clifford Rusch realized that if the city sold the TFAC building to a group of private investors and then leased the building back, it could save the city $1.2 million over 15 years. This option would still allow the city to buy back the TFAC building at its market value. Through the sale, the investment group could take advantage of income tax credits "associated with ownership and restoration of aging property and through standard depreciation credits" (Van Landingham 1999, 116). If the city held onto the building, it could not take advantage of the tax credits. But by selling the building and rebuying it later, it was passing on part of the cost of redevelopment to the federal treasury. By the mid-1980s, this tax loophole was repealed, and the city bought back the TFAC building in 1998 (Van Landingham 1999, 116).

All of these contextual variables—biophysical/material, community attributes, and rules—worked together to form the action situation of the TFAC revitalization project.

The Emergence of Polycentric Governance at the Torpedo Factory

The IAD framework helps illustrate the complexity of social coordination problems. The many contextual variables discussed here come together to produce the entangled political economy conditions preceding the TFAC's transformation. As discussed earlier in this chapter, the EBS-Cap framework helps us understand the adequate division of labor between government, markets, and civil society in any given collective action problem. This often means problems are more commonly solved by many overlapping layers of decision-making across these three institutional contexts rather than just one of them alone. Another way to describe this system is through the concept of polycentric governance.

In the eyes of individuals in the community, they saw two problems: (1) the underutilized TFAC building and waterfront area and (2) the lack of artistic community spaces. The way these problems were "solved" was through the interaction of many different individuals and groups in the community, or rather, through a "polycentric system."

To recall Ostrom's definition of polycentric, it means that there are "many centers of decision making that are formally independent of each other. Whether they actually function independently, or instead constitute an interdependent system of relations, is an empirical question in particular cases" (Ostrom, Tiebout, and Warren 1999, 31).

Before the TFAC was revitalized, the rundown waterfront area produced negative externalities for the community. What made the TFAC revitalization project successful was not that the government stepped in to internalize these negative externalities, but instead, that local artists discovered a more productive arrangement of resources through an entrepreneurial search (Kirzner 1997). They had a vision for a "preferred state of community affairs" and they worked to align their interests with others in the community in order to achieve this state of affairs (Ostrom, Tiebout, and Warren 1999, 35).

There was demand in the community for the torpedo factory buildings and the waterfront area to be redeveloped, but there was a constrained supply of ideas. The unclear property rights of the waterfront area until 1981 deterred

developers from stepping in, leaving more space for the artists to gain attention from city officials. The institutional landscape paved the way for the artists to propose their ideas and secure a three-year experiment for themselves.
It is clear they provided tremendous value to the community by entrepreneur-
ially identifying a use for the TFAC building and then revitalizing it.

Despite the onerous Architectural Review processes and limited resources,
the artists were able to successfully repurpose the old torpedo plant. The
interactions they had with the review board, city officials, planners, contractors, and developers is what paved the wave for further development of the
waterfront area. The cumulations of these interactions are what equates to
polycentric governance. It was not the Planning Commission's call for proposals, the artists' entrepreneurial effort, or the developers' resources alone
that produced the redevelopment outcomes.

Polycentric governance, originally formulated by Ostrom, Tiebout, and
Warren is best understood as a process (McGinnis 2019). Elinor Ostrom's
work exploring community-based commons management is the most popular
application of polycentricity (E. Ostrom 1990; E. Ostrom 2010; McGinnis
2019). Her main insight was that bottom-up resource management is most
likely to be sustainable if the rules governing them are nested within a broader
system of polycentric governance. This means we should not take for granted
the complex network of interactions that produce what we understand as
policy outcomes. McGinnis (2019, 52) writes: "in an ideal-typical system of
polycentric governance, a diverse array of public and private authorities with
overlapping domains of responsibility interact in complex and ever-changing
ways . . . "

Figure 4.1 displays a rough illustration of the many different groups
acting as centers of decision-making involved in the TFAC project. Each
decision-making center can be roughly grouped into one of three institutional
environments: (1) civil society, (2) government, or (3) markets. But some
groups and individuals do not fit cleanly in one institutional environment. I
illustrate this by making Marian Van Landingham's decision center overlap
both civil society and government, given her heavy involvement in both areas
over the years. There were many groups and individuals involved with the
TFAC project, but to list all of them would make the figure entirely too busy.
With the goal of creating a parsimonious illustration of polycentricity, I stick
to those included in figure 4.1 and also refrain from drawing explicit linkages
between each group. In reality, depicting all of the many complex relationships between each of the decision centers would be very difficult.

My goal has been to demonstrate that the transformation of the TFAC was
the result of these many different decision-making centers as they interacted
within the framework of the biophysical conditions, community attributes,
and rules-based contextual variables outlined earlier in table 4.1.

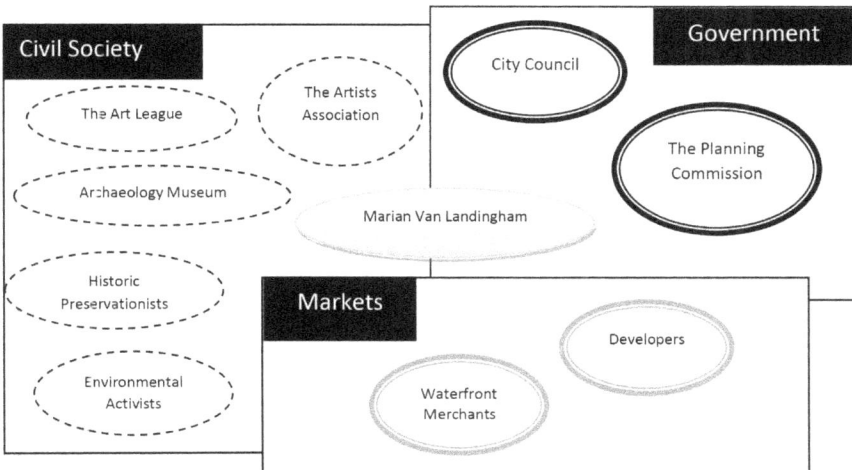

Figure 4.1. Polycentric Governance: Many Centers of Decision Making.
Source: Olivia Gonzalez.

The Many Hats of the Artists Here

Thus far, I have primarily referred to the TFAC artists as social entrepreneurs. A social entrepreneur is someone that exhibits the same characteristics as a "conventional" entrepreneur, but in many contexts that are not strictly market oriented. They often introduce "new products and services, utilizing new methods of production or delivery, exploiting new or untapped markets, employing new sources or kinds of raw materials, or developing new organizational forms" (Chamlee-Wright and Storr 2010, 151; see also Schumpeter 1934, 65). Entrepreneurship is a characteristic inherent to all human action. It is not something unique to a particular profession. Instead, the uniting theme among all social entrepreneurs is that their chief aim is "social transformation not monetary profits or political power. Though they may sometimes engage in business and political action, they have (short or long term) social change agendas" (Chamlee-Wright and Storr 2010, 151).

In the next few sections, I discuss the two different hats the artists wore in their community. The first is the hat of being a social entrepreneur. The artists clearly improved the community through very creative means. However, the line between social entrepreneur and interest group is an unclear one. Interest group dynamics are often highlighted in the public choice literature where each group is depicted as seeking the attention of politicians in order to gain their favor and obtain some sort of "rent," or privilege (Krueger 1974, Mitchell 2012). Although the traditional representation of interest groups, or rent-seekers as economists call them, is usually a greedy corporate lobbyist, this is also perhaps the most extreme example.

How do we distinguish the corporate lobbyist at Amazon seeking government subsidy for relocation of its headquarters from the group of artists seeking to improve their community? Theoretically, both meet the definition of "rent-seekers," but there certainly appears to be a qualitative difference. After discussing the general role of artists as social entrepreneurs, I will discuss the role of the artists as an interest group.

The Artists as Social Entrepreneurs

Applying Chamlee-Wright and Storr's insights from their (2010) paper on social entrepreneurship to the context of the torpedo factory, I argue that the artists in Alexandria similarly served three roles as social entrepreneurs in the community. The first role I have already discussed in great detail: the artists helped solve the collective action problem associated with finding a productive use for a dilapidated government surplus building. The artists also organized and engaged in community outreach in the community following the building's revitalization. Lastly, the artists provided art education and networking for the community.

The TFAC artists engaged in many entrepreneurial volunteer and fundraising activities. For the first few years of the TFAC's operations, the artists coordinated with the Alexandria Chapter of the Red Cross to staff the information desk with volunteers who were often local teenagers. It was a low-cost way to operate their front desk and it also gave young adults the opportunity to learn about art and gain professional experience (Van Landingham 1999, 28). The artists set out collection cans for visitors to deposit used soda cans to be recycled (Van Landingham 1999, 48). Many of these activities often served multiple purposes of keeping costs down while also improving their public image, and the community in the process.

Much of the TFAC's volunteer and community outreach events were originally informally organized but eventually were more formalized after the Friends of the Torpedo Factory organization was created in 1981. The Friends organization along with the TFAC's Art Association coordinated in leading many special projects and shows for the primary purpose of community outreach into the 1980s and 1990s (Van Landingham 1999, 132).

They hosted an art show in 1984 specially catered to be more accessible to handicapped individuals in the community. The Friends co-sponsored an annual show for senior citizens with the Alexandria Commission on Aging. A portion of the proceeds from one show was donated to the Alexandria Animal Welfare League. The TFAC continues to drive many community outreach programs to this day.

From the beginning, the artists at the TFAC worked to foster a supportive atmosphere. This included the sharing of art supply sources, exchanging technical knowledge, and collecting each other's work (Van Landingham 1999, 40). This provided a professional space for artists to network and learn from each other. It also provided an educational space for the public, either through watching artists do their work or by attending art classes hosted by the center's Art League. In the TFAC's 2020 Community Engagement Survey, city residents were asked why the TFAC is important to Alexandria's identity. The most popular response was that the TFAC was a "place for artists and arts education" followed by a "place to see art" (City of Alexandria, VA 2020, 52).

Artists as Another Interest Group

The artists do not represent the whole community. This, paired with the fact that they sought to influence the public based on their collective interests, makes them an interest group. This is not a particularly popular image to invoke because the artists contributed much to the community. Yet, the fact remains that they engaged in interest group behavior as they sought the attention of public officials.

The TFAC project was not unanimously supported by the community. Many citizens that opposed the center wrote letters to Council members in April 1974 asking that they not fund the $140,000 renovation in the upcoming annual budget. In response to this, Van Landingham went to City Hall to get copies of the letters so she could contact each sender and offer tours of the torpedo plant buildings. She hoped an explanation of the proposed use would help assuage concerns. This plan mostly worked; many people who attended her tours were more understanding of the project afterward (Van Landingham 1999, 8).

When businesses in the waterfront community were at first apprehensive about the TFAC's new presence, Van Landingham and the artists worked to ease the transition. They had buttons printed that had the Art Center's logo on them so they could wear them as they shopped and ate in the neighborhood. This was part of the artists' efforts to improve their public relations with the community to communicate they were not trying to compete. Instead, they envisioned their art center as attracting traffic that would benefit themselves in tandem with neighboring businesses. The remaining dissent was driven by citizens who passionately desired all of the torpedo plant buildings to be torn down so they could provide better access to the waterfront and more green space.

After the Alexandria Planning Commission issued a recommendation to the City Council in 1975 to have the whole waterfront area redeveloped, the

Artist Association commissioned a consultant group to conduct an economic analysis of the TFAC's contribution to the area (Van Landingham 1999, 53).

The report found that many of TFAC's visitors also visited restaurants and shops nearby (Marketing Research Group 1977). It also found 83 percent of those surveyed believed the TFAC enhanced the Old Town area. The artists attempted to use this report to back up their proposals for how to repurpose the torpedo complex buildings. They offered a plan that proposed minimal renovations for one of the buildings, with the artists repaying it all through their continued rental agreement.

The city ultimately went with the Alexandria Waterfront Restoration Group's proposal, which had competed with several other developer proposals. City Manager Doug Harman had actually favored another proposal put forth by the Redstone Development Corporation due to its superior legal, financial, and administrative arrangements. The Alexandria Group ultimately won the bid.

The artists and the developers who won the contract were both interests benefiting from the government's decision to work with them. Viewing the artists as an interest group is not incompatible with viewing them as social entrepreneurs. Although social entrepreneurs' chief aim is often social transformation and not monetary profits or political power, the latter two can sometimes be secondary aims. This is not the result of the malevolence of the artists. Instead, it is a result of the institutional environment that incentivized such behavior.

As soon as Alexandria City expressed interest in finding a purpose for the torpedo factory it was putting the community in a position to rent seek for the right to use it. The individuals that sought the attention of the city planners were expending entrepreneurial energies to obtain what economists call a "rent" or a benefit. The exclusive use of the building, as well as subsidized rents for tenants, were ultimately privileges provided by the Alexandria government. The energy devoted to securing this privilege amounted to social losses for the community because this same energy could have been directed to more productive uses absent the government's involvement (Tullock 1967).

Earlier I discussed how entrepreneurial opportunities can vary by institutional context. Before the clarification of property rights for the waterfront in 1981, the opportunity cost facing conventional entrepreneurs in the community was too high to invest time in redeveloping the waterfront. Because the property rights were unclear, they would have preferred diverting their entrepreneurial energies toward many other more secure alternatives. This created an opportunity for artists to fill in the space to compete for the city officials' attention.

Research has demonstrated that rent-seekers who use moral or social arguments to push for change in public society are often more successful

(McLaughlin, Smith, and Sobel 2019). Or rather, they are subject to less risk of being "caught" by the public's backlash for their rent-seeking behavior. As McLaughlin, Smith, and Sobel (2019, 212) write: "Rent seeking with no appeal to the public interest risks angering the public in a way that could more than offset any gains made through government support." They point to Amazon's cancellation of its plans to build their second headquarters in New York City due to public backlash about the $3 billion in public subsidies they would receive (Soper 2019).

The "bootleggers and Baptists" story originally told by Bruce Yandle depicts instances where concerns raised by Baptist congregations about alcohol were often accompanied by self-interested economic, or bootlegger, interest groups (Yandle 1983; Yandle 1999). Similarly, protectionist trade policies are more likely to be successful when they are framed as protecting jobs over improving the profitability of domestic industries (Hillman 2003).

The same interest group dynamics can hold true for the institutional context of public-private partnerships. The two main issues that can result are (1) favoritism involved with the initial contract award for the partnership and (2) suboptimal management of public resources due to incentive issues in the structure of the contract. My concern with the torpedo factory contract is less with the first issue and more with the latter.

Although there are benefits to public-private partnerships, their structure and institutional quality matter (Schomaker 2014). Research shows that when poorly structured, there is an increased risk of decreased public accountability (Forrer, Kee, and Boyer 2010) and an increased risk of rent-seeking behavior (Thillainathan and Cheong 2019; Hoppe and Schmitz 2013).

When it comes to the favoritism concern, research shows that rent-seeking does not always produce purely negative consequences. Instead, depending on the incentives at play, individuals may partake in public entrepreneurship that produces positive externalities for the community (Fuller and DelliSanti 2017). In the TFAC's case, the artists had a strong incentive to provide positive artistic and educational externalities for the community because doing so naturally furthered their own goals. The question that remains is whether these positive externalities are at the expense of more broad objectives of private citizens in the community. These objectives include the desire to have their taxpayer money efficiently managed.

Public-private partnerships usually start with a government entity selecting particular ends. Then the government entity solicits private contractors to supply the necessary means (Fuller and DelliSanti 2017). The TFAC project is unique because the artists in the community are the ones that identified services (art production and education) and then also proposed a means to deliver said services. Perhaps it could be said that the Alexandria government identified the need for a new use for the torpedo factory building, but they did not conduct a more official solicitation of requests for proposals until after the artists began their initial three-year experiment.

Next, I will discuss just how the structure of the TFAC public-private partnership has been holding it back from succeeding financially. There are better and worse ways of structuring these types of relationships and this chapter is an effort to encourage Alexandria to move toward the better. This is not to say that the artists do not bring value to the community, or that they have malintent. I want to draw attention to the reality that the incentives that institutions create do not change when interest groups happen to be artists or are more well-intentioned.

The TFAC can continue being an important part of Alexandria, but their future as a fiscally sustainable entity is dependent upon us deromanticizing artists' roles when it comes to how they manage resources. As soon as we're able to do this, we can move forward with making institutional changes that help the TFAC become more sustainable.

THE ONGOING SITUATION

Due to changes to the institutional landscape, the costs and benefits of the TFAC's current operations and lease structure remains an issue. Although the artists played an important entrepreneurial role in identifying a use for the building, it does not necessarily mean the current public-private partnership structure is the most efficient or best use of the torpedo factory space.

In 1981, City Manager Doug Harman said the artists' building on the corner of King Street "was too valuable commercially for the artists, (even though we had made it valuable)" (Van Landingham 1999, 97). The City Manager's concern is related to the opportunity cost of the torpedo factory building: is it the best use of the building?

The artists viewed their craft as vastly different from a strictly commercial pursuit. They planned to sell their art, but they equated their business model more with those employed by museums where the main focus is education. A 2010 report prepared by Management Analysis, Inc. echoed this sentiment: "Managing the art center building was never intended to be a major profit-making activity for the City, nor for the Torpedo Factory Artists' Association (TFAA)" (Management Analysis, Inc. 2010).

In 1977, the city was renting the studio spaces for $3–4 per square foot, while neighboring commercial spaces went for $12–15 per square foot (Van Landingham 1999, 65). City Council members cited this difference when expressing concerns about the financial viability of the TFAC.

This concern becomes more apparent when the city's budget is tight. This happened in 1993 when constrained coffers forced city officials to look for ways to "get more bang for their buck" with the TFAC (Hong 1993). They entertained several proposals for changes to the TFAC's operation and lease. These ranged from higher rents and shorter leases to expanded evening hours (Van Landingham 1999, 138). In late May 1993, a new lease agreement was approved that was considered a compromise between "artistic and financial interests" (Van Landingham 1999, 139). It raised the annual rent due from the Artists' Association from \$335,471 to \$365,496; this effectively reduced the city subsidy from 57 percent to 54 percent.

The artists often argued that the public subsidy calculations did not account for the sales, meal, and room taxes that were generated from visitors who come from outside of Alexandria to see the TFAC. It also doesn't take into consideration the larger economic benefits provided to the community, also known as economic multiplier effects.

A study conducted between 1993 and 1994 found that approximately 83 percent of the TFAC's visitors were from out of town (Frechtling 1994). These visitors spent nearly \$54.6 million on lodging, food, auto-related and other purchases while in the area, including an additional \$2.3 million in the actual TFAC building. This generated almost \$1.8 million in tax revenue for Alexandria. A 2010 report, commissioned by the City of Alexandria, concluded that the TFAC contributed about 2.3 percent to total visitor spending in 2009 (Management Analysis, Inc. 2010).

More recently, a report prepared for the TFAC Artists' Association, estimated the economic impact of the TFAC in 2016 (The Stephen S. Fuller Institute 2017). Visitors attracted to the area by the TFAC spent on average \$92.88, which totaled an estimated \$35.2 million for the whole year. This translates into an economic multiplier of 1.33, which means that for each \$1 out-of-town visitors spent in the area, Alexandria's gross city product gained \$1.33; a total of \$35.2 million.

As impressive as these numbers sound, they are not the full picture. Aside from the many assumptions required to calculate multiplier effects, they do not tell us what the community is forgoing by choosing to keep the art center in the torpedo building in its current form.

The 2010 Management Analysis report found that the "prime building space the art center occupies represents an estimated 'opportunity cost' of \$1.7 million each year for the City" (Management Analysis, Inc. 2010). The authors calculated this by comparing the TFAC's subsidized rents with market rents for comparable buildings in the area.

If the TFAC rented the entire 76,000 square foot building at \$40 per square foot, instead of for roughly \$3, it could generate \$3.04 million a year. The difference between this amount and the actual rent the city received from the TFAC in 2008 produces the opportunity cost figure of \$1.7 million.

In commercial leasing, the costs of space, utilities, interior decor and maintenance of common areas are typically factored into the rent. In the case of the
Torpedo Factory, these costs were factored into the master lease agreement
beginning in 1998 when the City bought back the building from private owners
and the seller agreed to a price determined by an independent appraiser of $5.4
million. At the time of the buy-back, there was an outstanding promissory note
from the original sale from the City to the private owner totaling $3,424,750.
Therefore, the net additional cost to the City to buy back the building was
$1,975,250. When the management of the Torpedo Factory was 'privatized' in
1998, this cost was divided over a 20-year period in order to determine a rental
rate in a manner that covered the City's projected costs. (Management Analysis,
Inc. 2010, 11–12)

The initial rental rate calculated based on the new arrangement was $3.19 per
square foot per year, starting in 1998. This rate incorporated many factors,
including the building's re-purchase costs, the interest on 62 percent of the
buy-back amount, and annual maintenance costs. The rate also accounted for
property taxes that would be paid by the Artists' Association.

Studio rents have gone up but are still far from competitive market rental
rates. According to the TFAC's website, all tenants pay $15.91 per square
foot per year.[2] This number incorporates utilities, marketing, programming,
maintenance, and staffing costs.

The true opportunity cost of the TFAC arrangement could be even higher
than $1.7 million. Opportunity cost is defined as what you are giving up when
making a decision. Comparable rents in the area are one way to narrowly
measure this, but there is even more to it. When the city continues to lease
the TFAC to the Artists' Association, it is choosing this arrangement above
many potential other arrangements, of which not all are known. Is there a
business or organization that could pay a higher rent and would also produce
benefits—economic and cultural—for the community? This exercise shows
what a higher rent would produce for the city, but it does not show what other
ways the torpedo building could benefit the community.

This means there are steps that the TFAC can take to improve its economic
viability. Although the building provides more than $16.2 million in direct
revenues and receives roughly 400,000 visitors annually, it is still dependent
on an effective subsidy to operate (Management Analysis, Inc. 2010).

The TFAC needs to become more cost effective. Some changes would
include generating more sales and becoming more customer-centric by
improving operating hours (Management Analysis, Inc. 2010). One planning
group recommended the TFAC improve its marketing efforts by implementing cross-promotional programs with businesses in the area (Gibbs Planning
Group, Inc. 2009).

Perhaps most importantly, the TFAC needs to adjust internal operations. Many of these changes will be hard to motivate, however, absent institutional changes that alter the incentives facing the TFAC.

Currently, the TFAC artists pay subsidized rents and utilities that do not vary by where they are located in the building or energy consumption. Studios on the first floor of the building are charged the same rental rate as studios on the second floor, despite differences in foot traffic. Moving to a system where studios that receive more foot traffic would better match rental rates with sales potential.

Reevaluating the percentage of utilities the city pays as well as allowing the portion that artists pay to vary with their consumption would significantly improve the incentives for energy consumption.

The most successful portion of TFAC operations is its after-hours building rental program. As of 2009, rental prices ranged from $4,000 to $5,000 for the first floor and $600 to $750 to add the second and third floors. These prices vary depending on the season. This means that although the artists do not want a tiered pricing rental structure applied to their studios, they have effectively implemented one for after-hour rentals. This has likely resulted from the fact that the Artists' Association financially benefits from this tiered system—they get all the proceeds from these events. Additionally, commissions to Artists' Association staff for event books are very generous which incentivizes sales volume.

If the Artists' Association wishes to keep rents low for artists, the after-hours rentals program points to their ability to support themselves with entrepreneurial pursuits. It begs the question of how things would change if the city lowered its subsidy of the building's total rent. Given the high event commissions, perhaps there is room to lower commissions and direct more sales toward keeping studio rents down in such a scenario.

Other than the period when the TFAC was owned by private investors, the building has primarily been owned by the city. Management of the TFAC, however, had originally largely been left to the Artists' Association. Concerns about TFAC's economic viability led to the creation of a new committee in 1993, the Art Center Working Group, to help streamline operations. In 2010, the City Council established a board to supervise the management of the art center, blurring the separation between ownership and management of the TFAC building that previously existed.

In 2016, Alexandria took steps to become even more involved in TFAC operations (US Fed News Service 2016). The leasing structure between the city, the Torpedo Factory Art Board, the Torpedo Factory Artists' Association, the Art League, and the artists was set to expire the same year, so the city decided to simplify things. Starting in October of 2016, the city provided new direct leases to the artists and galleries. The TFAC employees who were on the Board that was established in 2010 temporarily became city employees. This became permanent in 2018 when the City Council voted for permanent control of the TFAC (Schrott 2018).

According to Alexandria Times, there have been mixed responses to these changes (Schrott 2018). Some report artist morale falling since the management changes in 2016 and 2018. Other artists supported the move but were frustrated by how fast the decisions were made; they argued artists had largely been left out of discussions.

The main concern from an institutional perspective with this recent change is its influence on the incentives facing the TFAC artists and administration. As mentioned earlier, institutional quality matters for more efficient production of services through public-partnership arrangements. Strict governance is indeed important for protecting the public interest (Hodge and Greve 2017; Skelcher 2010). However, stricter governance does not always come from a stronger centralized presence. By becoming more involved in the management of the TFAC, city planners are discouraging risk-taking and innovation on the part of the TFAC artists and administrators.

LESSONS FROM THE TFAC REVITALIZATION PROJECT

Accounts of the TFAC project often portray a dichotomy between artistic and financial interests. It is true these interests create tensions for the TFAC project, but they are not always at odds, nor do they need to be. They could be more aligned if given the opportunity through institutional improvements that would better align the incentives of the artists with the city's concerns for the center's economic viability. Ironically, recent efforts to improve the management of the TFAC by the city have only worsened the situation by raising the costs of social and economic entrepreneurship.

When looking at the initial revitalization of the TFAC by local artists, it becomes clear this was a successful exercise in social coordination and public policy. The Art League artists in the early 1970s were able to identify a use for the torpedo plant building and follow through on their vision to revitalize it. In this initial phase of the project, the artists shined as social entrepreneurs, solving a collective action problem and providing many benefits to the community through outreach and art education.

When looking beyond the initial transformation of the TFAC building, our definitions of success evolve, of which the project surely fails to meet. The artists struggle with the continued efficient management of the building. This reduces the TFAC project's efficacy as a use of public resources. This is not the result of any entrepreneurial deficiency on behalf of the TFAC artists.

Instead, the leasing structure of the TFAC project has created suboptimal incentives for running an economically viable community center.

Improvements to the leasing structure would include reducing the subsidy of the TFAC, creating a tiered pricing rental structure, and adjusting utility charges to correspond to energy consumption. The TFAC's after-hour business rentals also demonstrate potential.

The institutional change that took place in 1981 should not be left underappreciated. It is true the artists' efforts helped improve the attractiveness of the waterfront area, but they did not do this alone. The 1981 settlement between the federal government and the City of Alexandria drastically improved the area's attractiveness for development due to its clarification of property rights along the Potomac River.

In an attempt to encourage more economic efficiency, Alexandria City officials have worsened the incentives facing the TFAC artists. This is because they tightened their grip by taking permanent control of the building's operations. To the extent that it is possible to reverse this decision, city officials should consider taking a step back while improving the leasing structure as this could generate the precise outcomes they desire: better stewardship of city resources.

There are other questions not addressed here but would be worth pursuing in future research. One such question relates to whether the TFAC artists could have operated absent public subsidy. This relates to the larger philosophical role for government in the provision of artistic and cultural amenities. Future research could explore how different polycentric arrangements either support or detract from the provision of these amenities for society. It is also worth exploring the fine line between socially beneficial public entrepreneurship and destructive entrepreneurship that produces high rent-seeking costs.

Additionally, future research would more systematically compare the institutional differences between the TFAC and other similar adaptive reuse projects. Conducting such an exercise would further elaborate the type of institutional diversity that is required for repurposing underutilized buildings. One particular extension could explore the efficacy of Adaptive Reuse Potential (ARP) models in accounting for institutions when predicting the potential success of different projects.

REFERENCES

Alauddin, Kartina, Mohd Fisal Ishak, Mohammad Nasharudine Shuib, and Halmi Zainol. 2016. "The Key Components of Knowledge Transfer for Problem Solving In Adaptive Reuse Projects: A Qualitative Study." *MATEC Web of Conferences* 66 (July): EDP Sciences, 00087.

Alexandria Archaeology. 2010. "Alexandria Waterfront History Plan." Office of Historic Alexandria, City of Alexandria, Virginia. https://media.alexandriava.gov/docs-archives/planning/info/waterfront/aacwaterfronthistoryplan.pdf.

Arief, Irdinal, and Harifuddin Thahir. 2020. "Adaptive Reuse to Concept of Land Use Planning and Design. Case Study: Independent Integrated City in Morowali, Central Sulawesi." *MATEC Web of Conferences* 331 (December): EDP Sciences, 07004.

Austin, Richard L., David G. Woodcock, W. Cecil Steward, and R. Alan Forrester. 1988. *Adaptive Reuse: Issues and Case Studies in Building Preservation*. New York, NY: Van Nostrand Reinhold.

Ball, Rick. 1999. "Developers, Regeneration and Sustainability Issues in the Reuse of Vacant Industrial Buildings." *Building Research & Information* 27 (3): 140–148.

Battiata, Mary. 1981. "Alexandria Approves Waterfront Agreement." *The Washington Post*. October 7, 1981.

Boettke, Peter J., and Christopher J. Coyne. 2009. "Context Matters: Institution and Entrepreneurship." *Foundations and Trends in Entrepreneurship* 5 (3): 135–209.

Bottero, Marta, Chiara D'Alpaos, and Alessandra Oppio. 2019. "Ranking of Adaptive Reuse Strategies for Abandoned Industrial Heritage in Vulnerable Contexts: A Multiple Criteria Decision Aiding Approach." *Sustainability* 11 (3): 785.

Brown, Garrett Wallace, Iain McLean, and Alistair McMillan (eds). 2018. *The Concise Oxford Dictionary of Politics and International Relations*. Oxford, UK: Oxford University Press.

Bullen, Peter A. 2007. "Adaptive Reuse and Sustainability of Commercial Buildings." *Facilities* 25 (1/2): 20–31.

Bullen, Peter, and Peter Love. 2011. "A New Future for the Past: A Model for Adaptive Reuse Decision-Making." *Built Environment Project and Asset Management* 1 (1): 32–44

Chamlee-Wright, Emily, and Virgil Henry Storr. 2010. "The Role of Social Entrepreneurship in Post-Katrina Community Recovery." *International Journal of Innovation and Regional Development* 2 (1/2): 149–164.

City of Alexandria, VA. 2020. "Torpedo Factory Art Center Community Engagement Report." https://torpedofactory.org/wp-content/uploads/2020/01/TFAC-Community-Engagement-Report.pdf.

City of Alexandria, Virginia. n.d. "The History of Historic Districts in Alexandria." https://www.arcgis.com/apps/MapJournal/index.html?appid=a76d020f1cda47a58121f6b72920e768.

Coase, Ronald H. 1937. "The Nature of the Firm." *Economica* 4 (16): 386–405.

Coase, Ronald H. 1960. "The Problem of Social Cost." *The Journal of Law & Economics* 3: 1–44.

Drucker, Peter. 1985. *Innovation and Entrepreneurship: Practice and Principles*. New York, NY: HarperCollins Publishers, Inc.

Forrer, John, James Edwin Kee, and Eric Boyer. 2010. "Public-Private Partnerships and the Public Accountability Question." *Public Administration Review* 70 (3): 475–484.

Frechtling, Douglas C. 1994. *Torpedo Factory Art Center Visitor Impact Study*. Alexandria, VA: Torpedo Factory Artists' Association.

Fuller, Caleb, and Dylan DelliSanti. 2017. "Spillovers from Public Entrepreneurship: A Case Study." *Journal of Entrepreneurship and Public Policy* 6 (1): 72–91.

Gibbs Planning Group, Inc. 2009. "King Street Retail Analysis." https://media .alexandriava.gov/docs-archives/planning/info/kingstreet/20090619finalgibbsking streetretailanalysis.pdf.

Goldman, Betsy Schein. 1989. "The Torpedo Factory Art Center." *American Artist*. February.

Günçe, Kagan, and Damla Misirlisoy. 2014. "Adaptive Reuse of Military Establishments as Museums: Conservation vs. Museography." *WIT Transactions on the Built Environment* 143: 125–136.

Hayek, Friechrich A. 1945. "The Use of Knowledge in Society." *The American Economic Review* 35 (4): 519–530.

Hillman, Arye L. 2003. *Public Finance and Public Policy: Responsibilities and Limitations of Government*. Cambridge, UK: Cambridge University Press.

Hodge, Graeme A., and Carsten Greve. 2017. "On Public-Private Partnership Performance: A Contemporary Review." *Public Works Management & Policy* 22 (1): 55–78.

Hong, Peter. 1993. "Artists Fear that Change Could Sink Torpedo Factory." *The Washington Post*. 6 May.

Hoppe, Eva I., and Patrick W. Schmitz. 2013. "Public-Private Partnership Versus Traditional Procurement: Innovation Incentives and Information Gathering." *RAND Journal of Economics* 44 (1): 56–74.

Jones, John C., and Karen A. Franck. 2019. "A brewery in a foundry, a winery in a strip mall: adaptive reuse by food enterprises." *Urban Design International* 24: 108–117.

Karim, S.B. Abd, K. S. Kamal, L. Ab Wahab, and M. Hanid. 2007. "Risk assessment and refurbishment: The case of Ipoh Railway Station Perak." Malaysia, Management in Construction and Researchers Association (MICRA) Conference. 28–29.

Kirzner, Israel M. 1973. *Competition and Entrepreneurship*. Chicago, IL: The University of Chicago Press.

Kirzner, Israel M. 1997. "Entrepreneurial Discovery and the Competitive Market Process: An Austrian Approach." *Journal of Economic Literature* 35 (1): 60–85.

Krueger, Anne O. 1974. "The Political Economy of the Rent-Seeking Society." *The American Economic Review* 64 (3): 291–303.

Kululanga, G. K., and R. McCaffer. 2001. "Measuring Knowledge Management for Construction Organizations." *Engineering, Construction and Architectural Management* 8 (5/6): 346–54.

Kurul, Esra. 2007. "A Qualitative Approach to Exploring Adaptive Re-use Processes." *Facilities* 25 (13/14): 554–70.

Lewis, Jo Ann. 1983. "Full Speed Ahead! The Torpedo Factory Opens Today." *The Washington Post*, 21 May.

Louw, Michael Paul. 2016. "The Adaptive Reuse of Industrial Structures: Revisiting the Thesen Islands Power Station Project in South Africa." *Journal of Engineering, Design and Technology* 14 (4): 920–40.

Management Analysis, Inc. 2010. *A Study of the Torpedo Factory Art Center.* City of Alexandria. https://torpedofactory.org/wp-content/uploads/2020/01/TFAC-A -Study-of-the-Torpedo-Factory-Art-Center-MAI.pdf.

Marketing Research Group. 1977. *Final Report: An Economic Analysis of the Impact of the Torpedo Factory on Lower King Street.* Alexandria, VA: Mount Vernon College.

Marriott, Michel. 1983. "Anticipating an Art Center in Alexandria." *Washington Post.* 3 April.

McGinnis, Michael D. 2019. "Beyond a Precarious Balance." In *Ostrom's Tensions: Reexamining the Political Economy and Public Policy of Elinor C. Ostrom,* edited by Roberta Q. Herzberg, Peter J. Boettke, and Paul Dragos Aligica, 19–72. Arlington, VA: Mercatus Center at George Mason University.

McLaughlin, Patrick A., Adam C. Smith, and Russell S. Sobel. 2019. "Bootleggers, Baptists, and the Risks of Rent Seeking." *Constitutional Political Economy* 30: 211–234.

Mehr, Shabnam Yazhani, and Sara Wilkinson. 2020. "The Importance of Place and Authenticity in Adaptive Reuse of Heritage Buildings." *International Journal of Building Pathology and Adaptation* 38 (5): 689–701.

Mitchell, Matthew D. 2012. *The Pathology of Privilege: The Economic Consequences of Government Favoritism.* Arlington, VA: Mercatus Center at George Mason University.

Mitchell, Matthew D., and Tad DeHaven. 2018. "Government Privilege: Contracting Abuses." *The Bridge.* 16 July.

Mohamed, Rayman, Robin Boyle, Allan Y. Yang, and Joseph Tangari. 2017. "Adaptive Reuse: A Review and Analysis of Its Relationship to the 3 Es of Sustainability." *Facilities* 35 (3/4): 138–154.

Murphy, Caryle. 1984. "Waking Up a Waterfront." *The Washington Post.* 29 November.

Nasta, Paula. 2019. "Adaptive Reuse: Parking, Zoning, and Shopping Malls." *The Routledge Companion to Automobile Heritage, Culture, and Preservation,* edited by Barry L. Stiefel and Jennifer Clark, 128–148. London, UK: Routledge.

North, Douglas C. 1991. "Institutions." *Journal of Economic Perspectives* 5 (1): 97–112.

———. 1990. *Institutions, Institutional Change and Economic Performance.* New York, NY: Cambridge University Press.

Olson, Mancur. 1965. *The Logic of Collective Action.* Cambridge, MA: Harvard University Press.

Ostrom, Elinor. 1990. *Governing the Commons: The Evolution of Institutions for Collective Action.* Cambridge, UK: Cambridge University Press.

———. 2005. *Understanding Institutional Diversity.* Princeton, NJ: Princeton University Press.

———. 2010. "Beyond Markets and States: Polycentric Governance of Complex Economic Systems." *American Economic Review* 100: 641–72.

Ostrom, Vincent, Charles M. Tiebout, and Robert Warren. 1999. "The Organization of Government in Metropolitan Areas: A Theoretical Inquiry." In *Polycentricity and Local Public Economics*, edited by Michael D. McGinnis, 31–51. Ann Arbor, MI: University of Michigan Press.

Parpas, Despo, and Andreas L. Savvides. 2020. "On the Determinants of a Successful, Sustainable-driven Adaptive Reuse: A Multiple Regression Approach." *International Journal of Sustainable Development* 15 (1): 1–13.

Rezaei, Naimeh, Mahsa Rasouli, and Bahareh Azhdari. 2018. "The Attitude of the Local Community to the Impact of Building Reuse: Three Cases in an Old Neighborhood of Tehran." *Heritage & Society* 11 (2): 105–125.

Sanchez, Benjamin, Mansour E. Esfahani, and Carl Haas. 2019. "A Methodology to Analyze the Net Environmental Impacts and Building's Cost Performance of an Adaptive Reuse Project: A Case Study of the Waterloo County Courthouse Renovations." *Environment Systems and Decisions* 39: 419–38.

Schliemann, B., J. Mullin, Z. Kotval-K, and Z. Kotval. 2017. "The Adaptive Reuse of Closed Military Bases in New England." *International Journal of Heritage Architecture* 1 (2): 216–225.

Schomaker, Rahel. 2014. "Institutional Quality and Private Sector Participation: Theory and Empirical Findings." *European Journal of Government and Economics* 3 (2): 104–118.

Schrott, Missy. 2018. "City Takes Permanent Control of Torpedo Factory." *Alexandria Times*. 20 November.

Schumpeter, Joseph A. 1934. *The Theory of Economic Development*. Cambridge, MA: Harvard University Press.

Shehata, Waleed Tarek Ali, Yasser Moustafa, Lobna Sherif, and Ashraf Botros. 2015. "Towards the Comprehensive and Systematic Assessment of the Adaptive Reuse of Islamic Architectural Heritage in Cairo: A Conceptual Framework." *Journal of Cultural Heritage Management and Sustainable Development* 5 (1): 14–29.

Shen, Li-yin, and Craig Langston. 2010. "Adaptive Reuse Potential: An Examination of Differences Between Urban and Non-Urban Projects." *Facilities* 28 (1/2): 6–16.

Shipley, Robert, Steve Utz, and Michael Parsons. 2006. "Does Adaptive Reuse Pay? A Study of the Business of Building Renovation in Ontario, Canada." *International Journal of Heritage Studies* 12 (6): 505–20.

Skelcher, Chris. 2010. "Governance of Public-Private Partnerships." In *International Handbook on Public-Private Partnerships*, edited by Graeme A. Hodge, Carsten Greve, and Anthony E. Boardman, 292–304. Cheltenham, UK: Edward Elgar.

Soper, Spencer. 2019. "Amazon Scraps Plan to Build a Headquarters in New York City." *Bloomberg*.

Spender, J. C. 1996. "Making Knowledge the Basis of a Dynamic Theory of the Firm." *Strategic Management Journal* 17 (S2): 45–62.

The Stephen S. Fuller Institute. 2017. "The Impact of the Torpedo Factory Art Center on the City of Alexandria's Economy." Prepared for the Torpedo Factory Artists' Association.

Thillainathan, R., and Kee-Cheok Cheong. 2019. "Malaysian Public-Private Partnerships—Incentivising Private Sector Participation or Facilitating Rent-Seeking." *Malaysian Journal of Economic Studies* 56 (2): 177–200.

"The Zoning Ordinance of the City of Alexandria, Virginia." Article X—Historic Districts and Buildings. https://library.municode.com/va/alexandria/codes/zoning ?nodeId=ARTXHIDIBU.

Torpedo Factory Art Center. 2022. "History." https://torpedofactory.org/about-us/ history/

Tullock, Gordon. 1967. "The Welfare Costs of Tariffs, Monopolies, and Theft." *Economic Inquiry* 5 (3): 224–232.

US Fed News Service. 2016. "City of Alexandria to Streamline Leases at Torpedo Factory Art Center." Washington, D.C.: HT Digital Streams Limited, 12 May.

Van Landingham, Marian. 1999. *On Target: Stories of the Torpedo Factory Art Center's First 25 Years*. Alexandria, VA: Marian Van Landingham.

Vardopoulos, Ioannis, Christos Stamopoulos, Georgios Chatzithanasis, Christos Michalakelis, Panagiota Giannouli, and Eleni Pastrapa. 2020. "Considering Urban Development Paths and Processes on Account of Adaptive Reuse Projects." *Buildings* 10 (73): 73.

Vecchio, Marcello, and Godwin Arku. 2020. "Promoting Adaptive Reuse in Ontario: A Planning Policy Tool for Making the Best of Manufacturing Decline." *Urban Planning* 5 (3): 338–350.

Wadland, Mary. 2018. "Did You Know Old Town Alexandria Was Only the Third Town in the Nation Named Historic District after Charleston and New Orleans?" *Zebra*. 16 July.

Wilkinson, Sara J., Craig Langston, and Hilde Remøy. 2014. *Sustainable Building Adaptation: Innovations in Decision-Making*. Oxford, UK: John Wiley & Sons.

Yandle, Bruce. 1999. "Bootleggers and Baptists in Retrospect." *Regulation* 22 (3): 5–7.

Yandle, Bruce. 1983. "Bootleggers and Baptists: The Education of a Regulatory Economist." *Regulation* 7 (3): 12–16.

NOTES

1. Acknowledgements: I would like to sincerely thank the editors and other authors of this volume for their very thoughtful feedback. Any remaining errors are my own. I would also like to thank my mom for taking me to the Torpedo Factory when I was younger and instilling in me a curiosity about adaptive reuse projects and the transformation of the art center.

2. As of October 2021. https://www.alexandriava.gov/recreation/arts/info/default .aspx?id=95569.

Chapter 5

Local Constituencies, Lobbying, and the Fight to Keep Local Bases Open during the 2005 Round of Base Closure and Realignment

Julie Thompson-Gomez

The United States has adopted a process known as Base Realignment and Closure (BRAC) to draw down on unnecessary infrastructure in an ostensibly technocratic and impartial manner. The last round of BRAC took place in 2005, despite numerous calls for additional closures since then. This lack of recent base closures suggests that some bases are easier to close than others. Why is this the case?

I explore an argument centered not on elected officials or representatives, but on what I call "local constituencies" who lobby to keep their bases open amidst the threat of closure. In some cases, base closures do not face opposition because the community believes it will benefit from closing the base. In other cases, base closures face strong opposition because the community believes it will suffer greatly from the loss of the base. My argument applies only in the latter case when the effected community rallies to keep the base, creating a local constituency. The question then becomes, how do local constituencies use social capital to keep their military bases? Using hundreds of letters from an online archive, I show how an organized league of local business owners known as the Committee of Fifty lobbied the BRAC Commission directly via a letter-writing campaign called Operation Keep Cannon to keep open Cannon Air Force Base in Clovis, New Mexico, after it was slated for closure during the 2005 round of BRAC. Mobilizing locals to write thousands of letters, the campaign succeeded, and Cannon Air Force Base was realigned to a new mission rather than being closed. Although the

Committee of Fifty was not created just for the mobilization of Operation Keep Cannon, it appears to have retained a good deal of organizational power in the Clovis community, leading some locals to refer to the committee as the "Shifty Fifty."

The rest of the paper will explain how my argument fits into the existing literature surrounding public choice and interest groups, followed by an explanation of the BRAC process and how it came to be. I will then discuss the existing arguments for why there has not been another round of BRAC and some of the reasons why localities are loath to lose their bases. I then bring in the case of Cannon Air Force Base and the Committee of Fifty's letter-writing campaign before concluding with policy recommendations.

STATE OF THE LITERATURE

The literature on social coordination has long recognized that civil society and other groups with a good deal of social capital which have special interests can effectively mobilize to lock in the benefits they have received from the government. Additionally, such groups may reorient themselves from mutual assistance to lobbying and rent seeking. For example, one study demonstrates how communities in New Orleans reoriented their social capital toward lobbying and rent-seeking after Hurricane Katrina (Chamlee-Wright and Storr 2011). As the federal government parceled out aid for redevelopment, community leaders were required to demonstrate their locality's viability to qualify for the aid. Communities with higher levels of social capital—that is, the "connections among individuals—social networks and the norms of reciprocity and trustworthiness that arise from them" (Putnam 2000, 19)—were able to mobilize mutual assistance to help their residents rebuild and recover more quickly. However, those same communities were also able to turn their efforts toward external rent-seeking, and many did so in varying cases. In other words, the "dynamic" wherein "community-based interest groups reallocate social capital away from mutual assistance and towards lobbying . . . may unfold in any context where significant government resources are offered on a community-wide basis." (Chamlee-Wright and Storr 2011, 183).

Although much of the popular literature on social capital in the social sciences highlights the benefits of societies with significant social capital (Putnam 2000), other research points to the "dark side of social capital" (Chamlee-Wright and Storr 2011, 168; see also Berman 1997). This acknowledgement that civil society can be used for good or ill seems simplistic but is deeply important for understanding how communities react and respond to political problems that may have ripple effects well beyond their original intentions. My argument demonstrates that it can be extremely difficult to reallocate or take away government rents from local constituencies that already have them but believe that their way of life depends on retaining the rents.

The Transitional Gains Trap is another helpful way of understanding the dynamic of rescinding rents once the government has given them. The trap occurs because "there are only transitional gains to be made when the government establishes certain privileges for a group of people. The successors to the original beneficiaries will not normally make exceptional profits; but, unfortunately, they usually will be injured by cancellation of the original gift" (Tullock 2004, 212). One such trap exists in agricultural subsidies in the United States; although the transitional gains have already been realized, "We are now stuck with the situation in which there are significant social losses [to the broader public], but a powerful political group would suffer transitional losses by the termination of the program" (Tullock 2004, 218).

I argue that the Transitional Gains Trap is relevant to the matter of closing excess military bases in the United States. Just as with agricultural subsidies and taxi medallions, "there is a large number of people who would suffer large transitional costs if the institutions [in this case, bases] were terminated." The costs—financial, political, and social—of closing some bases are "large enough so that compensation of the losers would impose upon society an excess burden which would be of the same order of magnitude as the cost of the present institution" (Tullock 2004, 221). Therefore, even though it may be beneficial for the federal defense budget to close a military base, local communities may feel that they will never be able to recover from the loss of the base and lobby to keep it even if the base brings less benefit to the locality than residents perceive.

Although the BRAC process was created to be objective and rational in order to avoid some of the costs of the Transitional Gains Trap, the fact is that BRAC has not been able to mitigate these costs in every case. Some localities can be convinced to give up their bases, but others remain caught in the trap and use their social capital to lobby to keep their local bases. The next section will explain how BRAC came about and the problems it was meant to address.

BRAC AND THE BASE CLOSURE PROBLEM

BRAC is the process by which Congress has allowed the U.S. Department of Defense (DoD) to close or realign military bases since 1988. Rounds of BRAC have taken place in 1988, 1991, 1993, 1995, and 2005 (Mann 2019, 2). As the DoD drew down after the end of the Vietnam War and began to close obsolete bases from World War II, Congress passed a law in 1977 mandating that "no action may be taken to effect or implement—(1) the closure of any military installation; [or] (2) any realignment with respect to any military installation" without public notice, Congressional notification, written justification from the Secretary of Defense, and several other stipulations (Military Construction Authorization Act 1978). This law applied to any U.S. state, the District of Columbia, Puerto Rico, and Guam, but not foreign bases, suggesting that the reasons for preventing base closure were domestic, not international. Indeed, the 1991 BRAC report claims that "In the 1960s and again in the 1970s, accusations were widespread that base closures were being used by the executive branch to punish uncooperative legislators," which led Congress to require such stipulations that "effectively prevented DoD from closing any major military installation" (Defense Base Closure and Realignment Commission 1991, 1–1). Interestingly, however, it is difficult to ascertain whether this is the real reason that Congress passed the anti-closure law. In fact, the *Washington Post* reported just a few months after the passage of the law that "The Carter administration is planning a major round of military base closures next year," suggesting that whatever hurdles existed to close bases, the Carter administration did not think they were insurmountable (Causey, 1977). Regardless of the reason the bill was passed, the result of the anti-closure law was that almost no bases were closed for a period of about ten years.[1]

By the late 1980s, although the structure of the military had changed a great deal due to a rapid increase in defense spending as well as the Goldwater-Nichols Act, "the base structure remained unaltered" (Defense Base Closure and Realignment Commission 1991, 1–1). In 1988, Secretary of Defense Frank Carlucci "chartered the Defense Secretary's Commission on Base Realignment and Closure, ordering it to conduct an independent study of the domestic military base structure and to recommend installations for realignment and closure" (Defense Base Closure and Realignment Commission 1991, 1–1). At the same time, Congress passed a new law that allowed the independent commission to then send their results to the president. If the president approved, the list then went to Congress. Neither the president nor Congress could amend the list, but "Unless Congress passed a joint resolution of disapproval within 45 days, the secretary of defense had the authority to carry out the closures" (Mayer 1999, 32). Each of the BRAC rounds has followed this format.

The criteria by which bases are selected for closure have remained remarkably similar throughout each round. Although BRAC is often marketed as a cost-saving measure, "potential costs and savings have been a consideration that have ranked below military value," and in fact, "No BRAC round has established cost savings targets, floors, or ceilings" (Mann 2019, 3).

The BRAC *Report to the President 1991*, for example, listed its priorities as follows:

MILITARY VALUE (given priority consideration)

1. Current and future mission requirements and the impact of operational readiness of the Department of Defense's total force.
2. The availability and condition of land, facilities, and associated airspace at both the existing and potential receiving locations.
3. The ability to accommodate contingency, mobilization, and future total force requirements at both the existing and potential receiving locations.
4. The cost and manpower implications.

RETURN ON INVESTMENT

1. The extent and timing of potential costs and savings, including the number of years, beginning with the date of completion of closure or realignment, for the savings to exceed the costs.

IMPACTS

1. The economic impact on local communities.
2. The ability of both the existing and potential receiving communities' infrastructures to support forces, missions, and personnel.
3. The environmental impact.

The later 2005 guidelines look very similar to the ones above from 1991 since "Congress amended the BRAC statute to require the Secretary to regard military value . . . as the primary consideration. Other factors, such as potential costs and savings, were explicitly categorized as lower priority" (Mann 2019, 4). The consistency of the base selection guidelines suggests that BRAC is structured to prioritize the technocratic needs of the DoD and to remove political considerations from the decision. This focus on technocratic needs should in theory lower the barrier to exiting the Transitional Gains Trap; that is, the architects of the BRAC process appear to have hoped that shifting political responsibility for base closures and turning a blind eye towards the social costs would be outweighed by the strategic and financial benefits of base closures. This turned out not to be the case, as the next section will demonstrate.

BRINGING POLITICS BACK INTO A
TECHNOCRATIC PROCESS

Despite the best efforts of BRAC's architects, politics have not been removed from decisions to close or realign domestic bases even though BRAC is designed to be an impartial, unbiased process. This is certainly evident in the ways that members of Congress have spoken about BRAC.

Although the earliest reasons for preventing base closure were based on Congressmembers' fears of being targeted by the executive branch, representatives' comments seem to focus a great deal more on how a base closure would impact their constituents. Of course, the logic behind the executive branch targeting a Congressmember's district by closing a base is that it would frustrate constituents who lose their jobs or livelihoods. Constituents would then take out their anger on their Congressmembers by voting them out of office. Therefore, Congressmembers see threats on two fronts: they must protect themselves from the executive branch while also protecting themselves from their constituents. It is unclear, however, whether BRAC removes or mitigates either of these threats. For example, in a Congressional hearing on the 1991 BRAC list, Representative Patricia Schroeder, a Democrat from Colorado, "noted that, of the 21 major bases slated to be closed, 19 were in districts represented by Democrats, and claimed that 99 percent of the civilian job losses from those closures were in Democratic districts," suggesting that the base closures were intended to target Democrats in the upcoming election (Sorenson 1998, 46). While it is hard to know whether this was truly an oversight or a calculated political move, the fact remains that suspicions of executive branch targeting did not evaporate simply because BRAC is meant to be a neutral, technical process.

As for concerns about constituents, Congressmembers appear confident that a delegative process for BRAC will insulate them from political harm at the ballot box. For example, at a 1985 Hearing Before the Subcommittee on Military Construction of the Committee on Armed Services that discussed ways to amend the law preventing base closures, Senator Phil Gramm, a Republican from Texas, gave the following testimony:

> Any proposal that gives discretionary powers is subject to abuse, but the problem is unless you give the Secretary power to be efficient, nobody is going to be efficient. The beauty of this proposal is that: If you have a military base in your district—God forbid one should be closed in Texas, but it could happen—under this proposal, I have 60 days. So, I come up here and I say, 'God have mercy. Don't close this base in Texas. We can get attacked from the south. The Russians are going to go after our leadership and you know they are going to attack Texas. We need this base.' Then I can go out and lie down in the street

and the bulldozers are coming and I have a trusty aide there just as it gets there to drag me out of the way. All the people in Muleshoe, or wherever this base is, will say, 'You know, Phil Gramm got whipped, but it was like the Alamo. He was with us until the last second.' The bottom line is the public interest will have been preserved. (Gramm 1985, 17)

Senator Gramm's words make it abundantly clear that he expected political blowback from his constituents regarding base closure, but also that he thought a BRAC-like process would help him save face. Interestingly, however, some quantitative empirical research suggests there is "little evidence that legislators suffered for BRAC-led closures, suggesting that electoral fears about the BRAC process may be unfounded" (Emrich 2021, 3). Although this could mean that "BRAC protected lawmakers from electoral fallout," it could also mean that "the fear of voter backlash was misplaced in the first place" (Emrich 2021, 15). In either case, it remains puzzling that there has not been another round of BRAC for so long despite DoD requests for one given that it is unclear whether BRAC helps or hurts politicians worried about bases closing in their districts.

Despite BRAC's initial relative success with closing excess bases, there has not been another round of BRAC since 2005. This is not for lack of the Pentagon's asking for additional base closures. The DoD has "requested a new BRAC round as a means of realizing greater efficiency and reducing excess infrastructure" every year between 2013 and 2017 (although not in FY 2019), and even reported in 2017 that 19% of its base infrastructure was "excess to its needs" (Mann 2019, 9; see also Maucione 2018). Moreover, the Acting Secretary of Defense for Energy, Installations, and Environment testified in 2017 before the Senate Appropriations Committee Subcommittee on Military Construction, Veterans Affairs, and Related Agencies that, "Savings from BRAC rounds are real and substantial. The last five BRAC rounds are collectively saving the Department \$12B annually. A new efficiency-focused BRAC could save the Department an additional ~\$2B annually (based on the '93/'95 rounds)."

If this is the case, what are some of the reasons Congress is reluctant to authorize another round of base closures? Surely fiscally minded conservatives and libertarians would want to reduce wasteful government spending, just as progressives would rather redirect excess military funds to social programs. Lawmakers might ignore calls for another BRAC round because they fear the executive branch will use it as an excuse to target their districts. If this is the case, we might expect to see members of the president's party calling for BRAC while the opposition blocks it, but this does not appear to be happening.

Another explanation for opposition could be rooted in problems from the most recent 2005 round of BRAC. Many Congressmembers' opposition could be, "based on the bad taste that BRAC 2005 left in people's mouths," as it focused much more on realignment rather than closure and turned out to be $21 billion more expensive than projected (Kendall 2013). The implementation of realignments turned out to be more expensive than expected and it therefore took much longer to recoup the costs of the BRAC round. There is, however, broad support from experts across the political spectrum who attest the mistakes of BRAC 2005 can be avoided and that another round of base closures is increasingly important given that the DoD predicted it would have 22% excess capacity by 2019 (*Defense360* 2017). In other words, Congress might be blocking base closures because it took longer than expected for the 2005 BRAC round to pay for itself, but the longer the DoD goes without closing any bases, the returns mount.

The final reason that Congressmembers may block BRAC is that they fear retribution at the ballot box. As discussed, there is some evidence that this argument does not appear to hold water, although more research should be conducted to explore to what degree these findings are replicable. Regardless, it is possible that there are other political constituencies at play, not just unorganized, individual voters whose concerns cannot be addressed by the current institutional structure of the BRAC process.

Given Congress's continued reluctance to authorize another round of BRAC, it appears that, "The resort to an independent commission is an attempt to take the politics out of politics and substitute a superficially rational process for a purely parochial one" (Mayer 1999, 38). However, the politics of reallocating defense spending on bases have not been substituted so much as misplaced—although BRAC has worked in the past, it may no longer be a viable option if it does not address the pressures local constituencies face when threatened with the loss of a major "special privilege" for their community.

ALTERNATE EXPLANATIONS

Other scholars have posited and tested reasons that Congress is reluctant to move forward with BRAC which are worth reviewing here, but they do little to address politics at the local level and how local constituencies influence BRAC decisions.

First, as previously mentioned, Congressmembers may not allow base closures because they expect blowback from their constituents. Mayer (1999, 35) notes, "The conventional wisdom in Congress was that a base closing foretold electoral disaster because newly jobless constituents would heap their frustration on the inept legislator who had failed to protect their well-being." Moreover, there are several mechanisms by which this is purported to occur, such as the executive branch targeting a Congressmember by closing a base, or a representative being insufficiently insulated from retribution at the ballot box by base closure. BRAC is meant to insulate politicians from this retribution by separating technocratic decisions from the political process. It is worth noting that this type of political insulation by delegation is not unique to BRAC but can also be seen in attempts to immunize independent central banks from political business cycles (Alesina and Summers 1993). Preliminary evidence, however, shows that this does not explain what is going on.

Regarding the short-term consequences of base closure, a RAND Corporation study conducted after the 1993 BRAC round examined the effects of base closures in California because the state "absorbed a disproportionate share of the closed bases and displaced personnel, losing 82,000 military and civilian personnel on 21 bases" (Dardia et al. 1996, 2). Focusing on three bases in particular that "were selected due to their large presence in the local community and to the fact that the communities were sufficiently isolated geographically that the effects could be expected to be both severe and measurable" (Dardia et al. 1996, xi), the RAND study still found that "While some of the communities did indeed suffer, the effects were not catastrophic [and/or] not nearly as severe as forecasted." Notably, the RAND study notes that, "Though the closures had noticeable effects, they are relatively localized and have been at least partly offset by other economic factors" (Dardia et al. 1996, xii-xiii), raising the possibility that the overall health of the economy may play a large role in the ability of localities to bounce back after a base closure. In any case, however, the RAND study demonstrates that the short-term effects of base closures even in areas that might be expected to be impacted a great deal are not as severe as doomsayers would claim.

The long-term consequences of base closure also prove the pessimists wrong. For example, examining the housing prices, municipal bond rating, tax revenue per capita, and population growth of Portsmouth, New Hampshire; Austin, Texas; and Philadelphia, Pennsylvania—all of which hosted bases closed by BRAC—reveals that each of the areas recovered in different ways, "reflecting more regional trends than national" (Knupp and Preble 2020). Similarly, a study conducted by the DoD in 2005 examining more than 70 localities "affected by a base closure and determined that nearly all civilian defense jobs lost were eventually replaced. The new jobs are in a variety of industries and fields, allowing communities to diversify their economies away from excessive reliance on the federal government" (cited in Smith and Preble 2018, 7). Just as the short-term consequences of base closure are not as apocalyptic as pessimists predicted, the long-term consequences of BRAC demonstrate that some localities may be even *better off* without the base than they were with it. These results throw cold water on the notion that constituents are likely to vote out any politician who supports BRAC; constituents may be disgruntled by change, but change may bring benefits sooner than expected and cool tempers. Based on this evidence, it seems unlikely that Congress has failed to approve another round of BRAC purely because they are afraid of voters kicking them out of office—after all, at least some voters could likely be swayed by more positive takes on base closure and the examples of localities that fared better after base closure.

A second argument that seeks to explain why Congress has not authorized another BRAC round maintains that defense contractors hold sway over policymakers as a hangover from the Cold War. Defense contractors might lobby Congress to prevent BRAC for two reasons. One is that the defense industry's main client is the federal government, and that this "requires defense firms to invest in politics to win contracts" (Gholz and Sapolsky 1999, 16). In other words, contractors would lobby to keep bases and programs open in order to have as many markets as possible.

A second reason defense contractors would balk at BRAC is that closing bases could mean losing money; "Defense contractors fear that sunk investment will be stranded if projects are cut—that is, their investment will not be adaptable for alternative uses except at great cost" (Gholz and Sapolsky 1999, 16). Some of these pressures may have been mitigated during the Cold War when "the high level of perceived threat placed a premium on military expertise, which checked the contractors' political influence. Now, without the Soviet threat, contractors have too much influence over defense procurement decisions" (Gholz and Sapolsky 1999, 16). This argument may be true for procurement or other defense decisions, but it does not on its own make much sense as an explanation for why BRAC has not occurred.

Given the federal government's reliance on contractors, the defense industry could argue *in favor of* BRAC if contractors expected to benefit from the changes brought about by BRAC. For example, during the 1995 BRAC round, when the list "included two large Air Force bases—McClellan Air Force Base in Sacramento, California, and Kelly Air Force Base in San Antonio, Texas—the White House announced its intention to keep most of the jobs there by turning the work over to private contractors" (Mayer 1999, 33). Under this plan, "the bases would close, officially, but the facilities and most of the jobs would remain in place and be transferred to defense contractors" (Mayer 1999, 36). At the time, this idea was viewed as a blatantly political move by the Clinton administration and was rejected, but both bases were closed in 2001 due to BRAC and have been realigned for other purposes. In other words, contractors might expect to be able to continue at least some of the work they were contracted to do before and after BRAC, depending on what type of closure or realignment occurs. Therefore, defense contractors may not have as much incentive to oppose BRAC as assumed. Given the murkiness surrounding the effects of base closure, it seems highly likely that political actors other than blocs of voters or defense contractors must be behind Congress's reluctance to authorize another round of base closures.

ROLE OF LOCAL CONSTITUENCIES

In contrast to existing arguments, I argue that bases create "local constituencies" that lobby to keep the base amidst the threat of closure.[2] Local constituencies are not individual, unorganized constituents, nor even blocs of similar voters. They are mobilized, organized actors from a wide swathe of backgrounds in a community who have an interest in the base remaining in the locality. They seem to start with active concerned citizens or even local groups that lobby the BRAC Commissions themselves to keep the base, though they may also enlist the help of their sympathetic elected representatives or appointed state government officials. Local constituencies overcome the collective action problem by emphasizing pessimistic predictions of what will happen to the locality once the base has been closed or realigned elsewhere. Local constituencies may become particularly active when they perceive that a base closure will do irreparable harm to the local community (i.e., the community will not be able to replace the benefits that the base supplies). This is important because if a local constituency believes that they will eventually see benefits from closing the base and returning the land to public use, then they will not lobby against the base closure. (After all, not every base closure faces opposition. If local constituencies believe that they will be better off because of a base closure, then my framework does not hold. It may apply only when local constituencies believe their communities will suffer greatly from base closure). Nevertheless, if the local constituency believes that they will not be able to easily replace the benefits a base brings, they will oppose BRAC by lobbying the BRAC Commission.

Local constituencies wish to keep the bases because of unique distributional consequences; although bases may be placed just about anywhere, the localities themselves are not mobile. Hosting a base not only ensures the flow of federal funds to localities, but also brings a steady flow of people to an area that otherwise may not attract many people. Growing or sustaining the population thus supports local businesses, schools, and the tax base. Although a military base may be consolidated elsewhere through realignment, this will not benefit the original community that lost the base. Indeed, once a base has been closed, it is not likely that another base will be placed there in the future.

This is the epitome of the Transitional Gains Trap in a military infrastructure context—the local constituency benefits from the base but will face a transitional loss if it is closed. If the local constituency believes the transitional loss will be enough to end their community and way of life as they know it, they will try to keep the base open by lobbying not just elected officials but more atypical decisionmakers like the BRAC Commission itself.

It can seem difficult to rebut this type of pessimistic viewpoint held by local constituencies because of complex interdependence between the locality and the base. Indeed, it can be especially difficult to disentangle how many jobs the military base supports in rural communities alone. One estimate said that Cannon Air Force Base contributed $98 million to the local economy before 2006 (KCBD 2006). Moreover, even if the number of jobs affected is known, there are complex dynamics at play that make it difficult to know exactly how the community will be affected. The aforementioned RAND report explains this very well:

> These difficulties [of estimating base closure impact] reflect the variety of outcomes that can follow base closure: residents who worked on the base and have lost their jobs can either look for jobs in the local labor market or leave the community to work elsewhere; local businesses (including rental property owners) may lose the portion of their revenues that came from now-unemployed workers or from relocated base personnel or base purchases, but some local business (notably in health services) may gain revenues from retiree demand redirected from base facilities; and vacancies that are created in jobs formerly held by military dependents who have relocated may create new job opportunities for remaining local residents. Thus, while many effects of base closure can serve to reduce local labor and service sector demand, there are other forces acting to increase demand. (Dardia et al. 1996, 9)

In other words, it is quite challenging to predict the economic effects of a base closure given that each base and local community are intertwined in different ways. This high degree of uncertainty is sure to make local constituencies nervous, especially if they perceive that they have much to lose from the base closure. They may then see lobbying against base closure as a fight for their livelihood, very squarely bringing politics back into the BRAC discussion without a clear way to alleviate these parochial, local concerns.

Other works have alluded to the influence of local constituencies but do not explicitly test them or attempt to generalize how and why they work more broadly. For example, the RAND report notes that, "Projections of the effects of the recent round of closures tend to be more pessimistic—often warning of the severe and wide-ranging nature of the anticipated effects. To some extent, this gloomy tone can be attributed to the fact that such studies are often commissioned by *local governments that are trying to lobby against closure*" (Dardia et al. 1996, 8, emphasis added). By the same token, Mayer points out that, "In each successive round, *cities and states* adopted more sophisticated advocacy strategies to protect their bases. In the 1995 round, *local governments and community groups* in southern California spent close to \$1 million to lobby the commission"; additionally, "*State and local governments* are now hiring Washington, D.C., consulting firms in anticipation of future BRAC rounds" (Mayer 1999, 36, emphasis added).

To put it bluntly, local constituencies lobby against BRAC because they perceive that they are fighting a political process that is not meant to work for them. Since BRAC is meant to grant political cover for Congressmembers and technocratic legitimacy to the DoD, it is not necessarily structured to weigh and account for the concerns of local constituencies who may believe that their lives and livelihoods are at stake based on the existence of a military base in their locality. Such a phenomenon has also been described in the literature as "distributional politics," or "who gets what," but distributional politics can become "existential politics," in which "the stakes are whose way of life gets to survive" (Green, Hale, and Colgan 2019). Since BRAC is not designed to accommodate the political concerns of local constituencies, the local constituencies will seek creative ways to influence the BRAC process from outside of the technocratic, impartial structure it was designed to have.

CASE STUDY: CANNON AIR FORCE BASE IN CLOVIS, NEW MEXICO

One such example of how an organized local constituency impacted the BRAC process to reverse their initial decision comes from Cannon Air Force Base in Clovis, New Mexico. On May 13, 2005, Secretary of Defense Donald Rumsfeld forwarded the Department of Defense's list of requested closures to the BRAC Commission. Local residents quickly learned that list included Cannon Air Force Base, which then was home to a mission that involved hosting F-16 aircraft. Just three days later, on May 16, 2005, The Committee of Fifty formed Operation Keep Cannon (KDFA 2006). Although the Clovis Army Air Field had existed since the early 1940s, it was only after it converted to Cannon Air Force Base in 1957 that local businessmen began to consider how they could develop a structured committee that could represent the community and collectively deal with matters relating to the base. By 1959, the Committee of Fifty, named for the fifty local businesses that had agreed to be part of the committee, was born (Committee of Fifty, n.d.).

Operation Keep Cannon probably consisted of many lines of effort, but there is evidence of at least two coordinated campaigns. One appears to be a public rally to demonstrate support for the base from the local community, as evidenced by New Mexico Governor Bill Richardson's comment, "People are waiving [sic] flags, showing their patriotism. They have dedicated their lives to Cannon." The same article where Governor Richardson is quoted mentions "1,200 people carrying signs to 'Keep Cannon'" as a sign that the community may be able to retain the base amidst closures (KCBD 2005a).

The second line of effort appears to have been a letter-writing campaign directed at the BRAC Commission itself. Between May and June 2005, hundreds of letters poured into the BRAC Commission's office in Arlington, Virginia, from residents of Clovis and other New Mexico towns nearby and from as far away as Amarillo, Texas, more than one hundred miles from Cannon Air Force Base. Other letters in support of keeping Cannon Air Force Base arrived later, but the bulk of them arrived just a month after Cannon was marked for closure. These letters are now part of the University of North Texas's archival collections, which include the documents, reports, and correspondence from the 1995 and 2005 BRAC Commissions.

Although there are a few examples of letters in the collection asking to close Cannon Air Force Base, the overwhelming majority favor keeping the base. Many of the letters use dire language to request the BRAC Commission reconsider the Department of Defense's suggestion to close Cannon. The majority of the complaints are economic, but others point out the geographical benefits of the area that would be of use to the military should the base remain. Though the arguments these concerned individuals make are interesting on their own, more remarkable is the repetition of narratives and arguments—typically word-for-word—across dozens of letters.

Sometimes the repetition comes from one person sending the same letter addressed to each of the members of the BRAC Commission, as in the case of State Representative Anne Crook, who wrote, "Of all the bases that are on the BRAC list, Cannon is the most heavily impacted with a loss of an estimated 4,700 jobs. This is approximately 20.5 per cent of the workforce. The next closest base impact was at 11.6 per cent," after mentioning that "The flying weather in Eastern New Mexico and surrounding area allows more flying days than perhaps other areas that are being considered" (Crook 2005). Others like Porfirio Delgado took a similar approach, writing several times:

I do not believe the Commission is fully aware of the unique attributes that Cannon offers to our national defense. These include an abundance of air space and no encroachment issues, a bombing range that is only seconds away, the airspace to fly at supersonic speeds, and ideal year-round flying weather, among many others. In addition to the military value to the nation, Cannon has been supported over the last 50 hears [sic] by the local communities like no other in the country. We consider Cannon a part of our family. The closure of Cannon will also have a devastating impact on our economy. It has been estimated that the area will lose at least 20 percent of its workforce, plus the ripple effect that we will have on our public and higher education systems. (Cannon Individual Letters—117, 2005)

Other letter authors took a more personal approach and hand-wrote their concerns, like Fawn Kirby, who wrote, "So if Cannon is closed our economy will suffer. Ask your self [sic], is there more to lose than gain" (Cannon Individual Letters—117, 2005).

In addition to these letters, there are compilations of correspondence in the collection that specifically designate themselves as part of "Operation Keep Cannon" with a stamp usually on the bottom right side of the page. Many of these letters recycle the same talking points in different orders and with different signatures, including lines like the following:

All city services will be reduced: City police, Sheriff, Hospital, Paramedics, Fire Dept., etc., as well as, tax revenues. The weather in Eastern New Mexico provides a year round training ability with the exception of a few windy days; this in turn is ideal for perfect flying weather. Money will become very tight (Buying, selling, borrowing, etc.) Cannon has the, [sic] facilities, and ramp space to accommodate surge force requirements in training and emergency situations, readiness as was evidenced by the recent joint training effort between Cannon and the US Navy. 20–40% of stores will close. Homes will decrease in value possibly 25–40%, property value will also drop. WE strongly urge you to reconsider your decision and "Keep Cannon." (Community Correspondence—Cannon AFB, 2005)

Although these letters demonstrate that many people were certainly concerned about their economic prospects if Cannon Air Force Base were to close, school-age children also participated in the letter-writing campaign and came up with their own twists on the economic messaging articulated by adults. There are two compilations that total just over one hundred letters specifically from children. One young boy who identifies himself as "Matthew Justus, age 10" writes, "I really think that you shouldn't close Cannon. There will not be any air force base for miles and miles. Also, it will affect the stores and population very much. Lots of people will lose their jobs. Alot [sic] of people will go bankrupt. Think of all the people you'll be takeing [sic] out of their homes" (Letters from Students in the Cannon AFB Area, 2005). Another letter from "your 2nd grade friend Raena L. Gallegos" asks, "Will you please not stop your business! If you stop people will leave my town will get small! Because people will leave Portales [a town near Clovis] it will may be as saml₁ [sic] as Ilida [sic, Elida, another town close to Portales]. So are you still going to close!" (Community Correspondence—Cannon AFB, 2005).

It cannot be mere coincidence that these same themes of economic doom and decline show up not only in letters written by adults opposing the closure of Cannon Air Force Base, but also those which children wrote. Taken together, these letters demonstrate that a local constituency with a good deal of social capital was likely behind the letter-writing campaign that successfully kept the base open. Although there are letters in the collection that advocate to keep other bases open, none of them appear to have such a such a wide variety in the types of letters while retaining consistent messaging. For example, the collection contains a compilation of letters in support of keeping a Niagara Falls Base. Though there are several hundred letters supporting the base in Niagara Falls, nearly all of them are form letters, some of which have been only slightly personalized. The base in Niagara Falls was realigned and remains open, as does Cannon Air Force Base.

Although the letter-writing campaign appeared to impact the BRAC Commissions decision, it would be a year before Operation Keep Cannon succeeded. After touring Cannon in June, the BRAC Commission voted in August to turn the base into an enclave, meaning that the F-16 aircraft would move to another base but that Cannon would remain open as long as it found a suitable new mission by 2010; the commission voted six to one with two abstentions and called Cannon the "'most agonizing decision' they made all day," (KCBD 2005b). The Department of Defense began considering new missions for Cannon in the autumn of 2005 as other bases marked for closure began to shut down. By June 2006, the Air Force had announced a new Special Operations mission for Cannon beginning in 2007 that remains today (KCBD 2006).

The Committee of Fifty's Operation Keep Cannon was successful in that it managed to retain the base, but the victory came with some costs for the group as it picked up the nickname "The Shifty Fifty." It is easy to find online posts from airmen who have received orders to work at Cannon Air Force Base asking about the group; one asked, "So I got orders to Cannon and to put it mildly I am not excited. I keep hearing about the 'Clovis Shifty Fifty' and how they pretty much run that town. Is this true? Anyone want to shed a little light on exactly what they [sic] or what they do?" ("What is the Cannon 'Shifty Fifty'?" 2014). In another post, a user expresses disdain for another base by saying, "At Least It's Not Cannon" ("Holloman AFB, A Preview 'At Least It's Not Cannon'" 2018).

The Committee of Fifty may not be doing itself any favors. As it tries to restyle itself as a liaison between the community and Cannon Air Force Base, the Committee of Fifty website contains material sure to raise eyebrows, including information about how its "new initiative is to be more transparent as a committee and let the community know who our members are in order to educate them on what we do." Even their Frequently Asked Questions section includes, "Does the Committee of 50 control what businesses do or do not come to Clovis?" and "Are rental prices controlled by committee members?" (Committee of Fifty, n.d.). Perhaps part of the Committee of Fifty's problem is that crony systems like what they are accused of being have occurred in other parts of the United States, such as the bubba system in the Florida Keys (Sloan 2020). Regardless of how individuals may feel about the Committee of Fifty, their ability to mobilize their local constituency to Keep Cannon was undeniably successful, as the base has remained—in 2019, the Association of Defense Communities named Clovis, New Mexico, a Great American Defense Community (KFDA 2019). If Cannon Air Force Base were slated for closure in future rounds of BRAC, it seems unlikely the base would close after successfully lobbying to remain open once before.

CONCLUSION

This chapter has demonstrated that local constituencies can lobby to keep their special privileges just as fiercely as other groups lobby to gain new government rents. In the case of Cannon Air Force Base's potential closure, a local constituency mobilized by the Committee of Fifty successfully managed to keep their base even as they remain stuck in the Transitional Gains Trap and may not have the ability to respond to the transitional losses of losing the base in the future. Nevertheless, base closure and realignment persists as an important issue that deserves attention and action both to cut back on unnecessary military spending and to prioritize a strong national defense that need not spread itself thin for parochial concerns. But, as Tullock himself wrote about the Transitional Gains Trap, "It is hard for an economist to recommend any positive action to deal with this kind of situation. It is, as the title of this article suggests, a trap" (Tullock 2004, 221). Thus, the best solution may still be a difficult one.

If the BRAC process no longer addresses the concerns the original institution was meant to allay, then the best course of action may be to revise the process to explicitly allow for social and community concerns to be part of the calculus in deciding which bases to close. After all, "Too many strategies for governance of local commons are designed in capital cities or by donor agencies in ignorance of the state of the science and local conditions. The results are often tragic" (Dietz, Ostrom, and Stern 2003, 1910). Making some exceptions to the BRAC process or allowing compromises could avoid a tragedy of the commons in which no one makes changes to their use of the local good and everyone loses (Hardin, 1968). This is to say that a top-down, one-size-fits-all approach to base closures may no longer be feasible, but that a process that involves community hearings, longer timelines for phasing out base functions, or cash incentives for constituents or small businesses affected by base closures may be effective in allaying local concerns. By definition, such a process would entail greater cooperation between local constituencies and the BRAC Commission. Although some bases important to their communities would still need to be closed, there may be options for mitigating the transitional costs of residents suffering from the closure of the base. Above all, however, the most important policy suggestion is to avoid getting caught in such transitional traps in the first place.

REFERENCES

Alesina, Alberto, and Lawrence H. Summers. 1993. "Central Bank Independence and Macroeconomic Performance: Some Comparative Evidence." *Journal of Money, Credit and Banking* 25 (2): 151–162.

Berman, Sheri. 1997. "Civil Society and the Collapse of the Weimar Republic." *World Politics* 49 (3): 401–429.

"Cannon Individual Letters—117." UNT Digital Archives. Last Accessed 31 October 2021. https://digital.library.unt.edu/ark:/67531/metadc17838/m2/1/high_res_d /BRAC-2005_04762.pdf.

Causey, Mike. 1977. "Carter to End Firings and Demotions; Guidelines on Reorganization," *Washington Post*, 15 December.

Center for Strategic and International Studies, "An Open Letter on BRAC," *Defense360*, 19 June 2017, https://defense360.csis.org/open-letter-brac/.

Chamlee-Wright, Emily, and Virgil Storr. 2011. "Social Capital, Lobbying and Community-Based Interest Groups." *Public Choice* 149 (1–2): 167–185.

Clovis/Curry County Chamber of Commerce. n.d. "Committee of Fifty." Last accessed 31 October 2021. https://www.clovisnm.org/about-the-committee-of-50/.

"Community Correspondence—Cannon AFB." UNT Digital Archives. Last accessed 31 October 2021. ark:/67531/metadc17093.

Crook, Anne. 2021. "Letter from Rep. Anne Crook to Commissioner Gehman/Turner/ Hansen/Bilbray/Coyle/etc." May 30. UNT Digital Archives. Last accessed 31 October 2021. https://digital.library.unt.edu/ark:/67531/metadc14766/m2/1/high _res_d/BRAC-2005_01071.pdf.

Dardia, Michael, Kevin F. McCarthy, Jesse Malkin, Georges Vernez, 1996. "The Effects of Military Base Closures on Local Communities: A Short-Term Perspective," National Defense Research Institute, RAND Corporation. https:// www.rand.org/pubs/monograph_reports/MR667.html

Defense Base Closure and Realignment Commission. 1991. *Report to the President 1991*. Washington, DC: US Department of Defense. https://digital.library.unt.edu/ ark:/67531/metadc25522/m2/1/high_res_d/BRAC-2005_13226.pdf.

Dietz, Thomas, Elinor Ostrom, and Paul C. Stern. 2003. "The Struggle to Govern the Commons." *Science* 302 (5652): 1907–1912.

Emrich, Colin. 2021. "The Electoral Effects of Closing Military Bases." *The Journal of Legislative Studies* 27 (3): 436–463.

Gramm, Phil. 1985. "Hearing Before the Subcommittee on Military Construction of the Committee on Armed Services." United States Senate 99th Congress, first session, 17, Available at https://play.google.com/store/books/details?id =IYXDqJogzo8C&rdid=book-IYXDqJogzo8C&rdot=1.

Green, Jessica, Thomas Hale, and Jeff D. Colgan. 2019. "The Existential Politics of Climate Change." *Global Policy Journal*. https://www.globalpolicyjournal.com/blog/21/02/2019/existential-politics-climate-change.

Gholz, Eugene, and Harvey M. Sapolsky. 1999. "Restructuring the U.S. Defense Industry." *International Security* 24 (3): 5–51.

Hardin, Garrett. 1968. "The Tragedy of the Commons." *Science* 162 (3859): 1243–1248.

"Holloman AFB, A Preview "At Least It's Not Cannon." @CloseHollomanAFB. 2018. Reddit. https://www.reddit.com/r/AirForce/comments/8ifzh9/holloman_afb _a_preview_at_least_its_not_cannon/.

KCBD. 2005a. "Clovis Citizens Show Support for Cannon Air Force Base." Published June 24, 2005, and updated December 14, 2014. https://www.kcbd.com/story/3518220/clovis-citizens-show-support-for-cannon-air-force-base/.

———. 2005b. "BRAC Votes to Temporarily Save Cannon AFB." Published August 26, 2005, and updated December 14, 2014. https://www.kcbd.com/story/3771762/brac-votes-to-temporarily-save-cannon-afb/.

———. 2006. "Changes Are In Store For Cannon Air Force Base," Published 21 June 2006, and updated December 14, 2014. https://www.kcbd.com/story/5062558/changes-are-in-store-for-cannon-air-force-base/.

KFDA. 2006. "Operation Keep Cannon: Mission Accomplished," Published June 20, 2006, and updated September 8, 2006. https://www.newschannel10.com/story/5057128/operation-keep-cannon-mission-accomplished/.

———. 2019. "City of Clovis named a 2019 Great American Defense Community." Updated January 3, 2019. https://www.newschannel10.com/2019/01/04/city-clovis -named-great-american-defense-community/.

Kendall, Frank. 2013. "A Tale of Two BRACS: Commentary," *Roll Call*, 21 November, https://www.rollcall.com/2013/11/21/a-tale-of-two-bracs-commentary /.

Knupp, James and Christopher Preble. 2020. "When Debating Base Closure, Look at the Data," *Cato at Liberty*, Cato Institute, 15 January, https://www.cato.org/blog/when-debating-base-closure-look-data.

"Letters from Students in the Cannon AFB Area." UNT Digital Collections. Last accessed 31 October 2021. https://digital.library.unt.edu/ark:/67531/metadc16542 /m2/1/high_res_d/BRAC-2005_03176.pdf.

Mann, Christopher T. 2019."Base Closure and Realignment (BRAC): Background and Issues for Congress," Congressional Research Service, 25 April, 1. https://www.everycrsreport.com/files/20190425_R45705_9e300ef394d6f4dabc78a7ef8fb bc33ef9bd01e7.pdf.

Maucione, Scott. 2018. "DoD skips BRAC request in 2019 budget," *Federal News Network*, 13 February, https://federalnewsnetwork.com/defense/2018/02/dod-skips -brac-request-in-2019-budget/.

Mayer, Kenneth R. 1999. "The Limits of Delegation: The Rise and Fall of BRAC." *Regulation* 22 (3): 32–38.

Military Construction Authorization Act, 91 U.S.C. § 1474 (1978). https://www .govinfo.gov/content/pkg/STATUTE-91/pdf/STATUTE-91-Pg358.pdf.

Putnam, Robert. 2000. *Bowling Alone: The Collapse and Revival of American Community*. New York City, NY: Simon and Schuster.

Sloan, David. 2020. "Bubbas and Chiefs." *Keys Weekly*. Last accessed 31 October 2021. https://keysweekly.com/42/the-bum-farto-files-bubbas-and-chiefs/.

Sorenson, David S. 1998. *Shutting Down the Cold War: The Politics of Military Base Closure*, New York: St. Martin's Press.

Smith, Adam, and Christopher Preble. 2018. "Another BRAC Now." *Strategic Studies Quarterly* 12 (1): 3–11.

Tullock, Gordon. 2004. "The Transitional Gains Trap." In *The Selected Works of Gordon Tullock, Volume 1: Virginia Political Economy,* edited by Charles K. Rowley, 212–221. Indianapolis, IN: Liberty Fund.

U.S. Congress, Senate Appropriations Committee, "Statement of Mr. Peter Potochney Acting Assistant Secretary Of Defense (Energy, Installations, and Environment) Before the Senate Appropriations Committee Subcommittee on Military Construction, Veterans Affairs, and Related Agencies Fiscal Year 2018 Department of Defense Budget Request for Energy, Installations, and Environment," 115th U.S. Congress, 1st session, June 6, 2017. https://www.appropriations.senate.gov/imo/ media/doc/060617-Potochney-Testimony.pdf.

"What is the Cannon 'Shifty Fifty'?" @redditearmiee. 2014. Reddit. https://www .reddit.com/r/AirForce/comments/2r2uf6/what_is_the_cannon_shifty_fifty/.

NOTES

1. Answering the question of why Congress halted base closures and realignment in the 1970s could apparently be its own separate research question, but it is unfortunately beyond the scope of this paper.

2. I borrow the term "local constituencies" from Mayer 1999, p. 38.

Chapter 6

Social Media and Social Movements

How Technology Has Aided Coordination

Ellen Hamlett

As technology rapidly evolves, so does the way we communicate with each other. Now, we can contact each other with the touch of a button or the click of a mouse, and we are inundated with information every time we so much as pick up our phones. This presents our society with innumerable opportunities for disseminating information to the masses. This chapter will explore how the internet has revolutionized organizing and mobilizing for social change through the lens of how information is distributed and how people communicate and organize.

In this chapter, I will first discuss the literature on social movements organizations (SMOs) broadly, describing the prominent theories on the ways SMOs structure themselves and how social movements are formed. Secondly, I discuss how the internet has helped to promote a new kind of social coordination by reducing transaction costs and assuaging the "knowledge problem." I argue that the internet has both considerably reduced the transaction costs of social coordination and has helped alleviate the knowledge problem that exists between individuals and coordinators through facilitating the streamlined exchange of information. Thirdly, I discuss the opportunities and challenges this streamlined exchange of information presents for SMOs in the digital era; highlighting how, in addition to new avenues for communication, there is concern over the rise of "slacktivism" and the proliferation of "fake news." Lastly, I explore these issues through the largest social movement of our time, the Black Lives Matter Movement, from its inception to the present, to understand how the internet has shaped this movement through the lens of transaction costs and the knowledge problem.

SOCIAL MOVEMENT THEORY

Scholars from across the disciplinary spectrum have sought to explain how social movements originate and evolve (Sen and Avci 2016, 125). Since the latter half of the twenty-first century, the United States has seen a flurry of social movements from the Civil Rights Movement to the Anti-Vietnam War Movement to the Occupy Wall Street Movement. However, social movements were thought to be disorganized and motivated by personal rather than political reasons. That is why social movements were typically regarded as a form of "collective behavior." This changed in the 1960s when the scholars made a social science breakthrough that changed the way social movement organizations (SMOs) were recognized. Scholars began to realize SMOs are in fact forms of "collective action" with highly organized social networks that are integrated into society (Goodwin and Jasper 2015, 155).

Collective action is often taken to solve a collective action problem, which emerge when individuals do not act in a way that benefits the public because it is personally costly. For example, in the wake of Hurricane Katrina many collective action problems arose when coordinating community recovery (Chamlee-Wright 2008). In the wake of this disaster, the Lower Ninth Ward was desperately in need of goods and services, however, despite the fact that it would benefit the community at large, many entrepreneurs were unwilling to take on the risk and cost of reopening.

As discussed in Emily Chamlee-Wright's chapter in this volume (see chapter one), collective action problems are often seen as a market failure. However, as Chamlee-Wright notes, just because a collective action problem exists, does not necessarily mean that government action is the most efficient way to solve the problem. Collective action problems can often be addressed through markets and civil society. In fact, many social movements are formed to solve a collective action problem.

How Social Movements are Structured

SMOs can vary widely—some are highly centralized and bureaucratic while others are decentralized and horizontally structured (Goodwin and Jasper 2015, 155). Typically, decentralized social movements are not institutionalized, where no individual or organization has control over the movement or any of its participants. According to Rich (2020, 432), decentralized SMOs "favor individual autonomy and consensus-based decision-making. Some even operate without a clearly defined leadership. Networks are decentralized in that they privilege communication and coordination at the local level overachieving national uniformity." We see this lack of defined leadership in the Occupy Wall Street Movement of the late 2000s (Calhoun 2013).

In contrast, centralized SMOs, often referred to as "federations," are hierarchical, with a small subset of individuals with decision-making authority for the movement. Typically, in the pursuit of effecting change, the decision-makers tend to develop relationships with government officials. Due to the nature of these relationships, with time these leaders become subject to the "law of oligarchy" and begin to adopt less radical goals for the organization. Over time, centralized SMOs tend to morph into interest groups, as they rely mostly on institutional methods to advocate for policy change, rather than disruptive tactics such as protesting (Rich 2020). The modern labor union is an example of how a federalized social movement formalized over time, where union leaders now work to achieve their goals mostly through collective bargaining and lobbying (Willems and Jegers 2012, 73).

How Social Movements are Formed

Just as the world is naturally complex and dynamic, SMOs are dynamic, complex, and evolving. While many theories have been proposed to explain how social movements come to be, two theories are generally accepted as the most prominent: the resource mobilization theory and the new social movement approach (Fuchs 2006, 104). The resource mobilization theory stems from rational choice theory: it considers the participants of SMOs as rational actors that are calculating the gains and losses that come from participating in SMO activity, such as protesting. This theory asserts that SMOs are the result of the "successful mobilization of resources and political opportunities by rational actors." typically brought on by the availability of resources to mobilize and to new political opportunities (Fuchs 2006, 106).

The new social movement approach is not a specific theory but a mix of several varied theories. This approach moves away from the traditional Marxist theories which focus on analyzing the emergence of SMOs from the perspective that socioeconomic class is the primary collective identity. The common chord between the new social movement theories is that they focus on additional collective identity factors—such as gender, sexuality, or ethnicity—as reasons to drive individuals to collective action (Sen and Avci 2016, 128).

However, neither of these theories is complete. The resource management theory helps explain how SMOs are formed but does not explain the motivations of an SMO. While the new social movement approach helps us to understand that SMOs are motivated by collective identities, it does not have a conceptual understanding of how SMOs are formed or how they behave. While there is no one explanation for how SMOs are born, a common thread through many of the prominent theories of social movements is that SMOs are born due to some combination of shared grievances, mobilized resources, and the right opportunity.

Social Movement Organizations and Entrepreneurship

Forming an SMO is, in many ways, similar to the groundwork necessary for entrepreneurial discovery. The entrepreneur's role in society, as Schumpeter (1942, 132) says, is to "reform or revolutionize the patterns of production." This is done by developing new products or methods of production, discovering new markets or resources, or developing new organizational methods for firms (Mitchell and Boettke 2017, 37). Like the organizer of a social movement, an entrepreneur must seek the right opportunity, at the right time, and with the right resources. In other words, they pursue opportunities to change the world.

In fact, there are several insistences where entrepreneurship is the key driver of economic development and community revival, especially in post-disaster circumstances. As community rebound after a disaster is a form of a collective action problem, like SMOs, entrepreneurs can spur community development if that entrepreneur is alert to opportunities that promote social change (Storr, Haeffele-Balch, and Grube 2015, 34). One of the most important roles that entrepreneurs play in post-disaster recovery is signaling to the community that a rebound is underway. According to Storr, Haeffele-Balch, and Grube (2015, 105), entrepreneurs accomplish this in one or more of four ways: 1) acting as first movers and accepting the risk associated with returning before a full recovery is made; 2) opening a business that provides goods or services that can aid the recovery process; 3) facilitating communication among displaced residents to aid in the recovery effort; 4) simply reopening their businesses to signal a return to normalcy.

For example, after Katrina devastated New Orleans, the severe destruction and concentrated poverty in the Lower Ninth Ward led many to believe that the neighborhood could not be rebuilt. After the storm, residents of the Lower Ninth Ward were prohibited to access their property for three months, delaying the restoration of property and signaling to the community that recovery would not occur. However, the community wanted to return. One entrepreneur, Casey Kasim, saw an opportunity to reopen his one-stop-shop with gas, groceries, laundry facilities, and more, to provide the community with the amenities needed to rebuild and recover. By reopening, Kasim not only served the community by providing it with goods and services, but he signaled to other entrepreneurs that it was possible to do business in the area and that recovery was underway, therefore drawing in more businesses (Storr, Haeffele, and Grube 2015, 115–116). In doing so, Kasim, "establish[ed] a centralized location that became the focal point for community recovery," driving community change by drawing community members and businesses back to the Lower Ninth Ward (Storr, Haeffele-Balch, and Grube 2015, 116).

Entrepreneurship—whether it be social, ideological, or traditional entrepreneurship—can spur social change through recognizing opportunities and acting on them. As articulated by Storr, Haeffele-Balch, and Grube (2015, 32),

> Social change, in the broadest sense, refers to any endogenous change in the social order . . . Entrepreneurs are a driving force behind these instances of social change. They are alert to opportunities to change society and are bold innovators who introduce new products, services, or ideas or establish new enterprises or revitalize existing ones to bring about social change.

Consequently, social change is a product of entrepreneurial action, whether through traditional entrepreneurship, such as Kasim providing goods and services to a community in need, or through a social movement formed with the explicit intention of solving a specific social ailment.

TRANSACTION COSTS AND THE KNOWLEDGE PROBLEM

Ronald Coase, determined to understand and develop a theory on why varying industries were organized in different ways, found himself asking the question: "How did one reconcile the views expressed by economists on the role of the pricing system and the impossibility of successful central economic planning with the existence of management and of these apparently planned societies, firms, operating within our own economy?" (Boettke, Haeffele and Storr 2016, 68). In his work, Coase found the answer to this question: transaction costs.

Coase discovered that there are costs to exchange, which can include finding a willing trading partner to negotiating prices to creating contracts. Coase argued that firms emerge to reduce transaction costs through coordination, otherwise the costs may be prohibitively high. If transaction costs are too high, it makes it difficult for people to participate in market exchange even if that exchange is mutually beneficial. For example, economic exchange can create negative externalities. Coase theorized that without transaction costs, having well-defined property rights would enable the externality creator and the externality victim to come to a mutually beneficial arrangement to both parties (Coase 2013). However, despite that two parties have the ability to reach a mutually beneficial arrangement, transaction costs, such as the cost of a lawyer, can be too costly for one or both parties, effectively making the bargaining process impossible.

Before his work, economists focused on the price mechanism as the only form of market coordination; however, Coase emphasized the role institutions play in the economic system. He argues that when firms coordinate in order to overcome transaction costs, this coordination creates institutional arrangements which control the process of exchange. For example, in his work, *The Institutional Structure of Production* (1992), Coase discussed how the emergence of the legal system has a "profound effect on the working of the economic system and may in certain respects be said to control it." He argues that the institutional setting in which an exchange takes place changes how firms or individuals reduce transaction costs.

Much of Coase's work was dedicated to applying this institutional analysis to better understand how individuals reduce transaction costs, whether it be through creating firms or developing legal structures, etc. In fact, Coase states, "a large part of what we think of as economic activity is designed to accomplish what high transaction costs would otherwise prevent or to reduce transaction costs so that individuals can freely negotiate and we can take advantage of that diffused knowledge of which Hayek has told us" (Coase 1992, 716).

In his seminal work, *Politics without Romance*, James M. Buchanan reminds us that the process of "political exchange" is much more complex than "market exchange," highlighting that transaction costs are just as pervasive in the political process. As Buchanan argues, "'political exchange' necessarily involves *all* members of the relevant community rather than two trading partners that characterize economic exchange," the transaction costs of political exchange are higher, and therefore coordination is more difficult to achieve (Buchanan 1999, 50, emphasis in original). As such, the transaction costs of collective action can hinder group formation, especially for large groups, which is often necessary for collective action (Olson 1971).

Dr. Mark S. Bonchek (1995) argues that, for those engaged in collective political action, there are three types of organizational costs (transaction costs): communication, coordination, and information. Communication costs concern the time and effort to craft and send messages. Coordination costs concern the time and effort to reach a group consensus. Information costs concern the time and effort it takes to "gather the information necessary to make a decision or communicate a message" (Bonchek 1995, 2.4). While the communication costs and coordination costs are relatively straightforward—both involve the work that can be done with the information an organization has—the information costs associated with collective action are more complex; it is not as simple as gathering information for the information must first be discovered. The challenge associated with discovering information is due to what Hayek (1945) calls the "knowledge problem."

In his paper "The Use of Knowledge in Society," Hayek describes a key challenge of economic coordination: that no single authority has all the knowledge necessary for central planning because knowledge is initially dispersed among many different individuals nor is the information shared among individuals to enable them to "dovetail their plans with those of others" (Hayek [1945] 2014, 95).

In the market process, information is shared through market exchange, and we rely on the price system as a mechanism for coordination. The political exchange process is more complex, but as technology advances and the internet becomes more ubiquitous, as Don Lavoie says, "we can expect these technological advancements to facilitate market transactions and thereby improve the coordination of plans" (Lavoie 2016, 55). I argue that this is true not only for market exchange but also for political exchange through the internet facilitating social coordination.

Prices convey information that enables millions of people to coordinate without any central authority or coercion (Hayek [1945] 2014). Just as Hayek described how prices convey information on the market that allows millions to "fit their plans with those of others," so too does the internet convey information that allows for people to coordinate (Mitchell and Boettke 2017, 35). As mentioned previously in this chapter, Buchanan notes that the transaction costs of political exchange are higher due to the simple fact that there are more people involved, and therefore coordination is more difficult to achieve (Buchanan 1999). However, the internet has created channels, specifically e-communication and social media, that allow individuals to convey information on a mass scale. This reduces the transaction costs that prevent the sharing of information, thus allowing for individuals to share the knowledge that is dispersed among themselves, enabling social coordination through individuals "dovetail[ing] their plans with those of others" (Hayek [1945] 2014, 95).

TRANSACTION COSTS, TECHNOLOGY, AND SOCIAL MOVEMENTS

All three types of transaction costs associated with collective action, as enumerated by Bonchek, can be reduced by increased access to technological advancements, more specifically, access to the internet. There is ample evidence to show how the internet has reduced transaction costs associated with collective action (Bonchek 1995).

As discussed previously in this chapter, Bonchek (1995) asserts that the internet—especially the role of computer mediated communication (CMC)—reduces the organizational transaction costs of mobilizing in three ways: speed, cost, and enabling coordination through asynchronous, intelligent communication.

Communication via the internet is both faster and cheaper than traditional media, allowing for communication between many people in many places. As Bonchek (1995, 4.6) writes, "When people and resources are dispersed in different times and different places, CMC can reduce the organizational costs involved in bringing them together to reach a decision and carry out a plan." Unlike traditional community organizing, the internet does not require that all activists be in the same room at the same time. By removing that requirement, the internet exponentially expands the pool of potential activists for any given campaign.

In the digital era, access and knowledge of technology have become a critical part of modern SMOs (Rolfe 2015). Technology can enhance a traditional social movement campaign by engaging activists online, then transitioning those activists to traditional, offline activism. A 2009 Survey by DigiActive found that social networking sites are the most frequent entryway for individuals to get involved in online activism (Harlow 2012). Social media allows organizers to mobilize activists in three main ways: 1) calls to action for offline activities such as participating in protests or giving testimony; 2) calls to action for offline activities that can now be done online, such as sending emails to government officials; 3) calls to action for online-only activities, such as social media information sharing (Harlow 2012).

Additionally, as Bonchek (1995, 4.6) describes, "for complex decisions requiring a face-to-face meeting, CMC is useful for gathering and distributing preliminary information and opinions. Once a commitment is generated, CMC is useful for coordinating actions among committed parties." Using the internet as a tool to facilitate communication significantly lowers the cost of finding, collecting, and analyzing the information necessary to a successful activism campaign. As articulated by Harlow (2012, 229), "when it comes to supporting traditional techniques of social movements, whether protests or signature drives, the internet, unlike any other medium, allows for fast, easy and cheap transnational action not limited by time, space or distance." In other words, the internet allows social movement organizers to engage more people for less cost, ostensibly revolutionizing modern activism.

While it is certainly true that the internet has reduced the transaction costs for communication, due to the lower cost of disseminating information there has also been an influx of unreliable information. The ability to create and disseminate information with a few clicks presents an opportunity for social movement organizers to spread information with ease but also presents an opportunity for disruptors to broadcast misinformation quickly and cheaply. While the dissemination of unreliable information is not new—misinformation has been spread for a variety of purposes since before the printing press—the internet has created an "attention economy" where misinformation is distributed and consumed rapidly and globally (Pennycook and Rand 2021).

Although social media was not created with the intention of being a conduit for disseminating information to the masses—for example, Facebook was famously designed as a site to connect Harvard students with each other—social media now plays a major role in how we communicate with each other and seek information. Despite that it was not the original design of social media to become a space where information is disseminated to the masses, it nonetheless has become so. The concept of a human behavior emerging not from deliberate design, but as the product of actions taken by many individuals trying to achieve their goals is not new (Mitchell and Boettke 2017, 38). Hayek defined this process as "spontaneous orders." Spontaneous orders are the result of human action, but not deliberate design. This phenomenon is explained by Mitchell and Boettke (2017, 38) with their "path in the snow" example:

> A student in the Midwest in January is trying to get to class quickly while avoiding the cold may cut across the quad rather than walk the long way around. Cutting across the quad in the snow leaves footprints; as other students follow these, they make the path bigger. Although the students' goal is merely to get to class quickly and to avoid the cold weather, in the process they create a path in the snow that actually helps students who come later to achieve this goal more easily.

In other words, spontaneous orders are the side effects of an action, not necessarily the goal (Martin and Storr 2008, 76). Typically, spontaneous orders are considered to be socially beneficial, like the path in the snow, not all spontaneous orders are. Spontaneous orders that are not socially beneficial are known as perverse emergent orders. The proliferation of misinformation is, in many ways, a perverse emergent order; while not planned, the rise of "fake news" has emerged as part of social media that is not socially beneficial.

This perverse emergent order presents a key challenge for social coordination in the digital age. Since it is easier to spread and receive information, users must now filter through waves of headlines, tweets, and broadcasts and discern what information is reliable. While the prevailing narrative is that people are deceived by false headlines due to their political preferences, studies show that while people are more likely to preferentially believe true headlines that align with their political beliefs, it is not the case for false headlines.

Rather than being "bamboozled by partisanship," people are more likely to believe false headlines when they fail to reflect on the veracity of what they see on social media (Pennycook and Rand 2021). However, this does not answer the question of whether the proliferation of unreliable information creates a burden for individuals seeking out information, since people now must take the time to discern if the information they come across is legitimate. The proliferation of "fake news" may have created a situation where the ease in which information can be accessed over the internet has significantly reduced transaction costs of disseminating information, but it has also made the transaction costs of finding legitimate information higher than before.

Additionally, due to the ease in which individuals can participate in online activism—through links that can send a prewritten email to your legislator with a click of the mouse or advertisements to sign an online petition—there is criticism that those that are involved in online activism are not as engaged as traditional activists, thereby "undercut[ing] a movement's value, creating a half-hearted, meaningless activism, or 'slacktivism'" (Harlow 2012, 229). Scholars define *slacktivism* as low-effort, nominal gestures, such as liking a Facebook post or signing an online petition, that do not, in effect, benefit the cause. Scholars argue that people engage in "slacktivism" are willing to perform a low-cost action to signal their support of a movement but are not willing to actively support a cause with the effort of a traditional activist (Kristofferson, White and Peloza 2014).

However, there is evidence to suggest that "slacktivism" does not undercut a movement's value and that online recruiting can engage high-commitment activists. Communications scholar Magdalena Wojcieszak (2008) conducted a study that examined the online behavior of neo-Nazi and radical environmentalist groups whose group indemnity was intensified by participating in online groups. She found that the more participation in online discussion forums increased, the more offline political activities increased; in fact, online participation was the strongest predictor of offline political activity. Economists Campante, Durante, and Sobbrio (2018) looked at the evolution of an Italian grassroots movement that began on the social media platform, Meetup.com, and successfully resulted in offline success as an electoral initiative. This study found that the availability of broadband internet was associated with these groups developing sooner and growing more quickly, resulting in an off-line movement with tangible electoral successes. Lastly, journalism professor Summer Harlow (2012) focused on the protests that followed the murder of a Guatemalan lawyer that was allegedly carried out by Guatemalan president Alvaro Colom. The accusations caused a flurry of online activity, for example, the creation of Facebook pages demanding justice. The author examined the relationship between interactions on Facebook and the offline protesting activity and found that the online activism on

Facebook successfully created a sense of community, which resulted in a movement that moved offline to protest the injustices on the streets of Guatemala. Therefore, there is little reason to believe that the use of social media results in a preponderance of "slacktivism" that undercuts the legitimacy of a social movement.

CASE STUDY: THE BLACK LIVES MATTER MOVEMENT

The Black Lives Matter movement (BLM) is likely the largest social movement in United States history (Buchanan, Bui, and Patel 2020). Emerging in 2013, the BLM movement is arguably the first of its kind; decentralized, geographically widespread, and organically started on the internet with the use of the hashtag, *#BlackLivesMatter*. Since its inception, the movement has inspired a great deal of literature examining the efficacy of the movement and how efficiently it operates, much of it concerning how the BLM movement uses social media to communicate with activists and vice versa. As noted by Tillery (2019, 318), "Most extant studies have highlighted the role that hashtags play in forming dialogs between core BLM activists and their adherents. These studies have led to considerable gains in our knowledge by demonstrating how these dialogs have boosted the movement's ability to disseminate information." Growing out of the unique opportunity to disseminate information and communicate via hashtags, the BLM movement has a unique structure founded on the principle of decentralized decision making.

History of the Black Lives Matter Movement

The Black Lives Matter movement began on July 13, 2013, when Alicia Garza, Opal Tometi, and Patrisse Cullors initiated the *#BlackLivesMatter* hashtag on Twitter to protest the acquittal of George Zimmerman in the shooting of Trayvon Martin. Over the next few years, the hashtag became more influential as advocates and activists used the hashtag to communicate on police reform issues. The hashtag gained even more traction in the wake of the shooting of Michael Brown in Ferguson, Missouri, when "Black Lives Matter" became the motto of the protests that swept the nation (Tillery 2019). Following these protests in Ferguson, organizers from 18 different cities formed BLM chapters in their communities, creating a network of organizers and activists that became the Black Lives Matter Global Network infrastructure, the decentralized guiding structure of the BLM movement ("Herstory").

In 2020, the BLM movement protests swept the nation and became the center of political discourse. In the wake of the death of George Floyd, among others, millions of Americans went to the streets to protest police brutality.

The largest day of demonstrations was June 6th, 2020, when over half a million protestors mobilized in nearly 550 cities and towns across the country. Polls, done in the weeks following the June 2020 BLM protests, found that anywhere from 15 million to 26 million people participated in the demonstrations, making it the largest movement in United States history (Buchanan, Bui, and Patel 2020). In contrast, despite the highly organized nature of the 2017 Women's March demonstration, which had an attendance of 3 to 5 million (Chenoweth and Pressman 2017), the BLM demonstrations far surpassed those numbers through organic recruitment via social media. A majority of the participants of the demonstrations were motivated to protest after they watched a video related to police violence—the videos that are typically shared via social media and hashtags (Buchanan, Bui, and Patel 2020).

Structure of the Black Lives Matters Movement

Despite sharing many similarities, the BLM movement, unlike the Civil Rights movement of the 1950s and 60s, does not rely on the traditional hierarchical structure but rather a decentralized structure. Furthermore, Milkman (2017, 23) notes, "BLM activists were also critical of the civil rights movement's reliance on hierarchical organizational forms and its centralized leadership . . . BLM instead strives for 'leaderful,' horizontal organizational structures." Rather than a small number of figureheads that travel around the country to mobilize activists, as was done in the Martin Luther King Jr. (MLK) era, the BLM consists of local chapters with leaders independent of centralized headquarters (Cobbina et al. 2021).

Scholars argue that the advancement in technology has facilitated these more horizontal structures, allowing for more participation for more members due to the ease with which organizers can communicate with activists. According to Goodwin and Jasper (2015, 191), "Technological change has reduced the need for such centralized and hierarchical structures. To sustain the voluntary participation of members, activist groups needed to find ways to satisfy a desire for more local autonomy." And the BLM movement has done just that. As Jennifer Cobbina-Dungy, an associate professor in the School of Criminal Justice at Michigan State University, explains, the decentralized structure of the BLM movement allows for local leaders to coordinate with each other based on a shared set of values "that prizes local connections and fast mobilization in response to police violence" (Daniel 2021). What makes this movement so responsive is its decentralized nature, rather than planning everything from the leadership down, it instead provides a framework, materials, and guidance to empower activists to participate in the movement however the individual or community sees fit.

Spreading Information and Building Community

Much of the decentralized and horizontal nature of this movement can be attributed to social media. Scholars agree that the BLM movement is most closely aligned with the New Social Movement approach, and a defining feature of this approach is its use of social media as a form of communication. In the case of the BLM movement, Twitter has become the basic infrastructure of the movement (De Choudhury et al. 2016). Unlike traditional media, social media is a platform for user-generated content. Consequently, social media is inherently a decentralized medium for creating and spreading ideas and information (Ince, Rojas, and Davis 2017). One study that examined how Twitter users interact with the BLM movement via hashtags notes, "social media is now an arena where social movements promote their message, articulate their core beliefs, and offer a frame to the public. Social media is also a forum where 'the average citizen' can directly interact with a movement" (Ince, Rojas, and Davis 2017, 1817). Social media, therefore, provides SMOs with a channel to disseminate information about their mission, goals, events, etc. In fact, a study, that looked at college students' discussions of the BLM movement, found that two-thirds of students in the study explicitly mentioned that they receive their information about the movement from social media (Cox 2017).

Social media has provided the movement with an opportunity to organically spread information, facilitate conversations for individuals to engage with the issue, and build communities around the BLM movement (De Choudhury et al. 2016). Unlike traditional communication methods, social media—in the case of the BLM movement, Twitter and Facebook—allows the public at large to interact with the movement, allowing the BLM movement to engage broad audiences, rather than just a core group of activists. Social media has also successfully aided recruitment to the movement (Ince, Rojas, and Davis 2017). As articulated by one of the co-founders of the movement, Patrisse Cullors, "because of social media we reach people in the smallest corners of America. We are plucking at a cord that has not been plucked forever. There is a network and a hashtag to gather around" (De Choudhury et al. 2016). Research shows that, unlike traditional community organizing, online collective action communities are far more personal (Bennett and Segerberg 2011). Furthermore, one study on the BLM movement notes, "Twitter emerged as an important platform of discourse and reflection for many individuals, allowing them to share stories, find common ground and agitate for police and government reform around racial issues" (De Choudhury et al. 2016). As explained by Mundt, Ross, and Burnett (2018, 9), "this occurs in terms of . . . using social media platforms to 'comment on' and engage with those issues in the process of information transmission. In other words, social media creates opportunities for developing interactive relationships with like-minded activists in ways that extend beyond traditional forms of coalition-based organizing." Social media creates a unique opportunity for activists to engage with each other in a meaningful way, creating a community that is not limited by the bounds of physical location.

Issue Framing and the Scaling of Social Movements

Additionally, online activism provides an opportunity to disseminate educational information and frame the issue. Harlow (2012, 228) writes that media frames can, "define an issue through selection, exclusion, emphasis, and elaboration—in other words, frames tell the audience how to think about something." Therefore, information sharing via social media networks allows organizers to mobilize activists online by framing a problem, determining solutions, and motivating people to engage offline. This is especially true for framing via the use of social media, which allows a movement to accomplish the above without relying on a figurehead of a movement to disseminate information. Rather, it allows for a large population to engage with the messages coming from a movement and create communities around it (Ince, Rojas and Davis 2017). Social media's ability to allow an SMO to shape a shared narrative among a wide population of individuals further illustrates the role social media can play in broadening and scaling a movement (Mundt, Ross, and Burnett 2018).

As mentioned previously in this chapter, the BLM movement is likely the largest in the United States history, turning out millions of protestors in June of 2020 (Buchanan, Bui, and Patel 2020). Scholars agree that the scale of this movement is remarkable. As Kenneth Andrews, a sociology professor at the University of North Carolina at Chapel Hill, notes, "The geographic spread of protest is a really important characteristic and helps signal the depth and breadth of a movement's support" (Buchanan, Bui, and Patel 2020). Like how technological change has facilitated the decentralized nature of the BLM movement, so too has technology facilitated the movement's ability to scale in size. A historical challenge for traditional social organizing has been scale; it is time-consuming and expensive to organize a large grassroots coalition of activists. However, as illustrated in this chapter, this is where the BLM movement has excelled. The literature surrounding social media and social organizing suggests that social media can facilitate framing, resource mobilization, and coalition building, which all contribute to a SMO's ability to scale up (Mundt, Ross, and Burnett 2018).

However, like how Kasim's decision to reopen his business in New Orleans' Lower Ninth Ward resulted in spurring community development, the use of social media by the BLM organizers was not necessarily originally intended to spur the scaling of the movement. Regardless, the movement grew organically. According to one study, the use of social media was imperative to the BLM organizing efforts in three ways: "(1) for mobilizing internal and external resources, (2) for building coalitions among and between BLM groups and other social movements, and (3) for controlling the narrative of the movement" (Mundt, Ross, and Burnett 2018, 6). As a movement whose roots are in social media, this has facilitated the BLM movement's ability to scale to the size that it has. For the reasons enumerated above—the ease with which SMOs can spread and frame information, communicate with organizers and activists, and build a community around an issue—the BLM movement has been able to scale to the largest and most geographically spread SMO in United States history.

Social Media, Transaction Costs and the Knowledge Problem

When transaction costs are prohibitively high, it can make participating in the market exchange too expensive, even when the exchange is mutually beneficial. Just as there are transaction costs for market exchange, so too are there transaction costs for political exchange and collective action. Nonetheless, Buchanan identified a key difference between market exchange and political exchange; that is, the transaction costs for political exchange are naturally higher due to the difficulty of coordinating all people in the relevant communities (Buchanan 1999, 50). However, the advent of the internet has helped to reduce the transaction costs of collective action by reducing the organizational transaction costs of mobilizing through making it cheaper, faster, and easier to coordinate and communicate with individuals, thereby allowing SMOs to grow larger and more quickly (Bonchek 1995). In fact, a study by Bennett and Segerberg (2012) shows that SMOs that use social media are typically larger, more flexible, and have scaled more quickly. We see this clearly in the case of the BLM movement. As evidenced in this chapter, social media allowed the BLM movement to create a framework in which they can mobilize activists efficiently and inexpensively, as social media can convey information with the click of a mouse and is free to use. The ability of the BLM movement to facilitate coordination, resource mobilization, and narrative framing through information sharing can be attributed, at least in part, to the reduction of transaction costs provided by the advent of social media.

In addition to reducing the transaction costs associated with collective action, social media has also provided organizers with a channel to not only communicate with the masses but for the masses to communicate with them. When breaking down Hayek's two-part description of the knowledge problem that (a) knowledge is dispersed among individuals which; (b) makes it difficult for people to coordinate and "dovetail their plans with those of others" (Hayek [1945] 2014, 95). We can see that the use of a hashtag, or other internet communication tools, can help facilitate the dispersion of information with the intention of coordination. Social media platforms allow for a smooth exchange of information by allowing individuals to share information bottom to top and allowing coordinators to disseminate information top to bottom, allowing individuals to coordinate plans.

We see this play out in the BLM movement through the communication between activists and organizers. The social media component allowed for organizers to quickly mobilize activists to participate in public demonstrations but also allowed the activists to communicate their on-the-ground needs to organizers. Furthermore, one study found that many of the BLM affiliated social media accounts, many were specifically dedicated to creating an online space for dialogue and communication (Mundt, Ross, and Burnett 2018). The facilitation of this dialogue via social media has helped to alleviate the knowledge problem, enabling mass coordination by allowing for individuals to share information from the grassroots, thereby allowing individuals to "dovetail their plans with those of others" (Hayek [1945] 2014, 95).

CONCLUSION

Technological advancements, such as the advent of social media, have entirely changed the ways social movement organizations operate. The ability to communicate social issues and coordinate plans with individuals across large geographic areas has created new opportunities for SMOs to support their mission. These technological changes and the ability to communicate with such ease have reduced the transaction costs of collective action, leading to new opportunities for knowledge sharing among activists and organizers.

However, these changes have brought on challenges of their own. For example, as demonstrated earlier in this chapter, online activism has had proven, tangible off-line results, but much of the literature surrounding this issue regards relatively short-term social movements. This begs the question: are activists that are recruited by an SMO online as dedicated to the issue as traditional activists? One study that analyzed how the use of Twitter promoted collective action around the BLM movement found that while some individuals engaged in perfunctory or one-time participation in the movement, others remained involved in online engagement over long periods of time (De Choudhury et al. 2016).

However, more analysis is needed to understand the longevity of activist commitment to offline activities. Additionally, while social media has revolutionized mass communication and reduced the transaction costs of collective action, a negative consequence has been the rise of "fake news." The internet and social media have proven to be a net positive for the ability of SMOs to organize and mobilize, but it is important to recognize that there are costs associated with using the internet as a tool to facilitate the dissemination of information.

Despite these challenges, the BLM movement has succeeded in using social media to become the largest social movement in United States history. This case study suggests that social media plays a major role in reducing the costs of social organizing. Two challenges that social organizers have faced throughout history are the cost of disseminating information and the difficulty of coordinating individuals. As demonstrated in the case of the BLM movement, social media has helped to assuage these challenges by facilitating communication between organizers and activists, and vice versa, in turn allowing the movement to build a community that can effectively coordinate activists.

REFERENCES

Bennett, W. Lance, and Alexandra Segerberg. 2011. "Digital Media and the Personalization of Collective Action: Social Technology and the Organization of Protests Against the Global Economic Crisis." *Information, Communication & Society* 14 (6): 770–99.

———. 2012. "The Logic of Connective Action: Digital Media and the Personalization of Contentious Politics." *Information, Communication & Society* 15. (5): 739–68.

Black Lives Matter Global Network Foundation. "Herstory." Blacklivesmatter.com. https://blacklivesmatter.com/herstory/.

Boettke, Peter J., Stephanie Haeffele, and Virgil H. Storr, eds. 2016. *Mainline Economics: Six Nobel Lectures in the Tradition of Adam Smith*. Arlington, VA: Mercatus Center at George Mason University.

Bonchek, Mark. 1995. *Grassroots in Cyberspace: Recruiting Members on the Internet*. Presented at the 53rd Annual Meeting of the Midwest Political Science Association. http://aom.jku.at/archiv/cmc/text/bonch95a.htm.

Buchanan, James M. 1999. *The Collected Works of James M. Buchanan, Vol 1: The Logical Foundations of Constitutional Liberty*. Indianapolis, IN: Liberty Fund.

Buchanan, Larry, Quoctrung Bui, and Jugal Patel. 2020. "Black Lives Matter May Be the Largest Movement in U.S. History." *New York Times*, July 3. https://www.nytimes.com/interactive/2020/07/03/us/george-floyd-protests-crowd-size.html.

Calhoun, Craig. 2013. *Occupy Wall Street in Perspective*. The British Journal of Sociology 64 (1): 26–38.

Campante, Filipe, Ruben Durante, and Francesco Sobbrio. 2018. "Politics 2.0: The Multifaceted Effect of Broadband Internet on Political Participation." *Journal of the European Economic Association* 16 (4): 1094–1136.

Chamlee-Wright, Emily. 2008. "Signaling Effects of Commercial and Civil Society in Post-Katrina Reconstruction." *International Journal of Social Economics* 35 (8): 615–26.

Chenoweth, Erica, and Jeremy Pressman. 2017. "This is what we learned by counting the women's marches." *Washington Post*, February 7. https://www.washingtonpost .com/news/monkey-cage/wp/2017/02/07/this-is-what-we-learned-by-counting-the -womens-marches/.

Coase, Ronald H. 1992. "The Institutional Structure of Production." *The American Economic Review* 82 (4): 713–19.

———. 2013. "The Problem of Social Cost." *The Journal of Law & Economics* 56 (4): 837–77.

Cobbina, Jennifer, Ashleigh LaCourse, Erika J. Brooke, and Soma Chaudhuri. 2021. "Protesting During a Pandemic: Narratives on Risk Taking and Motivation to Participating in the 2020 March on Washington." *Crime and Delinquency* 67 (8): 1195–1220.

Cox, Jonathan M. 2017. "The Source of a Movement: Making the Case for Social Media as an Informational Source Using Black Lives Matter." *Ethnic and Racial Studies* 40 (11): 1847–54.

Daniel, Verena. 2021. "How the BLM movement compares to the MLK Jr. era civil rights movement." *The State News*, January 18. https://statenews.com/article/2021 /01/blm-compared-to-mlk-era-civil-rights?ct=content_open&cv=cbox_featured.

De Choudhury, Munmun, Shagun Jhaver, Benjamin Sugar, and Ingmar Weber. 2016. "Social Media Participation in an Activist Movement for Racial Equality." *Proceedings of the Tenth International AAAI Conference on Web and Social Media* (ICWSM).

Fuchs, Christian. 2006. "The Self-Organization of Social Movements." *Systemic Practice and Action Research* 19 (1): 101–37.

Goodwin, Jeff, and James M. Jasper, eds. 2015. *The Social Movements Reader: Cases and Concepts*. Third edition. Chichester, West Sussex, UK: Wiley-Blackwell.

Harlow, Summer. 2012. "Social Media and Social Movements: Facebook and an Online Guatemalan Justice Movement That Moved Offline." *New Media & Society* 14 (2): 225–43.

Hayek, Friedrich, A. [1945] 2014. "The Use of Knowledge in Society." In *The Collected Works of F. A. Hayek, Volume 15: The Market and Other Orders,* edited by Bruce Caldwell, 93–104. Chicago, IL: The University of Chicago Press.

Ince, Jelani, Fabio Rojas, and Clayton A. Davis. 2017. "The Social Media Response to Black Lives Matter: How Twitter Users Interact with Black Lives Matter through Hashtag Use." *Ethnic and Racial Studies* 40 (11): 1814–30.

Kristofferson, Kirk, Katherine White, and John Peloza. 2014. "The Nature of Slacktivism: How the Social Observability of an Initial Act of Token Support Affects Subsequent Prosocial Action." *The Journal of Consumer Research* 40 (6): 1149–66.

Lavoie, Don. (1986) 2016. *National Economic Planning: What Is Left?* Arlington, VA: Mercatus Center at George Mason University.

Martin, Nona P., and Virgil H. Storr. 2008. "On Perverse Emergent Orders." *Studies in Emergent Order* 1: 73–91.

Milkman, Ruth. 2017. "A New Political Generation: Millennials and the Post-2008 Wave of Protest." *American Sociological Review* 82 (1): 1–31.

Mitchell, Matthew and Peter J. Boettke. 2017. *Applied Mainline Economics: Bridging the Gap between Theory and Public Policy.* Arlington, VA: Mercatus Center at George Mason University.

Mundt, Marcia, Karen Ross, and Charla Burnett. 2018. "Scaling Social Movements Through Social Media: The Case of Black Lives Matter." *Social Media + Society* 4 (4): 1–14.

Olson, Mancur. 1971. *The Logic of Collective Action.* Cambridge, MA: Harvard University Press.

Pennycook, Gordon, and David G. Rand. 2021. "The Psychology of Fake News." *Trends in Cognitive Sciences* 24 (5): 388–402.

Rich, Jessica Alexis Joliceur. 2020. "Organizing Twenty-First-Century Activism: From Structure to Strategy in Latin American Social Movements." *Latin American Research Review* 55 (3): 430–444.

Rolfe, Brett. 2015. "Building an Electronic Repertoire of Contention." *Social Movement Studies* 4 (1): 65–74.

Sen, Anindya, and Omer Avci. 2016. "Why Social Movements Occur: Theories of Social Movements." *Journal of Knowledge Economy and Knowledge Management* 11 (1): 125–130.

Schumpeter, J. 1942. *Capitalism, Socialism and Democracy.* New York City, NY: Harper & Brothers.

Storr, Virgil H., Stephanie Haeffele-Balch, and Laura E. Grube. 2015. *Community Revival in the Wake of Disaster: Lessons in Local Entrepreneurship.* New York City, NY: Palgrave Macmillan.

Tillery, Alvin B. 2019. "What Kind of Movement Is Black Lives Matter? The View from Twitter." *Journal of Race, Ethnicity, and Politics* 4 (2): 297–323.

Willems, Jurgen and Marc Jegers. 2012. "Social Movement Structures in Relation to Goals and Forms of Action: An Exploratory Model." *Canadian Journal of Nonprofit and Social Economy Research* 3 (2): 67–81.

Wojcieszak, Magdalena. 2008. "False Consensus Goes Online: Impact of Ideologically Homogeneous Groups on False Consensus." *Public Opinion Quarterly* 72 (4): 781–91.

Chapter 7

Stakeholder Primacy as a New Institutional Framework for the Entrepreneurial Market Process?

Mikołaj Firlej

Today, many argue that the market economy did not bring the efficiency properties that were expected from market process (Bugg-Levine and Shahnaz 2019). For example, in the last few decades more wealth has been created than in earlier times, but the gap between rich and poor has widened. Some blame the legal concept of shareholder primacy by pointing out that the requirement to maximize the shareholders' value is often realized at the expense of others, thus creating significant negative externalities such as air pollution, exploitation of public goods, and increase of wealth inequalities (Stout 2012). Thus, they argue to replace shareholder primacy with stakeholder primacy, according to which the objective of the business is to find an optimal balance of stakeholder interests rather than to maximize the sole shareholder value. Some practitioners argue that there are already countries, such as Canada, that have implemented the stakeholder primacy requirement in their corporate law (Liao 2014, 571).

This chapter explores the concept of shareholder primacy and its place in the legal systems of the U.S. and Canada. It explores whether indeed shareholder primacy is part of the legal system in these countries or rather a well-established social practice and legal provisions as such do not impose such a requirement. This assessment helps to shed more light on some important controversies associated with the concept of shareholder primacy, such as (i) whether the introduction or change of a particular legal rule, e.g., regarding the purpose of corporation justifies the move away from shareholder primacy and (ii) whether shareholder primacy is the result of a spontaneous market process or political process, i.e., in which rules are deliberately chosen for, and implemented in, a social community by some agent or agency.

In order to investigate these questions, I comparatively explore the corporate law in two countries: the U.S. and Canada. Both countries share a common legal ancestor, that is, British common law, but despite many similarities they are also marked by important institutional differences. Among the most relevant are the differing roles of federal versus state/provincial policymaking in the two countries. American corporate law has been strongly influenced by jurisdictional competition among the states, while Canadian law has instead been shaped by federal legislative activity, which resulted in the Canada Business Corporations Act (CBCA), a standardizing document regulating Canadian corporate law since 1975. Although superficially, Canadian corporate law appears to share a similar decentralized character to the U.S. as corporations are not required to be physically located in their "home" jurisdiction, significant jurisdictional competition between provinces has never emerged in Canada. Canadian corporate law has instead been characterized by increasing uniformity (Beck 1983, 152; Cumming and MacIntosh 2000, 159–60). The United States, on the contrary, has never adopted a national corporation law, leaving the formation and governance of business organizations to the laws of the individual states. This competitive system resulted in the rise of the state of Delaware which has become the most influential among corporations. One could argue that American corporate law can be identified de facto as the law of Delaware, given the share of legal incorporations in this state relative to others, particularly in recent years. Delaware is the domicile of choice for almost 70% of the Fortune 500 companies and approximately 93% of all U.S. initial public offerings are registered in this state (Delaware Department of State 2020). The Chapter thus takes a special notice of the legal developments in the state of Delaware, but it does not limit its scope to this specific state, particularly given important historical developments in other states in the discussed area. Further and importantly, Canadian corporate law differs from Delaware law in terms of fiduciary duties of directors. According to Delaware law fiduciary duties are generally owed to shareholders, while the CBCA points out that directors' duties are owed to the "corporation" and shareholders are not explicitly mentioned.[1] These similar yet contrasting approaches represent interesting comparative case which will flesh out the problem of the shareholder primacy in more detail.

THE WIDER DEBATE ABOUT
SHAREHOLDER PRIMACY

In the first part I outline the current debate about the concept of shareholder primacy. I argue that according to the shareholder primacy corporations do not have any social responsibilities and the narrowly conceived maximization of shareholder value may lead to the negative social return. Stakeholder primacy is a concept that responds to this criticism but it fosters a very different concept of fiduciary duty in which managers should balance interests of shareholders with other relevant parties and interests and the end result may not always ensure the greatest profit for shareholders.

Shareholder Primacy

The requirement of shareholder primacy is commonly defined as the view that managers' fiduciary responsibilities require them to maximize the shareholders' wealth and preclude them from giving independent consideration to the interests of other stakeholders (Lee 2006, 533). Thus, some authors argue that shareholder primacy is a legal concept encapsulating the assumption about the rational self-interest of individuals. This understanding, however, is questionable. Adam Smith's chain of "ownership, control, full access to profits, efficiency" (Ho 2009, 173; see Smith 1976) does not reflect fully today's corporate law, where professional managers represent the interests of shareholders.[2] Further, there are situations in which managers are conflicted between their own self-interest and shareholders' interests (Coffee, Jr. 1986, 13). Smith was aware of this potential agency-cost conflict and concluded that the managerial corporation could not effectively compete with singular owner entrepreneurs and would ultimately fail as a form of business association (Ho 2009, 173). Thus, in order to solve agency-cost problem identified by Smith, corporate managers must be required by law or otherwise become obligated to serve shareholder interests alone. However, one can further argue that such analysis misses a crucial point, that is the Smith's chain of "ownership, control, full access to profits, efficiency" does not fully capture the essence of shareholder primacy as it concentrates only on narrowly identified understanding of shareholders' objective, i.e., on the maximization of profits. While in the majority of cases in free enterprise private property system making profits is the key responsibility of executives, in some cases they may have different objectives. For instance, a group of individuals may want to establish a corporation for a charitable purpose, e.g., an educational foundation. The manager of such foundation will not have money profit as his objective but the rendering of certain services, e.g., providing the wider

possible access to higher education for people across the country. What is
common in both for profit corporations and not for profit organizations is the
principal-agent relationship between the owners and executives whereby the
manager is the agent of the individuals who own the organization (Jensen and
Meckling 1976, 305).

Thus, the principle of shareholder primacy should be defined as follows: (i)
the manager is the agent of the individuals who own the corporation and (ii)
the only responsibility of managers is to maximize the shareholders' interest
while (iii) conforming to the basic rules of the society, both those embodied
in law and those embodied in ethical custom (Friedman 1970). A final point
requires further scrutiny. One may argue that it is uncertain what the "basic
rules of the society" means as the law of a state may impose a number of
"social responsibilities" for the business owners such as to improve environment, reduce poverty and so on. Then the adherence to such "social responsibilities" by the managers may go against the shareholders' interest. Assuming
that a business owner has established a private corporation and is interested
in generating as much profit as possible, the managers spend of proceeds
for "social purposes," as required by law, goes against the business owners'
interest. Therefore, the mere existence of any social responsibilities of businesses, either in law or in ethical custom, limits the principle of shareholder
primacy.[3] Then, in the ideal free market economy "basic rules of the society"
would constitute only individual responsibilities, not social responsibilities
of companies (Friedman 1970). I will discuss this point later in the Chapter
in which I will explore whether the inclusion of stakeholder interests in the
legal definition of the purpose of a corporation undermines the concept of
shareholder primacy.

That said, the concept of shareholder primacy has dominated corporate law
discussions for decades (Hansmann and Kraakman 2001, 439–68). However,
in recent years the shareholder primacy has attracted a broad range of criticism. I will discuss two main arguments: (1) negative social return as a result
of shareholders' activity and (2) divergent shareholder interests.

A first argument is that the strict adherence to shareholder primacy might
create significant negative external effects for various stakeholders. The concept of shareholder primacy narrowed down to pursuing ever-greater profits
could lead to high profits to the capital provider which in turn are not always
a proxy for the efficient use of capital. For example, some corporations may
pursue profit at the expense of environment or employees' human rights.
Such a use of capital may provide profit to shareholders, but an overall negative return to society, e.g., in the form of air pollution or negative well-being
of employees (Alexander 2017, 307–08).

A second argument is that in the long term the concept of shareholder primacy also negatively impacts the shareholder themselves. Often shareholders'

interests vary in a given time horizon as owners may have different strategies in maximizing long-term value of a business, investors may have different expectations regarding the holding period, and different preferences regarding the return of invested capital. This problem is illustrated by the difference between value extraction and value creation among shareholders. Some shareholders may prefer to create longer term value by retaining earnings and reinvesting them in order to increase or strengthen the company's offering, e.g., through acquisition of innovative technologies. The owners can also choose to reinvest earnings by providing higher incomes and greater job security for employees, aiming at strengthening their motivation. Value extraction, on the other hand, occurs when earnings are immediately distributed to shareholders. The problem with shareholder primacy is that various shareholder may have very different perspectives regarding the use of earnings and building a longer-term value of corporation. Further, there might be a conflict even between current ("ex ante") shareholders and their future ("ex post") selves. The initial ex ante shareholders commitments may differ to ex post shareholders commitments particularly when existing shareholders have at some point an opportunistic interest in unbinding themselves from previous commitments and unlock capital to pursue other opportunities. This conflict between various commitments of the same investors in different time horizon puts corporations governed by the rules of shareholder primacy at a disadvantage when it comes to projects that require long-term firm-specific investments (Stout 2012, 85; Schwarcz 2005). Thus, some authors postulate to reject shareholder primacy, and instead inviting managers to consider independently the wider needs of a corporation in order to mediate between various parties, including the interests of employees, customers as well as ex ante and ex post shareholders (Alexander 2017, 307–08).

Stakeholder Primacy

The criticism of shareholder primacy has led many authors to seek an alternative model to guide the corporate activities. Recently, the Business Roundtable in the U.S. announced the adoption of a new Statement on the Purpose of a Corporation, signed by 181 well-known CEOs. In the Statement, CEOs argued to "move away from shareholder primacy" as a guiding principle of corporations and replace it by a "modern standard for corporate responsibility" that makes a commitment to all stakeholders (Business Roundtable 2019). Interestingly, since 1997 the Business Roundtable has advocated the principle of shareholder primacy, but according to the press release new Statement supersedes previous statements and "more accurately reflects commitment to a free-market economy that serves all Americans" (Business Roundtable 2019). According to a new model called often "the stakeholder primacy," shareholders are just one of several key stakeholders, together with a company's employees, customers, suppliers as well as broader societal interests, including the environment. The objective of the corporation is to find an optimal balance of stakeholder interests, of which shareholder wealth creation is important but not only variable of the equation.

Today many authors foster the concept of stakeholder primacy by advocating socially responsible investing (SRI).[4] This is a broad term that encompasses a different types of investment activities but based on a common premise to exclude investments in companies which maximize shareholder profit at the expense of other stakeholders. In the academic literature there are at least three types of SRI: (i) negative screening, (ii) best-of-breed, and (iii) impact investments.

Negative screening aims at avoiding investments in companies engaged in undesirable activities, such as tobacco, gambling, alcohol, or weapons manufacturing. Historically it was the original focus of SRI and it can be traced back to religious practice since at least 1800s. An example of the implementation of negative screening in the U.S. was The Sullivan Code, introduced by Leon Sullivan, pastor and member General Motors Board of Directors. The Code from 1977 introduced principles for the U.S. corporations to maintain their presence in South Africa by pledging equal treatment of nonwhite employees and respecting basic living condition as a response to the system of apartheid (McCrudden 1999,170).

Best-of-breed is more sophisticated practice than negative screening. Investment managers not only apply a negative selection, but also proactively evaluate each investment on the specific environmental, social, and other criteria. For instance, most recently private equity funds started to take into account environmental, social, and corporate governance (ESG) when investing in a company (Papadopoullos 2021). The specific ESG factors included may be selected according to materiality to financial performance of the portfolio and ESG integration is pursued as a means of improving investment performance.

Finally, impact investments are the most recent development in the SRI practice. Impact investments are investments made with the intention to generate positive, measurable social and environmental impact alongside a financial return. There are three elements that differentiate impact investing from ESG Investing that is (i) purposeful selection of assets with intent for impact, (ii) a contribution to the impact of the investee firm, and (iii) systematic measurement of that impact. For impact investors it is not enough to apply ESG criteria for their investment performance, but rather they focus on allocating capital to purposefully solve the world's most difficult problems, such as combatting climate change or eliminating poverty.

What is a common theme for all these types of SRIs is an evolving view of fiduciary duty. A foundational rule in the U.S. companies' law is that the board owes fiduciary duty "to the corporation and its shareholders."[5] Courts have interpreted this formulation as a vertical relationship in which the shareholder's interest is of the highest importance.[6] While both negative screening and ESG investing challenge the traditional concept of shareholder primacy where managers of for-profit corporations should focus only on financial returns, impact investing is going even further and it can be characterized as a clear implementation of stakeholder primacy.

However, despite the recent *Statement on the Purpose of a Corporation* presented by the Business Roundtable and increasing pressure to focus both on financial and social rate of return, impact investing alone has attracted relatively little capital. Although the wider ESG investing market is estimated at $12 trillion, impact investing accounts only for the range between $228–$502 billion with the caveat that the real number is probably lower as many financial institutions may not adequately report the amount due to the misunderstandings of what impact investing is (GIIN 2018, 21; GIIN 2019, 10). Further, the extent of private capital allocated to impact investing is also difficult to estimate, but the size is relatively low which is evidenced by the rather marginal participation of family offices capital accounting for nearly $2 billion, which is less than 1% of total assets allocated to impact investing (GIIN 2019, 15).

That said, one may pose the question: how does the fiduciary duty looks like in for-profit organization in today's world? With the wake of new regulatory guidelines that require funds to implement ESG criteria one may argue that the world is moving incrementally toward the stakeholder primacy, yet the data behind the impact investing shows otherwise—investors are not yet convinced that the pure manifestation of stakeholder primacy can generate positive financial returns. In the next section I intend to explore the place of shareholder primacy in the legal systems of USA and Canada.

IS THE PRINCIPLE OF SHAREHOLDER PRIMACY LAW?

In this section I argue that shareholder primacy is not a single rule of corporate law outlining the purpose of corporation. Rather, it is a legal principle, a generally observable standard that influences particular decision-making dilemmas. Despite the seemingly different formulations regarding the purpose of corporation in both U.S. and Canada, I argue that, in fact, Canadian corporate law as a whole is still deeply penetrated by the requirement of shareholder primacy. In the U.S. despite the fact that there is no statutory requirement, the concept of shareholder primacy serves as the guiding principle which helps to reduce law's uncertainty among various commercial rules and has been consistently used as such by courts.

U.S. Approach to Shareholder Primacy

Whether shareholder primacy is a part of the U.S. law is a complex matter because the principle has not been formally identified in a statutory law (Fisch 2006, 648). It means there is no rule with sanction in the form of an enforceable fiduciary duty. The company laws in the U.S., such as the corporate law in Delaware, contain only the fiduciary duties of care and loyalty which include the subsidiary duties of good faith, oversight, and disclosure. Duty of care requires informed, deliberative decision-making based on all material information reasonably available. Duty of loyalty requires that directors of a corporation in making all decisions in their capacities as corporate fiduciaries, must act with good faith and without personal economic conflict. The duty of loyalty can be breached either by making a self-interested transaction or taking a corporate opportunity. Some argue that the existence of duty of care and loyalty runs only to shareholders, which means that directors are only accountable to shareholders for their decisions.

However, under the corporate law in Delaware, the directors owe the duty of loyalty to both *the corporation and its stockholders*, without consideration to their self-interest. While the fiduciary duty to the shareholders [stockholders] may arise in specific factual cases (Coffee, Jr. 1986, 84–85), the company laws in the U.S., even in Delaware, is at best unclear whether there is a rule of shareholder primacy. It is because the interest of corporations is a broader term and may include other considerations beyond the maximization of shareholder value. This is explicitly stated in New York state's *Business Corporation Law*, which acknowledge that a director shall be entitled to consider, without limitation, both the long-term and short-term interests of the corporation, its shareholders, and a number of other constituents such as employees, retired employees, customers, creditors, and communities.[7]

However, while shareholder primacy is not a single rule and may not even be a fiduciary duty per se, it is still a law. This is because U.S. courts consistently recognize such legal obligation at least since the seminal case *Dodge vs Ford Motor Co* from 1919.[8] The case involved a dispute between Henry Ford and the Dodge brothers over whether Ford Motor Company, a corporation that Ford controlled, should pay dividends to shareholders in light of accumulation of significant capital surplus or rather the company should be permitted to make large capital investments in order to further increase production. Ford argued that the increase of production will help to build a greater long-term value of the company and that by employing more men he will "spread the benefits of this industrial system to the greatest possible number, to help them build up their lives and their homes."[9] However, the minority shareholders objected and demanded that Ford will distribute the capital surplus in the form of dividends. The Michigan Supreme Court held in favor of minority shareholders by arguing that:

> A business corporation is organized and carried on primarily for the profit of the stockholders. (. . .) The discretion of directors is to be exercised in the choice of means to attain that end, and does not extend to a change in the end itself, to the reduction of profits, or to the non-distribution of profits among stockholders in order to devote them to other purposes.[10] (Dodge v. Ford Motor Co.)

Similarly, in Delaware, court decisions have clearly established that the shareholder primacy rule applies. Despite the fact that duty of loyalty extends to both corporation and stockholders, according to the courts, directors have in fact a fiduciary duty to make their decisions looking solely to the best interests of shareholders. Delaware Supreme Court Chief Justice Leo E. Strine, Jr. has made his view clear where Delaware law stands on the subject: "A clear-eyed look at the law of corporations in Delaware reveals that, within the limits of their discretion, directors must make stockholder welfare their sole end, and that other interests may be taken into consideration only as a means of promoting stockholder welfare" (Strine, Jr. 2015, 768).

In the more recent case *eBay Domestic Holdings, Inc. v. Newmark* [2010], the founders of Craigslist, an advertisement website created adopted a poison pill plan to prevent eBay's attempt to acquire the company. They argued that the poison pill was necessary to protect Craigslist's social values and culture, which would be threatened by the acquisition by the large corporation such as eBay. The Delaware Chancery Court rejected the argument on the basis that managers of a for-profit company cannot deploy a rights plan to defend a business strategy that openly refrain from stockholder wealth maximization as it would be a violation of their fiduciary duty toward shareholders.[11] In another influential case, *Revlon*, the court held that "concern for non-stockholder interests is inappropriate when an auction among active bidders is in progress, and the object no longer is to protect or maintain the corporate enterprise but to sell it to the highest bidder."[12] Rather, in that context the directors were solely required to maximize shareholder value.

Shareholder primacy should however not imply that managers in corporations are absolutely bound by their shareholders. Interestingly, *Dodge* case has also established a business judgment rule which gives the board of directors or managers in a for-profit corporation a strong protection against ill-considered legal allegations about the way they conduct business. The business judgment rule is the offspring of the fundamental principle of the U.S. corporate law that is the separation of ownership and control and the primacy of managerial authority.[13] The business judgment rule recognizes that as long as board of directors and managers act in good faith, in the best interests of the corporation, and on an informed basis they are free to take risks associated with the course of business without a constant fear of lawsuits affecting their judgment from shareholders. A shareholder primacy rule with a duty to maximize profit would present a potential conflict between authority and accountability as profit-seeking is the core managerial function in a business while often shareholders have different and contested views of how to maximize value.

That said, although shareholder primacy is not codified as a rule that establishes an *explicit* fiduciary duty to maximize profit, the principle still creates an obligation. The difference between duty and obligation is that duty is related to the potential legal sanction for breach, while obligation is not attached to a sanction, although it is a form of law as it is generally observed.

The reason shareholder primacy can be considered as legal obligation is that U.S. courts have recognized and systematically embraced the concept of shareholder primacy, while *Dodge* has become a major point of reference (Hansmann and Kraakman 2001, 439–68). Thus, shareholder primacy exists as a meta-rule (legal principle) and is widely observed, not necessarily because of legal consequences for breach (although may happen) but because of internalization of custom (Rhee 2018, 2004).

Herbert Hart provides an influential account of obligations that become law. He argues that not all law is in the form of a general command backed by the coercive force of the threat of sanction (Hart 2012, 18–25). There are also 'secondary rules' that confer the power to change, modify, or enforce primary rules. One of such secondary rules is rule of recognition which helps to combat the problem of uncertainty of the law. The rule of recognition is a collection of standards that govern the validity of all rules. Thus, the rule of recognition confers power to new rules by validating them (Hart 2012, 95). One can then argue that this is exactly the role of shareholder primacy. Shareholder primacy does not exist as a single statutory rule in the form of an enforceable fiduciary duty backed by a threat of sanction, but instead it serves as the focal point of the larger architecture of the corporate law and market system. It helps to navigate various challenges that arise in the company's lifespan.

Courts do not always explicitly state the rule applied to recognize an obligation, but instead the decision frequently reveals the rule. As illustrated in *Dodge*, shareholder primacy helps to solve the uncertainty regarding the conflict of interest among investors and managers regarding the use of capital surplus. In *eBay* case shareholder primacy guided to maximize common stock value when the corporation is selling control. Based on these examples, one can argue that despite the fact that there is no single rule that mandates profit maximization, in a wide range of managerial decisions there is a meta-rule that steer managers toward the end of shareholder primacy even when corporate law empowers the managers with the primary authority (Rhee 2018, 2006, 2018).

Canada Approach to Shareholder Primacy

One of the important recent legislative developments in Canada was Bill C-97, which included changes to the *Canada Business Corporations Act* (CBCA). Bill C-97 states that when acting in the best interests of the corporation, directors and officers may consider, but are not limited to the interests of shareholders, employees, retirees and pensioners, creditors, consumers, and governments; the environment; and the long-term interests of the corporation.[14] This piece of legislation is consistent with the view held by Canadian courts according to which directors of corporations may consider various stakeholder interests and should not be limited to the short-term benefits of shareholders. In particular, the Supreme Court of Canada decision in *Peoples Department Stores Inc. (Trustee of) v Wise* (2004) (*Wise*) was instrumental as the court argued that directors should strive to make the corporation a "better corporation" and when assessing what is in the corporation's best interests, directors may look to the interests of, "*inter alia*, shareholders, employees, creditors, consumers, governments and the environment to inform their decisions."[15] Bill C-97 can be considered as a "codification" of *Wise* and in some instances it goes even further, e.g., in the inclusion of retirees and pensioners interests.

Some scholars argue that since *Wise* the Canadian jurisprudence has rejected the shareholder primacy and that Canadian courts are more stakeholder-centric which distinguish Canadian law from the U.S. companies' law, in particular in Delaware (Abols and Freelan 2020). One of the arguments which signals Canadian stakeholder primacy approach is that the CBCA states that directors may consider the "long-term interests" when deciding what is in the corporation's best interest and it does not mention of short-term interests.[16]

In the scholarly debate short-term value maximization is often considered as a feature of shareholder primacy as opposed to "long-term sustainability" of stakeholder primacy (Palladino and Karlsson 2019). A common example is the practice of stock buybacks which are justified under this shareholder primacy on the grounds that shareholders should be "returned" available cash when it has not found another productive use. The proponents of stakeholder primacy argue that this rationale does not take into consideration other types of corporate expenditures for stakeholders, including increased wages and it does not promote a long-term value creation (Palladino and Karlsson

2019). Another example is the case where a recently developed company has promised to bring a significant long-term value but it has quickly received a reasonably satisfying acquisition offer for the majority shareholders which is driven more by speculation rather than the assessment of internal value. In such cases, the advocates of stakeholder primacy argue that according to the concept of shareholder value, the managers should rather sell the business than strive to build a longer-term internal value.

I would however dispute the claim that shareholder primacy is necessarily associated with short-termism. First, even in Delaware the corporate law does not require directors to place short-term profits above long-term value. "The fiduciary duty to manage a corporate enterprise includes the selection of a time frame for achievement of corporate goals . . . " and further (. . .) "Absent a limited set of circumstances as defined under *Revlon*, a board of directors, while always required to act in an informed manner, is not under any per se duty to maximize shareholder value in the short term, even in the context of a takeover," the judges found in *Paramount Commc'ns, Inc. v. Time Inc.*[17] With narrow exceptions specified e.g., in *Revlon*, directors can exercise *their business judgment* in evaluating long-term initiatives.

Second, there are many real business case study situations in which it is more profitable for shareholders to adopt a longer-term perspective, so the adoption of a radical short-term approach would go contrary to the shareholders' maximization of value.

Finally, even though the CBCA explicitly refers only to long-term interests of corporation, the Canadian courts provided some further explanatory context. In the *BCE Inc. v 1976 Debentureholders* (2009) (*BCE*), the judges of the Supreme Court of Canada found a director's fiduciary duty is indeed not confined to short-term profit or share value. However, in the same judgment when the court considered a transaction's impact on debenture-holders, it argued that one would expect the directors, acting in the corporation's best interests, to consider the "short and long-term interests in the course of making their ultimate decision."[18] Thus, the sole consideration of "long-term interests" should be not regarded as the characteristic of stakeholder primacy.

Where indeed Canadian corporate law differs from Delaware is in the rule about the purpose of corporation which states that the directors owe fiduciary duty only to corporation, not to the corporation and stockholders; and that the directors in Canada may consider the interests of both shareholders and certain other stakeholders.[19] This view is echoed by a number of practitioners who agreed that the shareholder primacy is inconsistent with Canadian corporate law, even before the introduction of Bill C-97 (Liao 2014, 570). I argue however that when one considers the whole Canadian corporate law, it is still reflective of shareholder primacy, despite the more stakeholder-centric rule regarding the purpose of corporation. First, only the shareholders have an exclusive right to select board directors of corporation, thus it is likely that in practice board will be accountable to the shareholders who elect them (Marin 2013, 243–44). Second, both in Canada and USA courts have adopted a deferential approach to the directors' duty of loyalty (Marin 2013, 244). It means that it is up to the business judgment of directors to take into account shareholder and stakeholder interests in their day-to-day decisions. According to the "business judgment rule" any decisions made by directors are justified as long as they lie within a range of reasonable alternatives. Some argue that the broad scope of the duty of loyalty combined with a business judgment rule will nudge directors in Canada to adopt a more stakeholder-oriented approach (Lupa 2011, 15). However, this expectation has rather not materialized as Canadian courts has been reluctant to favor stakeholders at the expense of shareholders (VanDuzer 2009, 411). Third, in the context of buyouts, Canadian securities law protects only shareholder interests. Specifically, *National Policy 62–202*, issued by the Canadian Securities Administrators and adopted in several provinces, states that: "(. . .) the primary objective of the take-over provisions . . . is the protection of the bona fide interests of the shareholder of the target company."[20] Shareholders are the only party with the power to accept or reject a takeover bid. The *Policy* also states that directors should not interfere with shareholders' right to vote on a takeover bid by abusing defensive tactics.

Taking this more holistic perspective on the situation of stakeholders in the Canadian corporate law, one can argue that despite a more stakeholder-oriented rule regarding the purpose of corporation, the law still favors shareholder primacy. The sole change of the rule stipulating the purpose of corporation is not enough to change the incentives of shareholders and directors embedded in the whole legal system. In the Canadian model, directors have to consider the interests of employees and other stakeholders beyond shareholders, but despite this "consideration" the end result of deliberation will likely be in favor of shareholders. Stakeholders' primacy could only work in practice if there will be a number of additional rules, which would allow to substantially derive consequences from the stakeholder-oriented purpose of corporation. These should include rules regarding the election of board of directors, such as the proposal that a corporation would be required to elect a significant percentage of its Board of Directors through company employee vote or the proposal that the executive board should be complemented by non-executive directors who would be required to supervise executives' behavior to ensure that the corporation acts responsibly in society (Ellerman and Kay 2018). Another example will need to concern the takeover bids, e.g., the employees' representation should have a vote regarding the potential future of a corporation in the context of a takeover bid. The Canadian corporate law does not include these or similar rules, thus one can argue that, similarly to the U.S. companies' law, in Canada the shareholder primacy exists as a widely observed meta-rule (legal principle), not necessarily because of legal consequences for breach, but because of the way incentives are structed in the whole legal systems. Although the law allows managers to consider the interests of stakeholders as a means toward increasing long-term shareholder value, they may never prioritize the interests of employees or any others above the interests of shareholders.

SHAREHOLDER PRIMACY AS THE INSTITUTIONAL BASIS OF THE MARKET PROCESS

In earlier section I argued that, based on the analysis of Canadian and U.S. companies' law, shareholder primacy is a legal principle rather than a single legal rule regulating the purpose of corporation. In this section, I make a distinction between two levels of analysis, one related to entrepreneurial market process as such and another one which pertains to the institutional framework based on which individuals can coordinate economic activities and realize the gains from social cooperation under the division of labor. I argue then that the principle of shareholder primacy is part of the institutional framework of market process both in U.S. and Canada. However, the emergence of the principle of shareholder primacy is likely not the result of a spontaneous market process, but rather an outcome of legal and political process. In concluding remarks, I will discuss what are the implications of this analysis in the context of a debate about stakeholder primacy.

In the introductory remarks to this chapter, I mentioned that one of the influential lines of criticism of the market process as such is the concept of shareholder primacy which is considered as a legal exemplification of the assumption of rational self-interest of individuals. This is questionable on the grounds that the obligation to maximize the value of shareholders rest on directors whose interests may not always and necessarily be fully aligned with shareholders. This view is also questionable as it seems disregard the fundamental fact that there is no such thing as a "market as such." What is called "a market" is always a system of social interaction characterized by a specific institutional framework, that is, by a set of rules outlining certain restrictions on the behavior of the market participants, irrespective of whether these rules are informal, enforced by private sanctions, or formal, enforced by a particular governmental agency (Vanberg 1986, 75; Buchanan 1964, 218–19). One of the great promoters of free market, Friedrich von Hayek, recognized that there is no spontaneous market order "as such" that can be assumed generally to be "efficient" or "beneficial," irrespective of the rules governing the behavior of the market participants. He referred to them as rules of conduct and argued that such rules form an institutional system (Hayek 1967, 67–68). According to this rationale, spontaneous market processes cannot be expected to generate beneficial outcomes independent of the rules governing the behavior of the market participants.

This prompts the issue of what rules can be considered "appropriate" in order to allow for a beneficial working of the market mechanism. How to assess whether the principle of shareholder primacy or stakeholder primacy provide more appropriate framework for the development of entrepreneurial market process? Hayek did not provide a direct answer. He deferred attempts to define what "appropriate" rules are, because he thought that changing social and other conditions may require changing answers to the question. Rather, he turned attention to the process by which rules are generated and changed (Vanberg 1986, 79). According to Hayek both the emergence of market and an institutional framework serving as a basis for that order stem from the spontaneous evolutionary process. Individuals pursue their various particular interests and by doing so they create social mechanisms that coordinate individual actions. Pursuing individual interests may lead to the emergence of social macro structures. The rules of just conduct are not "designed" but rather "discovered" (Hayek 1982, 97–98).

Not all rules however constitute the social order. Social order only arises a result of adhering to rules of conduct and consequently only those rules of conduct survive if they result in successful social coordination. Those rules that prove to be unsuccessful in coordinating individual actions will be socially de-selected and cease materially affect the dealings of individuals (Hayek 1982, 98). In other words, Hayek argued that the principle of shareholder primacy is a result of evolutionary selection of the appropriate rule guiding the corporate affairs of individuals. Thus, the directors' obligation to maximize shareholder value cannot be simply assumed as one of the alternative arrangements, but rather needs to be understood as an accomplishment amidst a variety of competing ideas and interests regarding the nature of corporation expressed by various stakeholders and social actors. This rule of conduct has been selected and legitimized because it successfully contributes to the survival of social group order. As Hayek put it, "maximizing profit is socially desirable" (Hayek 1967, 308).

The concept of stakeholder primacy, on the other hand, constitutes a constructivist proposal that requires to change an important part of the institutional framework by the means of political process, i.e., in which rules are deliberately chosen for, and implemented in, a social community by some agent or agency, whether this is a legislative body or a judge. It is not to say that Hayek was against deliberate planning in the daily management of affairs. He was however against of constructivism, that is constructing social institutions in the form of a deliberate design (Hayek 1982, 5). As the principle of stakeholder primacy is not a part of institutional framework, it should be regarded as a policy project designed to alter the evolutionary outcome of individual human actions.

There is, however, a methodological problem with evolutionary explanation of shareholder primacy. Since rules of conduct such as shareholder primacy has been selected on the premise that they successfully contribute to the social group order, the existence of these rules is tied to the existence of the group. Thus, individual action is dependent on the existence of group order, it presupposes the existence of this order and at the same time it is creating this order (Gedeon 2015, 6). Hayek argued that the rules of conduct could change if the external conditions will change in such a manner that the existing rules will fail to bring about social order. In this case, he claimed, individuals may experiment with new rules of conduct. As a consequence of these experiments some of these new rules may be created and institutionalized and these rules will reflect a new social order. For Hayek the scheme of evolutionary change starts from the change of environment, then there is a change of individual actions, which finally leads to the change of social order (Hayek 1967, 71). Thus, the potential emergence of stakeholder primacy should start from individual entrepreneurs contesting the current corporate order based on general sentiment that the adherence to shareholder primacy does not lo longer satisfy a particular social group. The problem with this approach is that the social order is created by individual actions, but the existing social order determines whether a particular rule of individual conduct will survive or not. Only those rules of conduct may be institutionalized that fit into a given social order, and those individuals may survive in the process of evolution whose rules of conduct prove to be compatible with the existing order of group-level rules.

In his reasoning Hayek did however ignore important considerations regarding the institutional change. First, he did not provide a clear differentiation between rules and principles in the context of institutional change. Whilst Hayek generally considered principles are more general less articulated rules of just conducts (Hayek 1982, 60), he considered their role as a reference to assess whether a particular course of action (rule) is compatible with a social order. In that sense, he wrote about the role of judges in the common law system, who are tasked to assess compatibility of a particular rule with general principles of law. In the common law system, judges are tasked to assess compatibility of a particular individual action with general principles of law. As principles are purpose-independent, judges do not strive in their application to design particular social or economic ends. Rather, they reflect on the practices which have evolved in the spontaneous order and, as such, should conform to the expectations which the parties would have "reasonably formed because they corresponded to the practices on which the everyday conduct of the members of the group was based" (Hayek 1982, 96–97). Thus, specific rules can change by a judge who assessed, through the application of more general principles, that a given rule does no longer bring about social order. It is uncertain however how does the principles change.

Second, Hayek argued that the principles are mostly implicit (Hayek 1982, 66) and they are rather a mere "propensity or disposition to act or not to act in a certain manner" manifested as a "practice or custom" (Hayek 1982, 77). He insisted principles stem from our tacit knowledge ("knowledge how") and individuals are not able to specify all the rules which govern our perceptions and actions. This reasoning ignores the fact that principles can and often are concretized and operationalized by more specific rules over time and such operationalization makes the principles not only more explicit, but also more dependent on the collection of these rules.

Translating this insight into practical terms, even though there might exist a general social sentiment toward the stakeholder primacy rather than to the maximization of shareholder value, directors of public companies in the U.S. and Canada will likely not be able to defend in the court the decision to elect employees' representation in the Board or to reject the takeover bid because of the opposition from the employees' representation. This is because the general principle of shareholder primacy has already become operationalized, through both legislative and judiciary activity, into the collection of rules specifying the consequences of the potential adherence and non-adherence to shareholder primacy in many particular instances of a corporate life. If a particular individual would like to challenge the principle of shareholder primacy, he or she will need to challenge not just a single rule before the court, but the foundational part of a whole corporate legal system, according to other specific rules are evaluated. Moreover, this particular corporate order, underpinned by principles, has been created by individual actions and it determines whether a particular rule of individual conduct will survive or not. Therefore, in the context of highly operationalized principles even if an individual would like to consider other practices that might present to him/her as more attractive than those that are conventional in his/her respective group, it might be too disadvantageous for him/her to deviate from established conventions because of the cost associated with experimenting with entire legal system, not just with a particular rule. Therefore, it is because of this potential excessive cost of challenging the well-operationalized principle, a shift to a more appropriate institutional arrangement cannot, in principle, be expected to be brought about by an invisible hand process, but only by deliberate and organized action across the wide spectrum of operationalizing rules.

The conclusion from the above assessment is that the idea of evolutionary explanation of shareholder primacy do not provide a strong rationale to assume that there is some general spontaneous process at work on which we could rely for the generation of appropriate corporate institutions. The invisible hand explanation of market is an influential concept, but its application in the context of institutional framework is limited because, for systematic reasons, certain kinds of principles, such as the principle of stakeholder primacy, will likely not emerge from a spontaneous process. Thus, when addressing the issue of whether the principle of shareholder primacy or stakeholder primacy provide more appropriate framework for the development of entrepreneurial market process, there is no strong justification for appealing to the simple answer that, if only let alone, spontaneous forces would automatically generate "appropriate" rules. Rather, one has to engage in the more challenging analysis of how both frameworks affect the private incentives, choices, and social outcomes of entrepreneurial activity across broad spectrum of rules. This research is underdeveloped in the context of stakeholder primacy, yet it can help to bring compelling arguments whether one should indeed engage in the political process to reshape the established corporate framework.

CONCLUSION

Today many argue that we live in a pivotal moment in the history of corporate law where there is a change from shareholder primacy to more stakeholder-oriented model. Canadian corporate law is usually presented as a good example of how does the U.S. companies' law should evolve. In this chapter, I argued that both the U.S. and Canada are still deeply embedded in the principle of shareholder value, despite different rules regarding the purpose of corporation. I concluded that shareholder primacy is a foundational concept that is part of institutional arrangement of the market in both countries. I then argued that the principle of stakeholder primacy, for systematic reasons, cannot be expected to emerge from and to be enforced by a spontaneous process. This is because the principle of shareholder primacy is not a single rule, but it encompasses the whole legal system and is operationalised by many specific rules. Thus, the potential non-adherence to this principle by an individual entrepreneurial action would likely result in too excessive cost because one would challenge the foundational part of a whole corporate legal system according to which other existing rules are assessed. The analysis suggests that it is unlikely that the principle of stakeholder primacy will emerge from a spontaneous process, thus I postulate to engage in constitutional economics research and analyze how these two alternative frameworks affect private and public choices. Only then the principle of stakeholder primacy could gain a real traction.

REFERENCES

Abols, Gesta, and Brad Freelan. 2020. "Shareholder Governance, 'Wall Street' and the View from Canada." *Harvard Law School Forum on Corporate Governance*, February 16. https://corpgov.law.harvard.edu/2020/02/16/shareholder-governance-wall-street-and-the-view-from-canada/.

Alexander, Frederic. 2017. "Saving Investors from Themselves: How Stockholder Primacy Harms Everyone." *Seattle University Law Review* 40 (2): 303–20.

Beck, Stanley, Ed Iacobucci, David L. Johnston, and Jacob S. Ziegel. 1983. *Cases and Materials on Partnerships and Canadian Business Corporations*. Toronto, Canada: Carswell.

Buchanan, James. 1964. "What Should Economists Do?" *Southern Economic Journal* 30 (3): 213–22.

Business Roundtable. 2019. "Business Roundtable Redefines the Purpose of a Corporation to Promote 'An Economy That Serves All Americans.'" https://www.businessroundtable.org/business-roundtable-redefines-the-purpose-ofa-corporation-to-promote-an-economy-that-serves-all-americans.

Bugg-Levine, Antony, and Durreen Shahnaz. 2019. "Impact Investing's 'Third Phase': What New Challenges Lie Ahead?" *Knowledge at Wharton*, June 27. https://knowledge.wharton.upenn.edu/article/whats-next-for-impact-investing/

Coffee, Jr., John. 1986. "Shareholders versus Managers: The Strain in the Corporate Web." *Michigan Law Review* 85 (1): 1–109.

Cumming, Douglas, and Jeffrey MacIntosh. 2002. "The Rationales Underlying Reincorporation and Implications for Canadian Corporations." *International Review of Law and Economics* 22 (3): 277–330.

Delaware Department of State. 2020. "Annual Report Statistics." Accessed October 31, 2021. https://corpfiles.delaware.gov/Annual-Reports/Division-of-Corporations-2020-Annual-Report.pdf.

Ellerman, John, and Ira Kay. 2018. "A Proposed Alternative to Corporate Governance and the Theory of Shareholder Primacy." *Harvard Law School Forum on Corporate Governance*, September 12. https://corpgov.law.harvard.edu/2018/09/12/a-proposed-alternative-to-corporate-governance-and-the-theory-of-shareholder-primacy/.

Fisch, Jill. 2006. "Measuring Efficiency in Corporate Law: The Role of Shareholder Primacy." *The Journal of Corporation Law* 31 (3): 637–74.

Friedman, Milton. 1970. "The Social Responsibility of Business Is to Increase Its Profits." *New York Times*, September 13.

Gedeon, Péter. 2015. "Spontaneous Order and Social Norms. Hayek's Theory of Socio-Cultural Evolution." *Society and Economy* 37: 1–29.

Hansmann, Henry and Reinier Kraakman. 2001. "The End of History for Corporate Law." *Georgetown Law Journal* 89: 439–68.

Hart, H. L. A. 2012. *The Concept of Law*. Oxford, UK: Oxford University Press.

Hayek, Friedrich. 1967. *Studies in Philosophy, Politics, and Economics*. London, UK: Routledge and Kegan Paul.

———. 1982. *Law, Legislation, and Liberty*, Volumes 1–3. London, UK: Routledge and Kegan Paul.

Ho, Karen. 2009. *Liquidated: An Ethnography of Wall Street*. Durham, NC: Duke University Press.

Jensen, Michael, and William Meckling. 1976. "Theory of the Firm: Managerial Behavior, Agency Costs, and Ownership Structure." *Journal of Financial Economics* 3 (4): 305–60.

Lee, Ian. 2006. "Efficiency and Ethics in the Debate about Shareholder Primacy." *Delaware Journal of Corporate Law* 31 (2): 533–87.

Liao, Carol. 2014. "A Canadian Model of Corporate Governance." *Dalhousie Law Journal* 37 (2): 559–600.

Lupa, Patrick. 2011. "The BCE Blunder: An Argument in Favour of Shareholder Wealth Maximization in the Change of Control Context." *Dalhousie Journal of Legal Studies* 20 (1): 1–34.

Marin, Michael. 2013. "Disembedding Corporate Governance: The Crisis of Shareholder Primacy in the UK and Canada." *Queen's Law Journal* 39 (1): 223–72.

McCrudden, Christopher. 1999. "Human Rights Codes for Transnational Corporations: What Can the Sullivan and MacBride Principles Tell Us?" *Oxford Journal of Legal Studies* 19 (2): 167–201.

Mudaliar, Abhilash, Rachel Bass, and Hannah Dithrich. 2018. "Annual Impact Investor Survey." Global Impact Investing Network (GIIN).

Mudaliar, Abhilash, Rachel Bass, Hannah Dithrich, and Noshin Nova. 2019. "Annual Impact Investor Survey." Global Impact Investing Network (GIIN).

Palladino, Lenore, and Kristina Karlsson. 2019. "Towards Accountable Capitalism: Remaking Corporate Law Through Stakeholder Governance." *Harvard Law School Forum on Corporate Governance*, February 11. https://corpgov.law.harvard.edu/2019/02/11/towards-accountable-capitalism-remaking-corporate-law-through-stakeholder-governance/.

Papadopoullos, Chris. 2021. "Why Private Equity Has Started Taking ESG Seriously." CapitalMonitor. Accessed December 10, 2021. https://capitalmonitor.ai/asset-class/equity/why-private-equity-is-finally-taking-esg-seriously/.

Rhee, Robert J. 2018. "A Legal Theory of Shareholder Primacy." *Minnesota Law Review* 102 (5): 1951–2017.

Schwarcz, Steven. 2005. "Temporal Perspectives: Resolving the Conflict Between Current and Future Investors." *Minnesota Law Review* 89 (4): 1044–91.

Smith, Adam. 1976. *An Inquiry into the Nature and Causes of the Wealth of Nations*. Edited by R. H. Campbell and A. S. Skinner. New York City, NY: Oxford University Press.

Smith, N. Craig. 2009. "Consumers as Drivers of Corporate Social Responsibility." In *The Oxford Handbook of Corporate Social Responsibility*, edited by Andrew Crane, Dirk Matten, Abagail McWilliams, Jeremy Moon, and Donald S. Siegel, 281–302. Oxford, UK: Oxford University Press.

Stout, Lynn. 2012. *The Shareholder Value Myth: How Putting Shareholders First Harms Investors, Corporations, and the Public*. Oakland, CA: Berrett-Koehler Publishers.

Strine, Jr., Leo. 2015. "The Dangers of Denial: The Need for a Clear-Eyed Understanding of the Power and Accountability Structure Established by the Delaware General Corporation Law." Wake Forest Law Review 50 (3): 761–93.

Vanberg, Viktor. 1986. "Spontaneous Market Order and Social Rules." *Economics and Philosophy* 2 (1): 75–100.

VanDuzer, Anthony. 2009. *The Law of Partnerships and Corporations*. Toronto, Canada: Irwin Law.

Van Marrewijk, Marcel. 2003. "Concepts and Definitions of CSR and Corporate Sustainability: Between Agency and Communion." *Journal of Business Ethics* 44 (2/3): 95–105.

NOTES

1. *See* Canada Business Corporation Act, RSC 1985, c C-44, 122(1)(a); The Delaware Code, Title 8, Chapter 1, Subchapter IV, Directors and Officers § 141 (a); Dodge v. Ford Motor Co., 170 N.W. 668 (Mich. 1919).

2. *See* Delaware Code, *supra note* 1 at § 141 (a).

3. Some commentators point out that social responsibilities of businesses in fact may not limit the shareholder value but rather to increase it, e.g., in the case when consumers demand for companies' products increases with social responsibility (Smith 2009).

4. It shall be noted that some also argue that corporate social responsibility (CSR) programs are at odds with the principle of shareholder primacy and stem from the stakeholder primacy (Van Marrewijk 2003, 95–105).

5. Polk v. Good, 507 A.2d 531, 536 (The Supreme Court of Delaware 1986).

6. eBay Domestic Holdings, Inc. v. Newmark, 16 A.3d 1, 34 (The Delaware Court of Chancery 2010); N. Am. Catholic Educ. Programming Found., Inc. v. Gheewalla, 930 A.2d 92, 101 (The Supreme Court of Delaware 2007).

7. *See* New York Business Corporation Law, § 717 (3)(b).

8. Dodge v. Ford Motor Co., 170 N.W. 668 (Michigan Supreme Court. 1919).

9. *Ibid.*

10. *Ibid.*

11. eBay Domestic Holdings, Inc. v. Newmar, *supra note* 5.

12. Revlon, Inc. v. MacAndrews and Forbes Holdings, Inc., 506 A.2d 173 (The Supreme Court of Delaware 1986).

13. *See* Delaware Code, *supra note* 1 at § 141 (a).

14. Bill C-97, s. 1.1 (a-c).

15. Peoples Department Stores Inc. (Trustee of) v. Wise, SCC 68 (Supreme Court of Canada 2004).

16. Canada Business Corporations Act, RSC 1985, c C-44, Section 122(1.1) (c).

17. *Paramount Commc'ns, Inc. v. Time Inc.*, 571 A.2d 1140, 1154 (Del. Ch. 1989).

18. BCE Inc v 1976 Debentureholders, SCC 69 (Supreme Court of Canada 2008).

19. Bill C-97, *supra note* at s. 1.1 (a).

20. Take-over Bids-Defensive Tactics, OSC NP 62–202, 20 OSCB 3526 (4 July 1997), s 1.1(2).

PART III

Challenging Social Problems: Environmental and Natural Resource Applications

Chapter 8

Compliance Markets Without Romance

Lessons from the Renewable Fuel Standard

Arthur R. Wardle

Environmental problems are commonly cast as a counterpoint to the ability of markets to deliver efficiency, prosperity, and ongoing growth.[1] It is true that the institutions that enabled the Great Divergence left critical amenities unpriced, allowing early industrialists to lay waste to waterways, airsheds, and other environmental resources. The incentives that drive efficiency in the exchange of private goods go awry when economic activity produces social costs unpaid by the goods' producers or consumers. These costs, once irrelevant in the days before industrialization, ballooned intolerably as economies grew increasingly prosperous.[2]

Early environmental law attempted to resolve these problems with the heavy hand of government, requiring specific technological fixes or outright bans. These policies did achieve environmental gains, but at great costs that environmental economists argued could be mitigated by the use of market-based policies like compliance markets. Compliance markets allow regulated firms to "trade" compliance so that firms with cheap environmental cleanup options can sell excess compliance to firms without such simple abatement opportunities. With the price of permits coordinating compliance behavior, marked-based regulation minimizes costs in equilibrium. Unfortunately, the simplistic compliance markets of textbook environmental economics bear only a family resemblance to complicated real-world systems with their numerous "pressure valves," exemptions, and complications that

introduce scope for rent-seeking and undermine coordination. Issues stem-
ming from these design features persistently dog the administration of many
actual compliance markets.

To illustrate the deficiencies of real-world compliance markets, this chapter examines the Renewable Fuel Standard's compliance market, supplementing with occasional references to other markets where appropriate. The
Renewable Fuel Standard (RFS) sets mandates for blending biofuels, most
notably corn ethanol, into U.S. transportation fuels. The policy directs the
EPA to set mandate volumes yearly and distribute the responsibility to blend
ethanol among fuel blenders (typically petroleum refiners) throughout the
country. Biofuel blending generates a "Renewable Identification Number"
(RIN), a compliance credit that can be submitted to the EPA or sold to
another blender. The cost of a RIN, therefore, reflects the marginal cost of
compliance—a firm, in deciding whether to blend additional biofuels, compares the cost of doing so to the market prices of RINs. When blending costs
are higher than RIN prices, firms buy RINs for compliance. Otherwise, firms
blend additional biofuels, selling any excess RINs to other firms.

The RFS makes a good demonstrative example. Its market is mature, having been created in 2006. It features many of the deficiencies facing compliance markets generally in stark clarity (it is, in this sense, cherry-picked). It
mandates the consumption of a good without being well-tailored to an identifiable externality. It requires the EPA to predict gasoline demand and biofuel
availability, a task at which it repeatedly fails and frequently delays, introducing substantial volatility to the RIN market. It features numerous exemptions, which are frequently extended or retracted in games of political cat and
mouse. RIN fraud is frequent enough to require costly investments in quality
assurance and federal enforcement. In short, the RIN market illustrates both
the potential for compliance markets to limit costs and the unromantic political economy of compliance markets in practice.

This chapter proceeds with a brief introduction to the economic theory of
externalities followed by an introduction to the Renewable Fuel Standard's
compliance market. I continue by examining three issues facing RFS administration—the political economy of special exemptions, the prevention of
fraud, and the bureaucratic selection of optimal quantities—and explain how
these relate to broader political economy problems facing compliance markets generally. Finally, I summarize and discuss.

EXTERNALITIES AND THEIR SOLUTIONS

When an uninvolved third party is affected by the production or consumption
of a good (other than through price changes), economists refer to that as an

externality. Externalities can be positive (e.g., planting aesthetically pleasing flowers in my front yard benefits my neighbors) or negative (e.g., hosting loud concerts in my garage annoys them). Most environmental problems can be understood as negative externalities. Coal and natural gas power plants don't pay the costs of air pollution when generating electricity, farmers don't pay the costs of nitrogen runoff when applying fertilizers to their fields, and litterers don't pay the cost of cleanup when they discard trash onto the street.

Not all externalities call for a regulatory response. Coase's famous paper "The Problem of Social Cost" (1960) forcefully argued that, in the absence of transaction costs, people can bargain and arrive at mutually beneficial remedies. An oft-cited example concerns honeybees and apple orchards. Beekeepers produce a positive externality (pollination services) for orchards, but the efficient provision of honey and apples does not require government subsidy. It is sufficiently simple for orchard owners and beekeepers to contract among themselves that efficient pollination provision is possible without interventions (Cheung 1973).

Examples abound of "Coasean bargaining" being used to resolve environmental problems (Deryugina, Moore, and Tol 2021). Transaction costs do, however, limit the domain of problems for which Coasean bargaining offers an actionable solution.[3] The world's population at risk of displacement from sea-level rise cannot meaningfully bargain with all the worlds' carbon emitters. The scale of this and other environmental problems requires some form of organized, institutionalized governance. Historically, this has taken many forms, and institutional entrepreneurs have applied great ingenuity to handling varied environmental problems (Anderson and Parker 2013; Libecap 1989).

The advent of the environmental movement brought major legislation to deal with externalities and clean up the environment, relying heavily on bans and specific technology requirements. These laws paid little attention to the costs of pollution abatement. The Clean Water Act's stated objective was to *eliminate* pollution in navigable waterways by 1985, a laughably unachievable goal that was thankfully never determinedly pursued. Such laws can be credited with the cleanup of many pollutants but can simultaneously be blamed for requiring cleanups whose marginal abatement costs far exceeded any reasonable accounting of their social benefits (Keiser and Shapiro 2019).[4]

Environmental economists rapidly identified and advocated for regulatory approaches that took minimizing compliance costs seriously (Tietenberg 1990), and more recent laws frequently implement this advice (McGartland 2013; Hahn 1989).[5] One such approach is the Pigouvian tax—firms facing a tax on some pollutant will abate that pollutant until the costs of further abatement equal the cost of the tax. In the event that the tax is appropriately set to equal the pollutant's social damages, this leads firms to conduct the optimal level of abatement.

My focus, however, will be on compliance markets, a conceptually similar policy design that theoretically allows governments to achieve environmental improvements at a minimized cost. Rather than relying on bureaucrats to identify the optimal path of abatement options across all industries at once, compliance markets drastically restrict the administrative complexity of pollution regulation. Under a cap-and-trade system, for instance, a would-be regulator needs only set an overall pollution cap and allotment scheme for pollution permits. Firms can then trade these permits amongst themselves; those whose marginal pollution abatement costs are quite high can buy permits from firms with cheaper abatement opportunities.[6] Such exchanges enable high-value, high-pollution activities to continue were truly necessary while forcing polluters to pay the cost of abatement elsewhere. Firms that can abate cheaply are incentivized to do so by the market value of the permits they can open up for sale. Even better, "pricing" pollution, either through permits or a tax, can steer the entrepreneurial focus of competitive firms toward developing cleaner techniques or new abatement technologies. Markets, when properly designed and administered by a regulator, can themselves coordinate solutions to environmental problems.[7]

This is, anyway, the theory underlying arguments in favor of compliance markets. But the compliance markets of the real world diverge from textbook accounts in numerous ways that undermine their ability to deliver efficiency, even if they promise a move in the right direction. The entrepreneurial opportunities opened up by these markets are not limited to those that clean the environment; they extend to political entrepreneurship for special treatment, arbitrage of poorly designed market rules, and new, difficult to detect opportunities for outright fraud. To be perfectly clear: the theoretical argument for compliance markets is sound and they do offer important advantages when compared to command-and-control alternatives. For a certain class of environmental problems, compliance markets are probably the best governing institution yet conceived. But as with any real-world institution, economists must contend with how actual politicians design actual compliance markets (Buchanan [1979] 1999). Greater clarity about the weight of political economic considerations on compliance market operation can inform market design reforms and yield better outcomes.

The Renewable Fuel Standard

Transportation fuels are a mixture of refined petroleum and various fuel additives, which can be blended either at refineries themselves or by independent blenders. The RFS requires fuel blenders in the United States to include biofuels as part of their mix. There are separate, nested mandates within the policy, with the largest mandate belonging to easy-to-produce "conventional" biofuels, satisfied almost entirely with corn ethanol. Within this is a smaller mandate for "advanced" biofuels made from higher efficiency[8] feedstocks like sugarcane and a separate mandate for biodiesel. The smallest mandate is for cellulosic biofuel, a policy that lawmakers hoped would prompt innovation in turning the green parts of plants (e.g., corn stalks) into valuable fuels, but has instead required constant revision as cellulosic biofuel innovations lagged painfully behind regulators' expectations (Wardle 2019).

Mandates for biofuel blending under the RFS were intentionally set to be optimistic. Acknowledging that the industry may not be able to keep up with initial projections for biofuel production, Congress tasked the EPA with annual reviews of mandate levels. By November 30 every year, the EPA is supposed to release a final rulemaking defining mandate levels for the upcoming compliance year (e.g., 2021's mandates should have been announced by November 30, 2020). This deadline is routinely missed. The EPA then divides these overall mandates by projections for fuel demand to arrive at percentage targets. The compliance target for each blender is equal to that percentage of their realized fuel output.

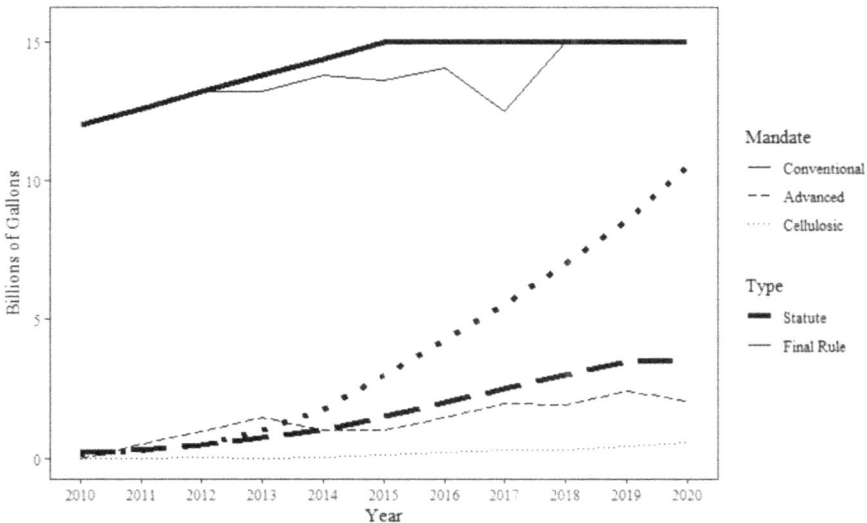

Figure 8.1. Renewable Fuel Standard Mandate Volumes: Statute vs. Final Rules.

Source: Data comes from Bracmort (2020), who includes supplementary information on which of these final rules were later vacated by courts. The value shown for the Conventional mandate is the cap on Conventional biofuels for each year, the Advanced mandate is the overall Advanced mandate minus the mandates for Biomass-based Diesel and Cellulosic. The Biomass-based Diesel mandate is not shown for ease of reading.

Figure 8.1 shows how the RFS mandates have developed over time, both as imagined in the original statute and in the final rules released by the EPA. In the statute, conventional biofuels' contribution to the overall mandate caps out in 2015, slowly outpaced, and eventually overtaken by cellulosic biofuel in 2022. In contrast, the final rules feature orders of magnitude less cellulosic biofuel. This isn't because regulators haven't pushed hard enough—the D.C. Court of Appeals struck down an EPA cellulosic biofuel mandate for being based on production projections that were "deliberately indulging a greater risk of overshooting than undershooting" (*American Petroleum Institute v. EPA* 2013). The grindingly slow progress in cellulosic biofuels, even with a mandate-driven guaranteed market for production, proves that lawmakers were overly optimistic about the technology's promise. If the final rule volumes for cellulosic continue growing at the same rate as they did 2016–2020, they will reach the 16-billion-gallon mark originally envisioned by Congress in the year 2234. In the meantime, the RFS mandate will continue to be dominated by corn ethanol, considered to be the "fuel of the future" by Henry Ford in 1925 (*New York Times* 1925).

The RFS compliance market affords blenders some flexibility in meeting their individual obligations. When biorefiners produce biofuels, they are assigned "Renewable Identification Numbers" (RINs). When blenders purchase these fuels, they "separate" the RIN, blend the fuel, and can then use those RINs for compliance with the RFS. The RINs can be traded among regulated parties. Firms for whom biofuel blending would be inordinately costly can buy RINs, and firms with cheaper blending opportunities can comply in excess to profit from RIN sales. Aside from other minor provisions (like the ability to bank a limited number of RINs for future compliance years), the fundamental structure of the RIN market is comparable to dozens of existing compliance markets.

The following sections highlight the political-economic issues facing different aspects of the RFS. Each draws comparisons to broader issues in compliance market administration, especially by reference to cap and trade, perhaps the most-discussed compliance market concept in the academic literature. Where possible, I make recommendations that would mitigate these problems in RFS reforms or future compliance markets. When it comes to special exemptions or special interest influence over mandate volumes, rules-based administration could replace subjective and discretionary bureaucratic decision-making, bringing greater certainty to biorefiners and fuel blenders alike. Other issues, such as preventing compliance credit fraud or selecting appropriate mandate targets, require higher-level changes but can serve as an object lesson to designers of future compliance markets.

Special Exemptions

The RFS includes provisions allowing the Secretary of Energy and Environmental Protection Agency to exempt small refiners who can demonstrate that RFS compliance would result in a "disproportionate economic hardship." Recipients of these exemptions are not generally made public, and the number of successful petitions has changed dramatically, from a low of seven in 2015 to a high of 35 in 2017, when the EPA did not deny a single petition (Environmental Protection Agency 2021b). Petitions for exemptions are considered at the refinery level rather than the firm level, allowing oil and gas majors like Chevron to successfully apply (Renshaw and Prentice 2018).

Administration of these exemptions is opaque. The recipients are not disclosed by the EPA—the general public only knows the identity of some recipients due to leaks or voluntary company disclosures. The exemptions are a frequent topic of RFS litigation and lobbying efforts. Even aside from the secrecy and unexplained variation in the numbers of exemptions granted year-to-year, there's good reason to suspect that the waivers aren't granted through a legitimate process. Mere hours before leaving office, the outgoing Trump administration granted two waivers to Sinclair's Wyoming refineries (Kelly and Pamuk 2021). A federal court later granted a motion that claimed the EPA did not adequately assess Sinclair's actual qualification for the waivers and required the EPA to reconsider. Sinclair did not even oppose the motion (*Sinclair v. EPA* 2021). The Government Accountability Office is now collecting information for an independent investigation into the propriety of RFS exemptions (Kelly 2021).

Special exemptions like these undermine the efficiency objectives of using a compliance market in the first place, though it's surprisingly tricky to understand exactly how. Recipients of small refinery waivers still get to separate RINs when they blend biofuel. They'll sell those RINs to other RFS obligated parties since the waiver means they have no in-house value. If the waivers were randomly assigned to different refineries, this means the overall efficiency benefit of the compliance market would be maintained. Even those exempted from the mandate will choose biofuel blending volumes that set the marginal cost of blending equal to the price of its associated RIN, the exact same optimality result as when nobody is exempt. The only difference is distributional: under this system, exempted refineries profit from biofuel blending. If overall mandate volumes are unchanged by the waivers, non-exempted refiners pay the difference.

In the broader context of cap and trade and other environmental compliance markets, this is known as the independence property. Stated differently, the amount of emissions reduction pursued by a given firm is independent of (i.e., unaffected by) the number of pollution permits they are freely granted.[9]

The only thing that matters is the overall market cap and the distribution of abatement costs among firms. In the market equilibrium, everyone will abate until the marginal cost of abatement equals the going price of the pollution permit. There is good quasi-experimental evidence that the independence property holds in real-world compliance markets (Fowlie and Perloff 2013).

However, the independence property is only true under certain assumptions that are not satisfied in many compliance market contexts including the RFS (Hahn and Stavins 2011).[10] Importantly, if permit allocations (or exemptions, in the RFS case) are manipulable by regulated firms, behavior is more complicated. One way of thinking about the decision facing firms is that they face two routes to compliance; either make the investments necessary to blend additional ethanol or make the political investments necessary to secure an exemption. Without knowing how RFS exemption decisions are made, it is difficult to get a sense of the scale of this problem, but costs incurred to seek exemptions waste resources and undermine the efficiency benefits of the whole compliance market (Tullock 1967; Baumol 1990).

The nature of the problem makes its own solution abundantly clear: either eliminate exemptions entirely, or issue them based on clear, objective, and non-manipulable criteria. This is diametrically opposed to the current administration of RFS exemptions, which is secretive and based on subjective findings about whether a refinery will face a "disproportionate economic hardship." Ambiguous criteria like these invite "trades" between politicians, bureaucrats, and regulated companies for their own mutual gain, generally at the cost of the general public (Holcombe 2018). If regulation is to bring about beneficial social coordination, transparency and predictability are critical.

FRAUDULENT CREDITS

The possibility of fraud exists in all markets, but the typical market process limits fraud's general pervasiveness. A used car salesman would love to obscure quality deficiencies, but car buyers' own self-interest forms the basis for many institutions that limit salesmen's ability to fleece their customers. Car buyers can benefit from quality guarantees, receive independent reports on vehicle history, or purchase from known, well-regarded dealers with reputations for fair dealing. These institutions unravel the salesman's inherent informational advantage and allow for the ongoing functioning of a used car market, even if they don't perfectly eliminate fraud (Akerlof 1970).

What if buyers don't care about quality? This would be a bizarre circumstance in most markets, but in a market for compliance credits, regulated parties only really care about complying with the regulation to the satisfaction of the regulators. If fraudulent credits are available and firms think their chances of being caught are reasonably low, there's little intrinsic reason for firms to prefer legitimate credits. Indeed, fraudulent biofuel producers have been uncovered multiple times since the RFS's inception. As an example, three companies generated enough fraudulent biodiesel RINs from mid-2010 through 2011 to make up 11% of the biodiesel RIN market despite never producing any biodiesel at all (Yacobucci 2013).

The early RFS handled this problem by holding blenders responsible for fraudulent RINs, forcing them to not only purchase new replacement RINs but also pay fines. For firms that were legitimately duped by fraudulent bio-refiners, this surely felt like being victimized twice. This system works to dis-incentivize the knowing purchase of fraudulent RINs but not without its own costs. Regulated parties under this system, keen on avoiding fraudulent RINs, need to invest in quality assurance for every RIN purchase they make or else face the risk of complete loss. This will be cheaper for high-throughput, established biorefiners, disadvantaging the nascent, small-volume experimental outfits that the RFS is supposedly designed to help. Validation is costly to firms, pushing up transaction costs associated with compliance and weighing on RIN liquidity. Even with these added costs, blenders cannot perfectly assess the legitimacy of each and every RIN and still get caught with fraudulent credits.

In 2014, the EPA developed a voluntary Quality Assurance Plan (QAP), whereby independent third parties could become RIN auditors and provide services to RIN market participants. RINs verified under a QAP become Q-RINs, which provide their holders an affirmative defense against fraud allegations.[11] It also modified rules regarding how many RINs would need to be replaced in the event of fraud and who would need to replace them. The efficacy and uptake of this program is unclear; a slideshow prepared by the EPA in 2015 reported that only 12 percent of RINs were Q-RINs, though that seemed to be increasing at the time (Bunker 2015). It hasn't stopped enforcement actions against new fraud schemes (Environmental Protection Agency 2021a), some of which are surprisingly sordid (Carr 2021). The EPA has already withdrawn one auditing firm's credentials for failing to adequately intervene after "glaring signs of RIN fraud" (Neeley 2019).

Fraud issues in the RFS's RIN market are an extreme example of a broader phenomenon that can make governing compliance markets challenging. Another example comes from carbon offset policies in cap-and-trade markets. Offset programs allow polluters to emit additional greenhouse gases without needing to purchase more permits if they can offset those emissions elsewhere. This can be formalized in an offset market, where established, specialist providers of offsets deal with many carbon market participants. When this functions as intended, offsets provide a way to cut the same amount of emissions at even lower costs than are possible within the narrow carbon market itself.

For offsets to work as intended, though, they must be "additional," meaning they must capture carbon that wouldn't otherwise have been captured. Selling an offset that promises to keep a forest from being logged when that forest was never at risk of being logged to begin with doesn't cut carbon emissions, and in fact it increases them since it relaxes the carbon cap in the market that buys the offset.[12] For many offsets, the true amount of emissions reduction is difficult to measure due to its dependence on complicated and dynamic environmental systems. Regulators have neither the time, resources, or expertise to carefully assess the quality of every offset purchased (Cullenward and Victor 2020, 93). When lower quality (i.e., less efficacious) offsets are cheaper to produce, this can unwind the whole market, even without outright fraud. Buyers of offsets have no reason to care so long as regulators are willing to accept the offsets, having little stake in their own emissions beyond the need to comply with cap-and-trade program rules. Solutions for these problems are difficult because the problem is inherent to a market borne out of compliance with regulation; participants have no inherent reason to care about quality.

Regulation coordinates effort around finding least-cost ways of satisfying the regulation, which may or may not line up with what regulators want. Making compliance market participants liable for fraudulent credits realigns incentives at the cost of saddling the market with transaction costs. Providing affirmative defenses to fuel blenders would grease the wheels of the legitimate market while eliminating important incentives for blenders to avoid known fraudulent producers. Regulators can iterate when they discover new schemes, just as fraudsters can iterate to avoid detection. One lesson is that enforcement needs to take center stage in policy design. How will the legitimacy of compliance credits be checked, how much quality control is feasible, and how do the costs of quality assurance weigh against the cost/ benefit ratio of the policy as a whole? To effectively minimize costs, designers of compliance market-based policies need answers to these questions. That being said, it may not be possible to foresee every potential way of gaming a market-based regulation. With compliance markets disadvantaged at the outset, realistic regulator expectations about the pervasiveness of fraud and difficulty in detecting it are paramount.

PICKING QUANTITIES

Lawmakers' misplaced optimism for cellulosic biofuels, described in the earlier overview of the RFS, is only one of the RFS's examples of the difficulty in picking the quantity of compliance permits to require. Nothing about the context of compliance markets makes governments any more capable of setting optimal quantities than they are in private goods, where the inability of central planning to determine optimal quantities is well-documented (Hayek 1945; Kirzner [1984] 2018). In fact, the dynamic complexity of environmental systems makes this problem far worse (Borenstein et al. 2019). This is reflected in the shortcomings of the EPA's Regulatory Impact Analysis for the Renewable Fuel Standard. That analysis, despite its complexity (e.g., estimating changes to production in 47 refining products in multiple regions), papered over important sources of uncertainty. The analysis held demand for vehicle miles traveled constant, relied on a single projection for future energy prices, and gave inadequate attention to technological constraints limiting higher blending volumes (Lade, Lin Lawell, and Smith 2018a).

The same informational deficiencies that led to over-optimistic cellulosic biofuel projections and the overconfident Regulatory Impact Analysis impact the day-to-day administration of the RFS too. Special interest groups with stakes in the EPA's decisions compete for influence over annual mandate rule-makings. With heavy thumbs on either side of the scale, decisions regarding RFS mandate levels come not from an optimizing social planner, but from the interplay between competing lobbyists operating under an overseeing court system. The outcome of this procedure is hard to anticipate; mandates announced in proposed and final rules are frequently out of step with market expectations, and stock prices for affected firms swing in response (Lade, Lin Lawell, and Smith 2018b; Wardle 2020). In fact, a great deal of the total volatility in RIN markets occurs around rulemaking announcements.

The political tightrope the EPA must walk in picking mandate volumes probably contributes to the excessive delays typical of RFS final rules. As mentioned previously, volume mandates for a given compliance year are supposed to be announced by November 30 of the previous year. Since 2010, this deadline has been missed by more than a month over half of the time, often by ridiculous margins. The final rule for the 2014 compliance year wasn't issued until November 2015, almost a full year after the compliance year had ended. The rule for the current compliance year (2021) is shaping up similarly—the outgoing Trump administration decided not to bother, and the Biden administration still has not issued a proposed rule as of this writing. The RFS has been around for over a decade, but this issue remains unresolved, and it is likely to get worse. The RFS statute only lists suggested volumes through 2022; after that, the EPA is fully in charge of setting volumes and compliance market participants won't even have a statute to guide their expectations.

That RIN prices swing so wildly in response to delayed announcements speaks to the depth of this problem for the efficiency of the RFS. A compliance market is supposed to minimize the costs of complying with a given objective, but its ability to do so is undermined when that objective is unknown to market participants and subject to continued lobbying efforts while the compliance year is underway. If firms are risk-averse, this uncertainty and its associated volatility violate the independence property by encouraging unexempted firms to overinvest in blending capacity as a hedge (Baldursson and von der Fehr 2004). On the other side of the market, policy-induced RIN price uncertainty erodes the incentive to invest in biofuel production and innovation (Markel, Sims, and English 2018).

Reckoning with these issues requires acknowledging that regulators are themselves the targets of special interest politics. This is to some extent unavoidable because regulators rely on information that only the industries they regulate can provide (Milgrom and Roberts 1986). This problem can be alleviated by designing compliance markets with less need for bureaucratic discretion. In the case of the RFS, eliminating the need for the EPA to revise mandate levels yearly is the most obvious way of doing this. Mandate levels could be based on explicit rules (automatic year-to-year adjustments based on progress towards targets). Even less radically, the stretches of time between discretionary reviews could simply be made longer.

Much of the bureaucratic discretion built into RFS administration is purported to limit the risk of excessive compliance costs. However troubling the EPA's mishandling of volume adjustments has been, the country is clearly better off than if the entire fuels industry had been held liable for failing to blend billions of gallons of non-existent cellulosic ethanol for the past decade. But there are better ways of setting up guardrails.

For any given compliance market policy, there are unstated maximum and minimum price levels, i.e., prices above or below which politicians will conclude that the policy has failed and reform the market, potentially by adjusting the number of permits required. Rather than leaving these levels unstated, lawmakers can add a price collar directly to the policy, directing regulators to sell infinite permits at some high price and buy infinite permits at some low price.[13] Collars transparently eliminate the possibility of excessively high compliance costs without needing to leave room for serious bureaucratic discretion over price levels (Pizer 2002). In fact, the RFS already makes some use of this idea for the cellulosic portion of the mandate. Firms can buy Cellulosic Waiver Credits for compliance at stated prices that change each year. In 2016, the year that regulated firms purchased the most credits, firms bought over 33 million credits at a price of $1.33 each (Environmental Protection Agency 2020). Price collars are not a perfect solution—government officials lack knowledge about where to set the collar just as they do for where to set the mandate. But in a world where "ideal" policy is not possible, there are still ways of avoiding subjectivity that opens the door to manipulation.

COMPLIANCE MARKETS FOR WHAT?

To this point, I've discussed issues with specific aspects of the RFS's policy design. But perhaps the most important way that the RFS differs from text-book accounts of compliance markets is in what the market is *for*. Theoretical treatments of compliance markets imagine they will be applied to mitigate an identifiable nuisance: water contaminants, air pollution, resource degradation, etc. To be sure, the logic behind compliance markets is that they minimize compliance costs for a given objective, and that remains true regardless of the sensibility of the objective. But in terms of maximizing economic efficiency, tacking some market-based cost containment provisions to a fundamentally flawed policy objective is hardly a win.

The major arguments touted by early RFS supporters focused on energy independence and environmental benefits. Concerns about dependence on foreign energy supplies, not exactly an externality to begin with, subsequently waned and became wholly irrelevant in 2019 when the United States achieved net energy exporter status. The environmental reputation of biofuels was never really deserved to begin with, and more recent research has only deepened our understanding of how they harm rather than help the environment (see Wardle 2018 for a review or this literature). Whether corn ethanol is less carbon-intensive than gasoline on a lifecycle basis is difficult to measure, and reputable researchers have published estimates on both sides. What is abundantly clear is that even if ethanol is slightly less carbon-intensive, it's a knife-edge difference (Hochman and Zilberman 2018). Meanwhile, making fuel from corn necessitates expanding farms and intensifying corn production, magnifying a litany of environmental issues already facing U.S. corn agriculture (Wardle 2018).

Of course, the RFS isn't just a corn ethanol mandate. The law includes mandates for cellulosic ethanol, which many hoped (and continue to hope) won't face the same environmental issues as corn feedstocks. One final justification for the policy, then, could be the inducement of innovation for better biofuel varieties (Acemoglu et al. 2012). But as discussed previously, the RFS is still by-and-large a mandate for corn ethanol. The surge in cellulosic biofuel has not come despite the intense effort and does not seem to be on the horizon; meanwhile, the corn ethanol portion of the mandate shows no signs of winding down.

Even if biofuel does avoid some of the gasoline's externalities, the RFS is not targeted to those externalities. The RIN compliance market, even ignoring the deficiencies mentioned so far, only coordinates minimizing the costs of biofuel blending, not the costs of abating the externalities themselves. There are a number of inefficiencies that result from this indirect targeting. Apart from the coarse distinctions between conventional, advanced, and cellulosic fuels, the RFS does not privilege cleaner biofuels over dirtier ones (Chen et al. 2021). Moreover, basing the compliance market on a performance standard for fuel inputs places an implicit subsidy on fuel output; to see this, consider that a firm can comply either by selling less low-biofuel blends or by selling additional high-biofuel blends (Helfand 1991; Fischer 2001).[14]

A recent cost/benefit analysis projected that net benefits for the corn and cellulosic ethanol mandates from 2016–2030 are negative across all examined scenarios, which included high and low social costs of carbon, high and low nitrogen runoff costs, and high and low prices of food and fuel (Chen et al. 2021). They found that agricultural producers are the primary beneficiaries of the policy, while U.S. consumers are the primary losers through higher food and fuel prices since blenders can easily pass on the costs of biofuels (Knittel, Meiselman, and Stock 2017). This is a familiar dynamic to political economists—the U.S. corn industry is well organized and connected, while "U.S. consumers" are such a broad group (with the aggregate cost of the policy spread so thinly) that organized resistance is essentially impossible (Holcombe 2018). It may be fair to say that the RFS minimizes the cost of getting 15 billion gallons of corn ethanol into U.S. fuel supplies annually, but for what purpose?

Questionable links between regulatory policies and the externalities that supposedly justify them are to be expected in special-interest politics. Individual voters lack the expertise, incentive, or time to closely examine the impact of every regulatory policy passed by democratically elected politicians. For rent-seeking firms and their friends in Congress, plausible connections to identifiable externalities are enough to obfuscate the real purpose underlying government transfers (Johnson and Libecap 2001; Holcombe 2018). Efficient policy design in service of inefficient, rent-seeking policy goals points to a countervailing pressure group attempting to mitigate costs (Becker 1983). Efficient mitigation of legitimate externalities will often involve a compliance market, but the presence of a compliance market says nothing about the legitimacy of the policy aim undergirding it.

DISCUSSION AND CONCLUSION

Compliance markets can be an effective tool for minimizing the costs of new regulations, but there are important divergences between idealized models of compliance markets and real-world execution. Many of these divergences are not new and have been recognized for decades in studies of more traditional command and control regimes. Extending this analysis to compliance markets reveals room for improvement. The Renewable Fuel Standard and its RIN market are a mature example of a real-world compliance market that typifies many of these issues.

While theoretical treatments tend to assume that regulators either know optimal quantities or can estimate them with reasonably small error, the RFS was off by orders of magnitude in projections for future biofuel availability. Rather than being tailored to a specific externality, it mandates the consumption of specific products with questionable justification. Yearly reviews of the overall mandate level garner heavy interference from both biofuel producers and RIN market participants, and the (often delayed) resulting mandates reflect this political tug-of-war. Much of the bureaucratic discretion afforded to the EPA is unnecessary and eliminating it from the RFS's regulatory design could mitigate these problems.

Likewise, special exemptions allow many firms, including large and well-established firms like Chevron, to evade some portion of their compliance. Procedures for granting these waivers are secretive and the source of multiple lawsuits. What little is known suggests the presence of below-board behavior by market participants and federal administrations alike. Again, these exemptions are not fundamental to market operation, and could easily be removed or reformed to mitigate political favoritism.

Outright fraud pervades the RFS simply because, unlike markets more generally, regulated firms have little reason to care about the legitimacy of their RINs so long as they can pass them off for compliance. This leaves regulators in the awkward position of needing to hold companies liable for purchasing fraudulent credits, even when those same firms are arguably the victims of fraudulent activity. Costs associated with assuring the validity of RINs count against the efficiency of compliance market systems, and the ability of regulators to adequately assure credit quality constrains the scope of problems that can benefit from compliance market regulatory schemes.

None of this is to say that compliance markets are bad in general, only that they suffer from many of the same political realities as any other regulation. All of the above-discussed issues are present and even exaggerated under command and control or tax-based regulatory systems. I have paid only minimal attention to the benefits of compliance markets (just enough to motivate my own arguments) because they are thoroughly explicated elsewhere. For many problems, compliance markets are the best-designed solution yet conceived.[15] Getting the most out of the social coordination provided by compliance markets requires acknowledging their political operation in the design stages. For some problems, this may tip the cost/benefit scale against a compliance market entirely, but for a broader set of problems it means limiting the scope of bureaucratic discretion and designing policies to work in a messy, political world.

REFERENCES

Acemoglu, Daron, Philippe Aghion, Leonardo Bursztyn, and David Hemous. 2012. "The Environment and Directed Technical Change." *American Economic Review* 102 (1): 131–66.

Akerlof, George A. 1970. "The Market for 'Lemons': Quality Uncertainty and the Market Mechanism." *Quarterly Journal of Economics* 84 (3): 488–500.

American Petroleum Institute v. EPA. 2013. 10th Cir., No. 12–1139.

Anderson, Terry L., and Dominic P. Parker. 2013. "Transaction Costs and Environmental Markets: The Role of Entrepreneurs." *Review of Environmental Economics and Policy* 7 (2): 259–75.

Baldursson, Fridrik M, and Nils-Henrik M von der Fehr. 2004. "Price Volatility and Risk Exposure: On Market-Based Environmental Policy Instruments." *Journal of Environmental Economics and Management* 48 (1): 682–704.

Banzhaf, H. Spencer, Timothy Fitzgerald, and Kurt Schnier. 2013. "Nonregulatory Approaches to the Environment: Coasean and Pigouvian Perspectives." *Review of Environmental Economics and Policy* 7 (2): 238–58.

Baumol, William J. 1990. "Entrepreneurship: Productive, Unproductive, and Destructive." *Journal of Political Economy* 98 (5): 893–921.

Becker, Gary S. 1983. "A Theory of Competition Among Pressure Groups for Political Influence." *Quarterly Journal of Economics* 98 (3): 371–400.

Borenstein, Severin, James Bushnell, Frank A. Wolak, and Matthew Zarazoga-Watkins. 2019. "Expecting the Unexpected: Emissions Uncertainty and Environmental Market Design." *American Economic Review* 109 (11): 3953–77.

Bracmort, Kelsi. 2020. "The Renewable Fuel Standard (RFS): An Overview." Congressional Research Service. https://fas.org/sgp/crs/misc/R43325.pdf.

Buchanan, James M. [1979] 1999. "Politics Without Romance: A Sketch of Positive Public Choice Theory and Its Normative Implications." In *The Collected Works of James M. Buchanan: The Logical Foundations of Constitutional Liberty. Vol. 1,* 45–59. Indianapolis, IN: Liberty Fund.

Bunker, Byron. 2015. "RIN Fraud & Compliance." https://www.epa.gov/sites/default/files/2015–11/documents/bunkerenergyconferenceslidedeck_09212015_final.pdf.

Carr, Donald. 2021. "Grease Thieves, Corn Oil and Fraud: How Biofuel Scam Artists Bilked U.S. Taxpayers of Billions." Environmental Working Group, May. https://www.ewg.org/ news-insights/news/grease-thieves-corn-oil-and-fraud-how-biofuel-scam-artists-bilkedus-taxpayers.

Chen, Louye, Deepayan Debnath, Jia Zhong, Kelsie Ferin, Andy VanLoocke, and Madhu Khanna. 2021. "The Economic and Environmental Costs and Benefits of the Renewable Fuel Standard." *Environmental Research Letters* 16 (034021).

Cheung, Steven N. S. 1973. "The Fable of the Bees: An Economic Investigation." *Journal of Law & Economics* 16 (1): 11–33.

Coase, Ronald H. 1960. "The Problem of Social Cost." *Journal of Law & Economics* 3: 1–44.

Costello, Christopher, and Robert Deacon. 2007. "The Efficiency Gains from Fully Delineating Rights in an ITQ Fishery." *Marine Resource Economics* 22 (4): 347–61.

Cullenward, Danny, and David G. Victor. 2020. *Making Climate Policy Work.* Cambridge, UK: Polity.

Currie, Janet, and Reed Walker. 2019. "What Do Economists Have to Say about the Clean Air Act 50 Years After the Establishment of the Environmental Protection Agency?" *Journal of Economic Perspectives* 33 (4): 3–26.

Deryugina, Tatyana, Frances Moore, and Richard S. J. Tol. 2021. "Environmental Applications of the Coase Theorem." *Environmental Science & Policy* 120: 81–88.

Environmental Protection Agency. 2020. "Table 6: Cellulosic Waiver Credits Purchased Annually." Annual Compliance Data for Obligated Parties and Renewable Fuel Exporters under the Renewable Fuel Standard (RFS) Program. https://www.epa.gov/fuels-registration-reporting-and-compliance-help/annual -compliance-data-obligated-parties-and.

———. 2021a. "Civil Enforcement of the Renewable Fuel Standard Program." https: //www.epa.gov/enforcement/civil-enforcement-renewable-fuel-standard-program.

———. 2021b. "Table 2: Summary of Small Refinery Exemption Decisions Each Compliance Year." https://www.epa.gov/fuels-registration-reporting-and -compliance-help/rfssmall-refinery-exemptions.

Fischer, Carolyn. 2001. "Rebating Environmental Policy Revenues: Output-Based Allocations and Tradeable Performance Standards." RFF Discussion Paper 01–22.

Fowlie, Meredith, and Jeffrey M. Perloff. 2013. "Distributing Pollution Rights in Cap-and-Trade Programs: Are Outcomes Independent of Allocation?" *Review of Economics and Statistics* 95 (5): 1640–52.

Hahn, Robert W. 1984. "Market Power and Transferable Property Rights." *Quarterly Journal of Economics* 99 (4): 753–65.

———. 1989. "Economic Prescriptions for Environmental Problems: How the Patient Followed the Doctor's Orders." *Journal of Economic Perspectives* 3 (2): 95–114.

Hahn, Robert W., and Robert N. Stavins. 2011. "The Effect of Allowance Allocations on Cap-and-Trade System Performance." *Journal of Law & Economics* 54 (4): S267–94.

Hayek, F. A. 1945. "The Use of Knowledge in Society." *American Economic Review* 35 (4): 519–30.

Helfand, Gloria E. 1991. "Standards Versus Standards: The Effects of Different Pollution Restrictions." *American Economic Review* 81 (3) (June): 622–34.

Hochman, Gal, and David Zilberman. 2018. "Corn Ethanol and U.S. Biofuel Policy 10 Years Later: A Quantitative Assessment." *American Journal of Agricultural Economics* 100 (2): 570–84.

Holcombe, Randall G. 2018. "The Regulatory State." In *Political Capitalism: How Economic and Political Power Is Made and Maintained*, 148–70. Cambridge, UK: Cambridge University Press.

Johnson, Ronald N., and Gary D. Libecap. 2001. "Information Distortion and Competitive Remedies in Government Transfer Programs: The Case of Ethanol." *Economics of Governance* 2 (2): 101–34.

Keiser, David A., Catherine L. Kling, and Joseph S. Shapiro. 2019. "The Low but Uncertain Benefits of US Water Quality Policy." *Proceedings of the National Academy of Sciences* 116 (12): 5262–69.

Keiser, David A., and Joseph S. Shapiro. 2019. "Consequences of the Clean Water Act and the Demand for Water Quality." *Quarterly Journal of Economics* 134 (1): 349–96.

Kelly, Stephanie. 2021. "U.S. EPA to Hand over Biofuel Exemption Documents to GAO Probe." *Reuters*, May 5. https://www.reuters.com/business/energy/us-epa-hand-over-biofuel-exemption-documents-gao-probe-2021-05-05/.

Kelly, Stephanie, and Humeyra Pamuk. 2021. "Trump's EPA Granted Sinclair Oil Last-Minute Biofuel Waivers." *Reuters*, January 21. https://www.reuters.com/article/us-usa-biofuelsexclusive/exclusive-trumps-epa-granted-sinclair-oil-last-minute-biofuel-waiversidUSKBN29Q2LT.

Kirzner, Israel M. [1984] 2018. "Economic Planning and the Knowledge Problem." In *Competition, Economic Planning, and the Knowledge Problem*, 75–86. Indianapolis, IN: Liberty Fund.

Knittel, Christopher R., Ben S. Meiselman, and James H. Stock. 2017. "The Pass-Through of RIN Prices to Wholesale and Retail Fuels Under the Renewable Fuel Standard." *Journal of the Association of Environmental and Resource Economists* 4 (4): 1081–1119.

Lade, Gabriel E., C.-Y. Cynthia Lin Lawell, and Aaron Smith. 2018a. "Designing Climate Policy: Lessons from the Renewable Fuel Standard and the Blend Wall." *American Journal of Agricultural Economics* 100 (2): 585–99.

———. 2018b. "Policy Shocks and Market-Based Regulations: Evidence from the Renewable Fuel Standard." *American Journal of Agricultural Economics* 100 (3): 707–31.

Libecap, Gary D. 1989. *Contracting for Property Rights*. Cambridge, UK: Cambridge University Press.

Markel, Evan, Charles Sims, and Burton C. English. 2018. "Policy Uncertainty and the Optimal Investment Decisions of Second-Generation Biofuel Producers." *Energy Economics* 76: 89–100.

McGartland, Al. 2013. "Thirty Years of Economics at the Environmental Protection Agency." *Agricultural and Resource Economics Review* 42 (3): 436–52.

Milgrom, Paul, and John Roberts. 1986. "Relying on the Information of Interested Parties." *RAND Journal of Economics* 17 (1): 18–32.

Montgomery, W. David. 1972. "Markets in Licenses and Efficient Pollution Control Programs." *Journal of Economic Theory* 5 (3): 395–418.

Neeley, Todd. 2019. "Genscape Must Replace RINs: Biodiesel Fraud Identified Early, but EPA Alleges Auditor Dropped Ball." *DTN Progressive Farmer*, August 7. https://www.dt npf.com/agriculture/web/ag/news/business-inputs/article/2019/08/07/bio diesel-fraudidentified-early-epa.

New York Times. 1925. "Ford Predicts Fuel from Vegetation," September 24.

Newell, Richard, William Pizer, and Jiangfeng Zhang. 2005. "Managing Permit Markets to Stabilize Prices." *Environmental & Resource Economics* 31 (2): 133–57.

Pizer, William A. 2002. "Combining Price and Quantity Controls to Mitigate Global Climate Change." *Journal of Public Economics* 85 (3): 409–34.

Renshaw, Jarrett, and Chris Prentice. 2018. "Chevron Granted Waiver from U.S. Biofuel Laws at Utah Plant—Source." *Reuters*, November 20. https://www.reuters .com/article/ususa-biofuels-chevron-exclusive/exclusive-chevron-granted-waiver -from-u-s-biofuel-lawsat-utah-plant-source-idUSKCN1NP2E6.

Schmalensee, Richard, and Robert N. Stavins. 2019. "Policy Evolution Under the Clean Air Act." *Journal of Economic Perspectives* 33 (4): 27–50.

Sinclair v. EPA. 2021. D.C. Cir., No. 21–9528, Order to Grant Motion for Vacatur and Voluntary Remand.

Song, Lisa, and James Temple. 2021. "A Nonprofit Promised to Preserve Wildlife. Then It Made Millions Claiming It Could Cut down Trees." *ProPublica*, May 10. https://www.pr opublica.org/article/a-nonprofit-promised-to-preserve-wildlife- then-it-made-millionsclaiming-it-could-cut-down-trees.

Stavins, Robert N. 1995. "Transaction Costs and Tradeable Permits." *Journal of Environmental Economics and Management* 29 (2): 133–48.

Tietenberg, T. H. 1990. "Economic Instruments for Environmental Regulation." *Oxford Review of Economic Policy* 6 (1): 17–33.

Tullock, Gordon. 1967. "The Welfare Costs of Tariffs, Monopolies, and Theft." *Western Economic Journal* 5 (3): 224–32.

Wardle, Arthur R. 2018. "A Review of the Environmental Effects of the Renewable Fuel Standard's Corn Ethanol Mandate." Policy Paper 2018.002, Center for Growth & Opportunity at Utah State University. https://www.thecgo.org/wp-content/ uploads/2020/10/A-Review-of-the-Environmental-Effects-of-the-Renewable-Fuel -Standards-Corn-Ethanol-Mandate-1.pdf.

———. 2019. "A Reset for the Renewable Fuel Standard?" *Regulation* 42 (3): 22–25.

———. 2020. "Industry Compliance Costs Under the Renewable Fuel Standard: Evidence from Compliance Credits." Working Paper.

Yacobucci, Brent D. 2013. "Analysis of Renewable Identification Numbers (RINs) in the Renewable Fuel Standard (RFS)." Congressional Research Service. https:// nationalagla wcenter.org/wp-content/uploads/assets/crs/R42824.pdf.

Yandle, Bruce, Maya Vijayaraghavan, and Madhusudan Bhattarai. 2002. "The Environmental Kuznets Curve: A Primer." Property & Environment Research Center. https://www.pe rc.org/wp-content/uploads/2018/05/environmen tal-kuznets-curve-primer.pdf.

NOTES

1. Arthur R. Wardle is a PhD student at the University of California, Berkeley's Department of Agricultural & Resource Economics. This research was funded by the Mercatus Center as part of the Bastiat Fellowship Program. I thank the editors of this

volume, participants in the 2021 Bastiat Fellowship Research Sequence, and Camille Wardle for comments. All errors are the author's.

2. Note that this is not true across the board for all forms of environmental degradation. The Environmental Kuznets Curve, which hypothesizes an inverted-U shaped relationship between income and environmental quality, applies in an important subclass of environmental problems (Yandle, Vijayaraghavan, and Bhattarai 2002).

3. Note, however, that cap-and-trade programs aren't antithetical to Coasean bargaining. If free rider problems are not too severe and a cap is set higher than the victims of pollution would like, bargaining can take place within the cap-and-trade market itself. By buying permits with the intention of leaving them unused, green advocates can reduce the effective cap. Cap-and trade-schemes only cease to be Coasean when free rider problems inhibit environmentalists from unifying to participate in the market (Banzhaf, Fitzgerald, and Schnier 2013).

4. The Clean Water Act's benefit/cost ratio is estimated to be particularly low (Keiser, Kling, and Shapiro 2019); laws governing other environmental goods, like the Clean Air Act, look much better on average (Currie and Walker 2019). But the point that technical standards and bans do not equalize marginal compliance costs and can therefore result in socially destructive abatement remains.

5. This also applies to new programs under existing environmental laws, like the 1990 amendments to the Clean Air Act (Schmalensee and Stavins 2019).

6. Economic theory predicts, and empirical analyses confirms, that while allocation schemes matter in terms of who benefits from regulation, the permits themselves are traded until they reach their highest-valued use. "Equilibrium outcomes in an efficient emissions permit market will be independent of how the emissions permits are initially distributed" (Fowlie and Perloff 2013). Complications with this result will be discussed later.

7. For a theoretical treatment, see Montgomery (1972).

8. In terms of the engineering difficulty of turning feedstock to fuel.

9. A small refinery exemption can be thought of as an allocation of free RINs equal to the compliance target that refinery would have otherwise faced.

10. Other important underlying assumptions not discussed here are (a) no transaction costs (Stavins 1995) and (b) no market power (Hahn 1984).

11. That is, the purchaser of a Q-RIN is protected from government sanctions, even if that RIN is later discovered to be fraudulent.

12. A particularly brazen example involves the Massachusetts Audubon Society, which sold an offset to the California cap-and-trade program promising not to log a property it was already managing as wildlife habitat (Song and Temple 2021).

13. Alternative policy choices can achieve the same goal without requiring regulators to directly buy or sell permits (Newell, Pizer, and Zhang 2005).

14. Formally, the fuel blending performance standard that results in the socially optimal blend rate will result in RIN prices equal to the optimal Pigouvian blending subsidy, output prices that are lower than is socially optimal, and therefore output that is suboptimally high.

15. To provide a specific example, I would classify the Individual Transferable Quota (ITQ) approach to fishery regulation this way, though even these require careful design considerations (Costello and Deacon 2007).

Chapter 9

A Calculus of Communication

Deliberation, Knowledge, and Public Choice in the Context of Water Management

Emil Panzaru

Deliberative democracy is a type of "communication that induces reflection on preferences, values, and perspectives in a non-coercive fashion" resulting in a "decision binding on the participants or on those for whom the participants are authorized to speak" (Mansbridge et al. 2010, 65). The quote suggests that deliberative democracy is a policy-making process by which people try to argue with one another based on logic rather than force, where force means A making B do what he/she would otherwise not do (Mansbridge et al. 2010, 65). In doing so, individuals try and make coherent arguments in support of their positions that could either be a preference (a descriptive statement on the topic stated in the form of "opinions" or "likes"), a value (statements committing to concepts such as liberty, equality, fairness, justice and so on), or a perspective (the societal/ecological condition and the understanding of that societal condition summed up as life experiences) (Bohman 2006, 178–79). The second sequence in the quote suggests the purpose of this deliberation. Namely those different individuals will converge on the same result derived from the soundest reasons, which represents the common "decision" referred to above (Gaus 2008, 26–7). Moreover, the result will have to be respected by participants at all times and will inform all their subsequent political behavior, which is what makes it "binding" (Gaus 2008, 27).

When applied to policymaking, deliberation selects for policies based on two criteria: how reflexive the process of adopting policies is and whether the policies being discussed are arrived at via consensus. On the one hand, reflexive policies are those which can be consciously and rationally evaluated as appropriate or inappropriate; this is made possible under deliberation by the fact that each person's preference, value, or perspective when it comes to policies is communicated to one another. In using this knowledge, individuals reflecting on these measures arrive at a general notion of their performance and then shape them based on that performance (opting either for reforming, maintaining or removing them entirely) (Dryzek and Pickering 2016, 1). Even more so, because deliberation results in a common decision, individuals are capable of reconciling each of their private interests regarding policymaking to the wider general interest that is meant to be satisfied by these policies. And because that decision is binding, participants in deliberation can rest assured that other individuals will comply with said measures. In practice, the method would involve deliberative mini publics favoring redistributive solutions from the better off to the poor in terms of time, skills, consumption, and status.

The deliberative method is then contrasted to a market-based approach. The reason why the market method is considered inappropriate for selecting policies by deliberative democrats is that it fails both in respect to reflexivity and in terms of creating and complying to a general interest. Firstly, markets do not feature the relevant knowledge to, in the words of John Dryzek, "collectively contemplate the reasons for failure" (Dryzek and Pickering 2016, i). This means that the knowledge they possess is merely that of private actors and not that of articulable values, statements, or preferences; as such, they never attempt to arrive at general conclusions about policies the way that deliberation does. And markets are based around private economic preferences that manifest as "tangible rewards for particular interests" rather than rational arguments aimed at persuading other people (Dryzek 1995, 16). Because of this, markets are likelier to be dominated by certain private interests (businesses, or private lobbyists) and thus fail to arrive at a solution that is in fact in the general interest. Finally, because of the dominant position these market actors are in, they have no reason to comply to any other-regarding decisions. As such, deliberation suggests that market mechanisms are to be discouraged in favor of a policymaking solution based on discourse.[1]

The debate thus arrives at the current text's research question: Can deliberative democracy serve the same role as markets when it comes to a particular public policy question—water management? I will represent the two arguments of reflexivity and general interest. The first one is that reflexivity poses an epistemic advantage because it leads to a deeper understanding of one's own position by having to verbally justify oneself. At the same time, the discussion helps people discover the diverse perspectives of others, including groups which are routinely marginalized. The resulting measures will thus be informed by preferences, values and perspectives that would thus not have been available otherwise. The second argument for deliberation is motivational. It implies that deliberation makes people think in more altruistic ways. It does so by removing the added costs of strategic reasoning (e.g., self-interested attempts by individuals to benefit themselves at the expense of others) which makes in turn means it is able to guarantee mutual trust between participants. This ensures that any policy that will result from deliberation will be in the general interest and will be fully complied with by those involved.

However, both these reasons have their flaws. I will expand on Gerald Gaus's (2008) critique of deliberation and note how the epistemic perspective does not grapple with the full implications of the knowledge problem as formulated by Friedrich Hayek, referring to the fact that no individual or group of individuals can possess general knowledge of an entire system in order to articulate the kind of rational and conscious decisions that deliberation expects from policymaking (Gaus 2008, 35). In particular, the knowledge problem manifests as a problem of subjectivity. This means that individuals could only come to know their own perspectives, values, or preferences better and not those of others. In turn, this merely allows them to personally agree or disagree with the result of the deliberation and to agree or disagree with others when debating public policy. What their knowledge does not imply is that they also possess an understanding of how deliberation will promote good or bad policies in any general other-regarding sense; after all, they do not possess knowledge of the totality of conditions that shape policies in order to know that any choice is generally applicable or not (Gaus 2008, 36). By contrast, markets are successful at overcoming the knowledge problem. Rather than try to derive a single, comprehensive response, they opt for a decentralized structure which makes use of everyone's existing personal knowledge to leave everybody better off than they were before. Subsequently, markets are in fact more reflexive than deliberation.

The second premise is also flawed when judged from the perspective of public choice and in light of the first issue. Due to the lack of general knowledge, participants to deliberation will have to decide whether they wish to implement the results of the discussion via vote. If that is the case though, then even the most well-intentioned and non-strategic participants have to worry about the dynamics of voting. After all, each method of voting has to balance external costs against decision-making costs/transaction costs. If the method of voting was settled in advance to be supermajority (or a system of unanimity), as the deliberative idea of convergence on the same reason would suggest, then the external costs would be low (no strategic maneuvers are possible) but the decision-making costs might be too high. Thus, altruism is neither sufficient nor necessary to establish that deliberation will be successful.

If, on the other hand, deliberation settles for a simple majority system of voting to decide on policies, then it has to consider the possibility of external costs again, since it is easy for a majority to impose their conditions on a minority, while only having to guarantee benefits to a sufficient number of people to achieve a small majority. And this would, of course, contradict the spirit of convergence which is supposedly the hallmark of deliberation due to the fact that the losing side has no motive to fully comply with policies it did not choose. This is by contrast to markets which, owing to thinking in marginal rather than absolute terms (any consumer or supplier can be "vetoed" by another consumer or supplier) represent a form of unanimous choice while also lowering decision-making costs.

Having shown how these issues apply generally to deliberative democracy, I then use water management as a case study of these very problems. Thus, an empirical example in water management will highlight both the knowledge and public choice problems faced by state-sponsored discussion circles whose aim is to promote equitable water access.

The text will follow the above argument in three separate sections. The first section will look at the deliberative literature focused on transformative convergence (as opposed to other branches of democratic theory focused on aggregation of votes) and note its shortcomings when it comes to engaging with the Austrian and public choice literatures.[2] The second section goes into a more detailed breakdown of the critiques presented above, and juxtaposes them with an account of the price mechanism and entrepreneurial profit and loss as the elements that make the market system both more reflective than deliberation and unanimous without having to worry about decision-making costs the way discursive democracy has to. The third section then takes the theoretical discussion and applies it to a concrete case study of Kenyan water management in riverine forests. It then describes the results of official government and academic attempts to manage existing water reserves which encountered the limits of building a strategy based on the personal knowledge of local participants and/or technical knowledge, as well as difficulties with corruption and compliance to rules derived from a simple majority system. Finally, it compares these with the successful functioning of a local market in land sustained by indigenous traditions that has created methods of conflict resolution that do not involve voting when conflicts arise between different groups and makes decentralized use of people's experiences with different soil and water conditions.

LITERATURE REVIEW

The epistemic merit of democracy is widely cited in the deliberative literature, especially in contrast to aggregative democratic procedures (Cohen 1986; Dryzek 1995; 1996; Habermas 1996; Bohman 2006; Gaus 2008; Bohman 2009; Dryzek and Pickering 2016; Benson 2018; 2019). Aggregation theories focus on taking the preferences of individuals as given and argue that democratic results are superior to alternatives when they add up all the stated preferences of citizens as voters. An example of an aggregation theory of democracy is the Condorcet jury theorem which suggests that, if beliefs that individuals hold are likely to be correct, then the more individuals vote, the higher the likelihood that the outcome will be a correct judgment (Knight and Johnson 2011, 153). However, this judgment depends on the quality of individual judgments (such that the reverse is also true where the worse people are at judgments, the worse the end result too). Unlike the Condorcet theorem, deliberative democracy aims to treat the process of deliberation itself as relevant and not just the result. As Jonathan Benson (one of the academics who is most keen on drawing parallels with other traditions and engaging with the classical liberal critiques of deliberation) claims, "it involves a process of critical reflection in which preferences and opinions can be considered and challenged and alternative values can be held up to scrutiny." (Benson 2019, 77–8).

The element of reflexivity on what oneself does and what others are doing is hence what ultimately makes deliberation epistemically relevant. By putting people in a position to articulate their preferences, values, and perspectives, it helps people discover their own opinion better, revealing aspects of their thinking that they did not dwell on at a previous time and how different their own position is compared to those of fellow participants. Furthermore, by confronting them with the logical demonstration of other people's preferences, values, and perspectives, they can learn things they might not have known. Consequently, those debating on the same topic can understand another's values and preferences better when they hear somebody from the same perspective, meaning that a person from a similar social background might understand why others came to logically see things the way that they did in terms of policies, even if they disagree with them (Bohman 2006, 179). Alternatively, they can acknowledge a different perspective on policies based on shared values and beliefs (when they hear somebody comment on their life experience of public policies from a freedom or equality basis for example) (Bohman 2006, 179). Individuals thus can arrive at a mutual understanding precisely because of the assumed epistemic benefits of deliberation.

Moreover, these opinions, values or perspectives, deliberative democrats contend, would not be available in arenas like markets. Communication in a market space happens through the price system which transmits information about the scarcity of certain resources, and technological possibilities of using said resources to myriad buyers and sellers. In so doing, the price system does not just affect but is also affected in turn by those who are buying or selling on the market (who transmit their preferences via their purchases to other buyers and sellers) (Boettke 2012, 288–9). However, deliberative democrats like Benson or Dryzek argue, prices are not perfect conveyors of the knowledge involved in decision-making. That is because they can only speak about self-regarding preferences, values, or perspectives (ones that target oneself in terms of well-being) and not other-regarding ones (things that people value for the sake of others and not for their own sake) (Benson 2019, 82). In terms of values for instance, there is no accounting for what the right thing would be to do with the resources embedded within the price mechanism. Assets are treated purely as resources because some individuals are willing and able to pay for them, even though this might go against the preferences of people who see the same sites as having cultural or religious value (Benson 2019, 82). Markets thus lack an equivalent to the verbal communication that gets realized in the case of deliberation—individuals can always bring up other regarding reasons, understand each other in those terms, and reach a common reason to endorse them.

However, such a judgment means that the existing literature has not fully internalized the influence of the knowledge problem on determining other-regarding preferences or values through conversation and thus underestimates the potency of the critique of deliberation derived from the Austrian economics literature (Pennington 2001; Gaus 2008). The problem refers on the one hand to the fact that spoken knowledge is considered sufficient for policymaking. In reality, knowing whether a policy is successful or not can only be known through people's personal experiences in specific places and at certain times in their lives. This would make it impossible for any one individual (be they a deliberative participant or a market buyer/seller) to command total knowledge since such an institutional agent would have to be simultaneously present in the lives of multiple people at multiple points in time. Because of this, it is not clear how or why deliberation is able to generate other-regarding reasons that are also common reasons (as it wishes them to be).[3] In fact, the next section will clarify that deliberation is unable to do so.

However, there is another justification in the literature for deliberative democracy: namely, that participants in deliberation tend to be altruistic and not self-centered. This is because, scholars claim, they are engaging in communicative rationality. Communicative rationality is understood as language focused around understanding through the power of reason alone rather than conversation oriented toward success (Habermas 1996; Knight and Johnson 2011, 132). In so doing, it excludes the use of power, or its offshoots like manipulation (making them do what you would want them to do without them being aware of this) or emotion (swaying them to adopt a perspective purely based on rhetoric, and/or on the emotional pull of life experiences/ values) (Mansbridge et al. 2010, 66–67).[4]

Communicative rationality thus leads to a growing sense of trust among the participants. By contrast, "communicating for success" through power, emotion or manipulation encourages every individual to benefit personally but only by tricking everyone else (Austen-Smith 1992, 49). The individual strategy involves deception (in the case of emotional appeals or manipulation) or coercion (in the case of power) for gain but results in nobody wanting to contribute to the discussion. Because of the fear of being deceived or coerced, every person will want to stop contributing. And if everybody does so, this would result in a worse situation where one cannot be exposed to other people's preferences, values, or perspectives (Austen-Smith 1992, 49). Communicative rationality is therefore a solution precisely because it connects individuals back to the overall interest. On the positive side, it rewards logical interventions with approval from the other participants and with benefits like personal acceptance of one's opinions. This re-establishes the trust for people to take part. At the same time, by discouraging discourse for success, it punishes the individuals who would otherwise benefit from corrupting the practice of policy-making.

This emphasis on mutuality seems at odds in the eyes of those doing deliberation with the approach championed by neoclassical economics. Neoclassical economics is focused not on communicative rationality, but on instrumental rationality, where the latter refers to the right selection of means toward an end (Habermas 1996; Dryzek 1995; Pennington, 2001). The problem with instrumental rationality is that it treats individuals not as social beings but as pure atoms, which means that the values, preferences, or perspectives they seek cannot change (Pennington 2001, 173). This in turn means that individuals under a neoclassical framework are left to be as manipulative or coercive as they want to be (any of their positions are good as long as the right means are selected, and their positions cannot change). Rather than being the solution to problems through efficient policymaking, the neoclassical approach ends up generating the very problems it sought to address (by encouraging individuals to behave in the very way that leads to mutual distrust). The solution for policies cannot therefore be found in the economic approach and has to be sought out through communicative rationality.

However, upon closer inspection, the deliberative critique of the economics literature is not as robust as it seems. The criticism of the neoclassical approach tends to conflate the analytical assumptions that the theory makes with normative pronouncements. Focusing on individualism and means-ends is not the same as suggesting that only individuals matter or that the purpose does not matter; on the contrary, it provides a robust method of thinking through how one can achieve good public policy and what would be required to do so. This is most represented by the public choice tradition which applies the insights of economics to political decision-making (Buchanan and Tullock 1990, 11). It does so while assuming that individuals will act on the incentives put in front of them, where incentives are understood as the advantages and disadvantages that people can obtain from an institution (Buchanan and Tullock 1990, 12). For example, if deliberative democracy were to work, it is because people would derive more benefits than costs from communication with each other and from formulating a common purpose. In this sense, public choice is no different from deliberative democracy itself. While it starts with a focus on individualism (in that only individuals, and not groups or nations, are the ones that can be described as actors with preferences, values, or perspectives), public choice aims to describe the conditions under which individuals would come to a shared agreement. And as we shall see in the next section, public choice is aware of some of the significant costs involved with reaching such an agreement via communication that deliberation has remained unaware of.

DELIBERATION, KNOWLEDGE, AND PUBLIC CHOICE

On the one hand, deliberation cannot know general knowledge from the particular knowledge of each participant's preferences, values, or perspectives. For example, one might not be aware there was a certain activity that changed one's idea of what their social background can do, a tradition that reframed the same values in a radical light or an opinion shaped by daily routines—all actions which fall outside the purview of the conversation because they are actions that often involve no sort of spoken component at all. As such, they cannot be described simply under the category of liking something, nor do they contain values that could be specified in the manner that participants could understand them (since they are not sets of articulable beliefs so much as actions), nor would they fall under one perspective (because they are multifaceted in kind). What deliberation is left with is simply the importance of verbal knowledge to the individuals participating in the deliberation themselves.

Moreover, these same participants are not just ignorant of the knowledge that other people outside of deliberation might possess. They do not even have a grasp of the totality of resources one might need to achieve good policy. These would include knowledge of time, money, social skills, and social background relevant for water management that is not included in the conversations either. Hence, individuals cannot know the simultaneous transactions across multiple individuals, nor understand all the various variables that led to these transactions and how they complemented each other. The epistemic upshot of this is that deliberative actors cannot reliably tell whether a resource is valuable for enacting certain policies or not (since its true value is practical and not captured in deliberation), and what might be purely accidental and not causal for the same policy (since any of these other factors could be a temporary element in practice, or a background could be advantageous in a person's life and only disadvantageous within communication). The only thing they do grasp is the importance of resources to deliberation itself—i.e., the verbal skills (being able to state one's case in a coherent and concise way), money investment (necessary to gather everyone together), social background (those who were brought up with an understanding of debates versus those who were not) that are relevant to creating a deliberative space.

Not only do participants to deliberation miss out on this general knowledge, but the process might be perpetuating the lack of knowledge by destroying opportunities to discover new insights. Dedicating time, space and money to deliberation means missed opportunities for resource relationships since it takes away time, space and money from these other activities that might matter more for water management. Less money, skills and time dedicated to outside activities and more to deliberation could mean less chances to cultivate one's identity and/or adapt over time to new water reserves. Moreover, discourse participants thus do not know what other uses the resource could have, hence they miss the practical context these resources were used in. Even more so, having everyone participate in deliberation means they have even fewer chances to participate in a tradition, habit or activity that would serve as a general source of knowledge.

Markets succeed where deliberation fails. Instead of trying to create a general account of all knowledge and then fall short, markets provide institutional mechanisms for individuals to make use of their existing knowledge for mutual benefit and discover new knowledge in the process. Applied to our case, this means that prices do not try to communicate the moral judgment that one would like to adopt (the way deliberation wanted prices to) since, as we have established, that knowledge is not possible to convey. On the contrary, by providing an opportunity to know whether the conditions behind the exchange have changed, one does not have to think about why this is the case. In his famous tin example in the "Use of knowledge in Society," Hayek (1945) makes exactly this point—nobody need know there has been a natural disaster which has made tin scarce; all they must do is look at the changes in price which will enable them to make the right decision and buy or sell. In turn, this new knowledge will then be reflected back in the form of a higher price for goods, which allows individuals to adjust their own consumption of tin until the price goes down again (which constitutes new knowledge conveyed by the price mechanism).

This lack of knowledge also means that deliberation is not a sufficient condition for good policymaking after all. As we have seen, individuals cannot know whether or not what they have agreed on constitutes a true policy of "common reason" based on general knowledge. Yet because individuals in a deliberation in an operational sense are supposed to select for a policy (or as Habermas puts it, a process that is "decisive"), they will have to use the only benchmark they do know (the number of people's likes and dislikes, the median of values or the quantity of perspectives on offer) (Habermas 1996, 8). In so doing, deliberation falls back on aggregate processes meant to gauge the numerical support for each policy, which is why it will have to subject any policy to a vote (Habermas 1996; Gaus 2008). By doing so though, deliberation opens itself up to the issue of the costs involved with aggregative decision-making processes like voting. On the one hand, there are the external costs of the decision. These represent the externalities (or the costs that were not included in the voting process itself). Some of these are private externalities, meaning actions which do have an effect on the other participants, but which have not been subjected to policy regulation. In the worst case, the vote itself creates such external costs. For instance, there is the possibility that some people will win, and others will lose, where the losing side has to comply even though they do not agree with the proposition. Even more so, there are the transaction (or decision-making costs) involved with the act of voting itself, referring to the difficulties in organizing such a vote, the difficulty of negotiating a common voting position, the time and effort expended to finish the vote itself and so on.

The issue is that deliberation cannot escape these costs and the incentives they produce no matter what decision-making system is in place. If unanimity is preferred, then we have a situation where the external costs are minimal, given that almost nobody will find themselves on the losing side of the aisle and because private preferences fully coincide with the adopted policy (Buchanan and Tullock 1990, 107). At the same time though, the decision-making costs are maximized, resulting in extensive strategic negotiations (Buchanan and Tullock 1990, 167). However, this combination of low external but high decision-making costs defeats the idea of a non-manipulative and non-emotional space, since participants are incentivized to use strategic tactics during negotiation. For example, they can exaggerate their commitment to one value or preference in order to obtain concessions from others (up to the point which reflects their true preferences rather than their supposed preferences) or use their power to "veto" any offer until they receive their preferred options. They do so even as altruistic individuals, since any altruistic individual is still a rational individual and will find it rational to behave in ways that promote what they see as the best values, preferences, and perspectives (Buchanan and Tullock 1990, 167). This shows that the altruistic assumption is neither sufficient nor necessary to prevent public choice considerations.

On the other hand, if deliberation adopts a simple majority-based voting system, then decisions would be arrived at easier (given that it would only require a minimum number of individuals to change their minds about a policy to win). In doing so though, they open the way to higher external costs, since a significant minority would find itself on the losing side in the face of a very slim majority. Moreover, this slim minority would be able convince a tiny "tiebreaking" percentage of participants to win in turn, meaning that these individuals are incentivized to abuse their powerful position within the voting process to their own ends. Now the problem becomes one of logrolling, where participants will start exchanging likes and dislikes in order to pass certain policies in exchange for others adopting the policies that they are most attached to (Buchanan and Tullock 1990, 135). This means that any minimum-winning coalition will have to appease the tiniest number of winning members (who receive concentrated benefits from the arrangement) in exchange for everybody else suffering the dispersed costs of keeping these potential defectors happy—an example of such a situation is when water supply is only upgraded for a couple of individuals as political favoritism. The only way to avoid such an outcome would be to institute means of side-compensation for the losing side (which imposes an extra disadvantage on those who might be tempted to join a coalition and thus disincentivizes them from logrolling); yet this simply transforms the deliberative arrangement into a market through vote buying and selling.

Indeed, it is markets which can avoid the issues of external costs and decision-making costs. That goes back again to the emphasis in market relations not on total costs and judgments, but on relative costs and judgments. From the public choice point of view, this translates to a marginalist analysis—decisions in markets are unanimous because they are only made for each individual by definition. Unlike what deliberation claimed, this is a positive element of markets—individuals are not incentivized to resort to manipulation like vote-trading since there are always other water providers to go to if one does not like the current offer and there are always other potential buyers to convince out there (which means no individual can impose their costs on another and no individual has to suffer negotiations that are too costly). Individuals in markets thus are incentivized to be entrepreneurial (i.e., to identify opportunities for gain which translate into profit when successful and loss when unsuccessful); this entrepreneurship in turn benefits other parties.

THE CASE OF INDIGENOUS WATER MANAGEMENT
OF RIVERINE FORESTS IN KENYA

The water management case of riverine forests in Kenya is particularly suited to examining the case against deliberation. On the one hand, the Kenyan pastoralist communities have a generations-long tradition of using a community-backed property rights system creating a market in riverine lands in the form of the ekwar system (Stave et al. 2007, 1482). On the other, the Kenyan state (with support from international organizations and Western governments) has tried to replace the ekwar system via a modern-day deliberative mini public, whereby indigenous pastoralists would enter into a dialogue with other ethnic groups and experts. The hope was that the resulting discussion would lead to the adoption of contemporary large scale irrigation practices based on the modern articulated knowledge of geology (focusing on the unique claylike soil composition of riverine forests and aquatic flora/fauna living in proximity to the great rivers) and on the establishment of sedentary agricultural organizations motivated to preserve indigenous heritage. However, state efforts at deliberation soon raised the very epistemic and incentive questions that my analysis has presented—namely, mere input from other populations and scientific knowledge were not sufficient to articulate the general knowledge that was necessary to look after riverine forests (and which the locals had known through age-old practices and customs). Moreover, the arrangement resorted to simply majority voting and thus suffered from public choice problems which gave urban outsiders to the community the power to impose their costs on the indigenous population.

Thus, from the epistemic perspective, the deliberative mini publics were only able to relate to the spoken knowledge of indigenous people, other groups, or scientists. For example, the hope was that mountain ethnic tribes (which tended to be richer and more dispersed than the pastoralists) would share water management techniques which would contribute to a growing common understanding of irrigation, soil cultivation, aquatic life and so on. However, the reality was that the two groups could only state their own preferences; sedentary mountain folk favored grazing because it is an integral part of the cycle of life for coniferous plants whereas pastoralists shunned it because it damaged clay soil and riverbeds (Stave et al. 2007, 1484). Moreover, general knowledge of other practices was not even linguistically available for the indigenous groups. The Turkana language that nomads speak features specialized language that pertains to their natural environment and soil (ng'akipi nakaperok alokwap is one such example referring to saltwater and freshwater) and which features 113 different types of wood species but no equivalent for types of soil (Stave et al. 2007, 1474). Conversely, scientific knowledge could not serve as a global source or knowledge either, because it could not pronounce itself on reseeding after storms, tending to livestock, and/or checking for soil humidity (all activities which were not of the form that the pastoralist nomads themselves could articulate) (Stave et al. 2007, 1484). On the contrary, what happened was that the application of scientific knowledge led to the loss of local knowledge and practices. This was the case with hydrology specialists and mountaineers who are falsely assumed to be superior to local techniques because they have a vast articulable database of information on hydrology and damming. In reality, their performance has been much worse than local groundwater measures for riverine forests; expert irrigation done in a style fit for Western agriculture ended up eroding riverine forest soil (Stave et al. 2007, 1474). As expected, the specificity of the knowledge made it impossible for the mini publics to succeed at articulating general knowledge.

The shortcomings of mini publics confronted with the knowledge problem sit in contrast with the indigenous water management system referred to as the ekwar. The term ekwar denotes the ownership by local herdsmen and women of riverbank areas (complete with the location's vegetation and soil) which allows pastoralist-owners to experiment with new agricultural techniques on their private territory without interference from other pastoralists and to exchange land with fellow ekwar owners (Barrow 1990, 167). At the same time though, the system limits the powers of land possessors to usufruct rights, meaning that landlords or landladies only enjoy private property as long as they can demonstrate that they have put their riverbank plots to good use. If they fail to do so, locals are allowed by tradition to ignore any encirclement and utilize the space themselves (including collecting and keeping fruit or trees) (Barrow 1990, 168).

By allowing individuals to acquire private property and engage in exchange, the ekwar creates a working market in riverbank areas capable of overcoming the knowledge problem. It does so by enlisting local knowledge via the price mechanism, meaning the price of riverine soil is left to fluctuate in accordance with its use. Consequently, the ekwar system is capable of mobilizing the know-how of all parties involved in the trade at both high and low ends of the price without having to construct a common knowledge pool. If prices are lower, then this lowering acts as a signal to those who require more land to purchase new territory. Simultaneously, since prices will be cheaper for water amenities, pastoralists who otherwise would not have had access to water amenities are consequently able to enjoy such goods. Yet a higher price is not a disadvantage either. On the one hand, it might communicate to outsiders the cultural value that these pastoralists attach to the riverbanks. On the other hand, a higher price attracts new potential investments in the ekwar market by owners wishing to reap the rewards of more valuable riverbanks (helping to lower the prices in turn when they are successful in spreading their findings, thus coming full circle).

Contrary to the expectations of the Kenyan government then, one does not require modern agricultural practices to be able to consolidate water management into larger and more efficient units. Due to the usufruct nature of the ekwar system and its price mechanism, such a consolidation will occur via a process of self-selection—by eliminating unreliable owners and/or pricing them out of the market, the system ensures that riverbanks are often concentrated in the hands of a few (most capable) local individuals (thus reaping the benefits of economies of scale). Moreover, individuals will be able to discover new ways to tend to riverine forests when the need is transmitted by the price system. A higher price subsequently leads individuals to discover more inventive ways to make use of the groundwater soil they do own in the area or improve their agricultural yields while also preserving local forests (Stave et al. 2007, 1482).

Having been unsuccessful in establishing common knowledge, the governmental discussion then turned toward establishing a voting procedure for deciding on water policies in the mini-public, which only added public choice issues to the equation. The rule that was settled on was that of simple majority vote following deliberation; however, simple majority merely brought forth the issue of high external costs, in that a "tiebreaking" majority of rich Kenyan urbanites originating from Nairobi were able to overpower the wishes of the Turkana and impose their costs on the pastoralists. They did so by exploiting their higher income, access to educational opportunities (the Turkana have a total rate of literacy of 13.9% compared to that of Nairobi at 91.6%) and existing political connections in the capital (Ngugi 2017, 488). These advantages allowed them to engage in logrolling, securing the assent of enough agricultural groups and private corporations to gain the upper hand in negotiations (Stave et al. 2007, 1473). In turn, the Nairobi elite were able to use this newfound majority to impose their agenda in discussions and committees on the very large minority of Turkana pastoralists. Rather than address the pollution problems that the Turkana faced (including some which were due to urban dwellers spoiling the countryside), meetings encouraged spending on large scale projects like the Turkana Gorge Dam that ultimately provided water for urban areas at the expense of local projects like the ekwars (Stave et al. 2007, 1473). Even more so, the committees themselves became tools for rich urbanites who sought to bolster their own wealth and status by gaining a seat at these meetings, corruption thus being allowed to run rampant. In fact, 20 billion US dollars are estimated to have been lost precisely due to such corruption in Kenya (and countries like Kenya) (Plummer and Cross 2006, 6).

These abuses occurred at the expense of the Turkana, who were forced to pay extra costs on their own ekwar projects via property taxes and subsidies siphoning their wealth to government malfeasance. For example, the state of Kenya requires any riverbank installation to be compliant with the 17 UN Sustainable Development goals covering acceptable levels of water acidity, health and safety standards for water pumps and other such factors (Hope et al. 2020, 172). Yet these measures are so strict that they raise the price of water pumps and similar equipment to as much as 20,000 dollars, a figure that is higher than the price of similar technology in New York (Hope et al. 2020, 172; Panzaru 2022). This redistribution from bottom to top disincentivized locals from wanting to participate in deliberative water management in the first place—since, unsurprisingly, the latter have seen their resources dwindle over time in favor of rich commuters (Stave et al. 2007, 1474).

By contrast, the ekwar market system managed to address water management externalities and thus prevent abuse of the ekwar property rights system. That is because it employed the mechanism of profit/loss whereby individuals were rewarded with more control over water management items like fish, charcoal, lumber, soil and so on and higher status (by engaging more with the elders of their community) when they managed to come up with ways that provided more energy for less resource use and conversely lost these benefits when they failed to do so (Stave et al. 2007, 1473). This further acted as a way of deterring outsiders who were there to pollute or otherwise impose the costs of their private water consumption onto others. That is because ekwar owners were incentivized by the possibility of profiting from clear riverbanks (and disincentivized by the losses incurred from the activities of such urbanites) to keep unwanted outsiders at bay and to seek out more environmentally conscious clients. In turn, local pastoralists were incentivized by the price mechanism to look for the most profitable riverbank area for them and thus avoid local areas that were polluted in favor of those that were better at water management. All the while, neither urban newcomers nor locals lost out in the water arrangement—due to the marginalist nature of the arrangement (with different private landowners allowing for more or less lax relations), urban dwellers were not banned from appealing to locals who were willing to deal with them, while indigenous individuals could always seek out arrangements in Nairobi if they so pleased. Unanimity was achieved without one voting. Lastly, there is no opportunity for logrolling in this system since no single property owner depends on another property owner to set these rules as they do in the case of voting.

SUMMARY AND FUTURE POSSIBILITIES

In conclusion, the theoretical argument was held up by the case study in question. Section III looked at the case of water management in Kenyan riverine forests. It then described the results from official government and academic efforts to manage existing water reserves which encountered the limits of building a strategy based on the personal knowledge of local participants and/ or technical knowledge, as well as difficulties with corruption and compliance to the rules derived from a simple majority system. Finally, it compared these with the successful functioning of a local market in land sustained by indigenous traditions which had generated methods of conflict resolution that did not involve voting when conflicts arose between different groups and made decentralized use of people's experiences with different soil and water conditions. This buttressed the points made in section II, where deliberation was critiqued both along the lines of epistemology and public choice, while juxtaposing these critiques with an account of the price mechanism and entrepreneurial profit and loss as the elements that made the market system both more reflective than deliberation and unanimous without having to worry about decision-making costs the way discursive democracy had to. And that critique was ultimately possible due to the lacunae identified in the existing deliberative literature. Hence, section I examined deliberative democracy as a form of transformative convergence (as opposed to other branches of democratic theory focused on aggregation of votes) but whose properties were susceptible to criticism from the Austrian and public choice literatures.

Within the larger volume, this chapter, like my earlier work (Panzaru 2022), has striven to demonstrate that the question of incentives is not logically separable from that of the knowledge problem. I thus noted in the text that the epistemic argument had a direct effect on the motivational argument for deliberation—it is because one cannot know when decisions have to be made through general knowledge alone that deliberation has to appeal to voting instead. However, the reverse is also true in that incentives can compound the knowledge problem: where individuals do not have an incentive to engage with one another on these terms, then there is no willingness for them to discover new knowledge that might be relevant to water management. In terms of the wider literature engaged in the volume, this shows how the Austrian and public choice approaches complement each other, and not just in their general classical liberal orientation (the shared focus on individualism, the limits of power, the preference for voluntary organization, the invisible hand mechanisms of the market). Both traditions seek to analyze the conditions under which successful human cooperation occurs; the focus on uncertainty in one leads to the analysis of individual choice in another and vice-versa.

Moreover, future texts could go beyond the limits of my analysis. My analysis did not comment on the constitutional level of decision-making, meaning the choice of the fundamental rules of the game that inform both markets and the political process (Buchanan and Tullock 1990, IX). In that sense, I have not queried the importance of deliberation for the adoption of the rules of a constitutional system. If, as Buchanan and Tullock (1990) have argued, the best rules within a constitutional selection process are those that everyone would agree to, then deliberation could make a positive contribution in spite of decision-making costs. For this, one would have to employ an argument for why face-to-face deliberation is the easiest way to unanimity by once again looking at its transformative capacities. Paralleling Buchanan and Tullock's (1990) initial argument, it can either analyzed as a game theoretic repeated game of trust, or a Pareto-optimal move toward a different set of Pareto-optimal or non-optimal conditions.

As a corollary of not discussing constitutional arrangements, I took for granted the existence of such things as property and individual rights within the market system, without which it would not be possible to talk about individual decisions, prices, or profit/loss in the first place. Thus, I never discussed the non-state mechanisms by which this property system is sustained beyond a passing mention of elders being important to one's status. But the reality is that institutions like the ekwar are sustained by a social group of elders who act as judges in a dispute, arbitrating in case the dispute cannot be settled directly (Stave et al. 2007, 1473). It could very well be that this social arrangement itself is deeply oppressive in that it benefits the elders to the exclusion of everybody else, or it is unsustainable in that it is based on traditions that are no longer valuable today. In order to establish whether this is the case or not, more research should look at the social arrangements that make market mechanisms work (Is it a matter of trust toward elders? A matter of obedience or authority?) and how they compare to the deliberative alternative.

REFERENCES

Austen-Smith, David. 1992. "Strategic Models of Talk in Political Decision Making." *International Political Science Review* 13 (1): 45–58.

Barrow, Edmund G. C. 1990. "Usufruct Rights to Trees: The Role of Ekwar in Dryland Central Turkana, Kenya." *Human Ecology* 18 (2): 163–76.

Benson, Jonathan. 2018. "Environmental Law and the Limits of Markets." *Cambridge Journal of Economics* 42 (1): 215–30.

———. 2019. "Deliberative Democracy and the Problem of Tacit Knowledge." *Politics, Philosophy & Economics* 18 (1): 76–97.

Boettke, Peter. 2012. *Living Economics: Yesterday, Today, and Tomorrow*. Oakland, CA: The Independent Institute.

Bohman, James. 2006. "Deliberative Democracy and the Epistemic Benefits of Diversity." *Episteme* 3 (3): 175–91.

———. 2009. "Epistemic Value and Deliberative Democracy." *The Good Society* 18 (2): 28–34.

Buchanan, James M. and Tullock, Gordon. 1990. 2nd ed. *The Calculus of Consent: Logical Foundations of Constitutional Democracy*. Indianapolis, IN: Liberty Fund.

Cohen, Joshua. 1986. "An Epistemic Conception of Democracy." *Ethics* 97 (1): 26–38.

Dryzek, John S. 1995. "Political and Ecological Communication." *Environmental Politics* 4 (4): 13–30.

———. 1996. "Foundations for Environmental Political Economy: The Search for *Homo Ecologicus*." *New Political Economy* 1 (1): 27–40.

Dryzek, John. S. and Pickering, Jonathan. 2016. *Deliberation as a Catalyst for Reflexive Environmental Governance*. Canberra, Australia: Center for Deliberative Democracy and Global Governance.

Gaus, Gerald F. 2008. "The (Severe) Limits of Deliberative Democracy as the Basis for Political Choice." *Theoria: A Journal of Social and Political Theory* 117 (1): 26–53.

Habermas, Jurgen. 1996. *Between Facts and Norms: Contributions to a Discourse Theory of Law and Democracy*. Cambridge, UK: Polity Press.

Hayek, Friedrich A. 1945. "The Use of Knowledge in Society." *The American Economic Review* 35 (4): 519–30.

Hope, Rob, Patrick Thomson, Johanna Koehler, and Tim Foster. 2020. "Rethinking the Economics of Rural Water in Africa." *Oxford Review of Economic Policy* 36 (1): 171–90.

Knight, Jack and James Johnson. 2011. *The Priority of Democracy: Political Consequences of Pragmatism*. Princeton, NJ: Princeton University Press.

Mansbridge, Jane, James Bohman, Simone Chambers, David Estlund, Andreas Follesdal, Archon Fung, Christina Lafont, Bernard Manin, and Jose Luis Marti. 2010. "The Place of Self-Interest and the Role of Power in Deliberative Democracy." *The Journal of Political Philosophy* 18 (1): 64–100.

Ngugi, Margaret. 2017. "Participation of Kenyan Nomadic Pastoralists in Non-Formal Education." *European Journal of Education Studies* 3 (10): 486–515.

Ostrom, Elinor. 1990. *Governing the Commons: The Evolution of Institutions for Collective Action*. Cambridge, UK: Cambridge University Press.

———. 2012. *The Future of the Commons: Beyond Market Failure and Government Regulation*. London, UK: The Institute of Economic Affairs.

Panzaru, Emil. 2022. "Impure: Ideal theory, Non-Ideal Theory and Institutional Justification in Water Management." PhD diss., King's College London.

———. 2022. "Environmental Justice, Incentives, and the Unknown: Knowledge Problems, Institutional Incentives, and Responses to Natural Disaster Scenarios." In Rosolino A. Candela, Rosemarie Fike, and Roberta Herzberg, *Institutions and Incentives in Public Policy: An Analytical Assessment of Non-Market Decision-Making*, Chapter 9. London, UK: Rowman & Littlefield International.

Pennington, Mark. 2001. "Environmental Markets vs. Environmental Deliberation: A Hayekian Critique of Green Political Economy." *New Political Economy* 6 (2): 171–90.

Plummer, Janelle and Piers Cross. 2006. *Tackling Corruption in the Water and Sanitation Sector in Africa: Starting the Dialogue*. Washington, DC: Water and Sanitation Program.

Stave, Jorn, Gufu Oba, Inger Nordal, and Nils Christoph Stenseth. 2007. "Traditional Ecological Knowledge of a Riverine Forest in Turkana, Kenya: Implications for Research and Management." *Biodiversity Conservation* 16 (1): 1471–89.

NOTES

1. This might seem to be too strong of a dichotomy between markets and democratic approaches. After all, one can think about an approach like Elinor Ostrom's (1990) polycentric model, which argues that elements of both models are important at different levels of governance. Thus, democratic deliberation might be more fitting for a closely knit community where everyone is already familiar with one another but not suitable at the global level at which point organizing such a debate on policies might prove unmanageable. Moreover, the very same community might use a mix of democratic and market processes in order to organize water management. Nevertheless, there are several rejoinders to this objection. For one, it is not clear that Ostrom's model (and institutions inspired by the model) should be seen as a mix between two approaches and not in fact a third approach in its own right, something which Ostrom could be interpreted to have thought based on her belief that polycentricity was "beyond markets and states" (Ostrom 2012, 68). Even if this were treated as a mix though, it is not clear that the deliberative argument is incompatible with the Ostromian position. After all, the argument is restricted to the operational level of policies and leaves open the possibility that markets are viable institutions beyond this level. It does not consequently present itself as a "universal panacea" of the type that Ostrom warned against (Ostrom 2012, 84–5).

2. The public reason approach is more characteristic of Rawls's model of deliberation in which discussion is not meant to transform people's opinions and convince them all to adopt the right reason (since everybody retains what Rawls would refer to as their conceptions of the good which would the equivalent of preferences, values, and perspectives in my formulation). Its role is to make people who otherwise disagree on matters of justice endorse the same principles for justice, even though these principles might be personally embraced for very different reasons.

3. For that matter, the idea of establishing full understanding with others even just within deliberation seems to be in question as well since one would have to be understood fully in one's context by other people without error (mistaking one person's perspective for that of another) and would (even more so) have to be able to understand others simply through that personal experience.

4. Authors like Habermas use language theory to describe the types of communication that they believe promote communicative rationality and those oriented toward success: drawing on John Searle, they would classify emotional displays and rhetoric as perlocutionary acts (i.e. doing something—in this case trying to win political favor—by saying something comical, tragic, diverting the discussion to other issues, rhetorical barrages) and communicative rationality as illocutionary acts (i.e., doing something in saying something—in this case, displaying the respect for reason by listening to others) (Knight and Johnson 2011, 133). I have not referenced this discussion. The differences it lays out between different types of speech have no bearing on my argument.

Chapter 10

Entrepreneurial Discovery in Land-Use Planning

M. Nolan Gray

If economics can be distilled down to the study of how individuals and societies allocate scarce resources, land-use planning can be distilled down to the study of how individuals and societies allocate scarce land. Unique among other commodities, land is fixed in space, highly inelastic, and its use will invariably impose externalities on neighbors—whether positive or negative. The social project of how we allocate and develop land has thus emerged as a major industry in the form of real estate, a key responsibility of local governments in the form of public land-use planning, and a lively field of study for students of social coordination across various disciplines, with deep implications for the form that human settlement may take.

If you crack open a book on land-use planning, you will quickly learn of the outsized role that the state plays in this space (Berke et al. 2006; Steiner and Butler 2007). Land-use planning is often treated as synonymous with zoning, a system of regulation whereby local governments assign land to districts with permitted land uses and densities (Hirt 2015). Yet before a single building is built, visions and standards set out in street plans and subdivision ordinances will detail the permissible form that new neighborhoods may take (Southworth and Ben-Joseph 1996). Underlying this framework is a theory of rational planning in which the public planner is to assemble all of the relevant information, produce a comprehensive plan rationalizing urban growth, and execute its provisions over a 10- to 50-year timeframe (Brooks 2002).

For students of the Austrian School of social theory, critiques of this theoretical framework should flow rather naturally: The knowledge needed to rationally order a society cannot be centered in a single individual or commission but is dispersed across the many thousands of actors who comprise a community (Hayek 1948). This knowledge is often highly subjective, existing in a form that cannot be easily aggregated (Polanyi 2015). To discover and leverage this knowledge, societies require a large sphere of decentralized planning, within which entrepreneurial discovery can test out new ways of allocating resources (Kirzner 2013). As Gray (2019) argues, teasing out the parallels between F. A. Hayek (1948) and urban theorist Jane Jacobs (1961, 1969), these critiques of broader economic planning apply with ease to land-use planning. Yet both standard rational planning theory and Austrian critique overlook the extent to which contemporary land-use planning practice depends on entrepreneurial discovery. Through mechanisms like zoning relief, private forms of land-use regulation, and development beyond the reach of conventional land-use ordinances, public planners can learn about changing conditions and incorporate this new knowledge into their plans (Gray and Millsap 2020; Nelson 2005; Talen 2012). Indeed, such spheres of decentralized planning are necessary to explain the persistence of public land-use planning; as a market process theorist might recognize, without the knowledge generated by entrepreneurial discovery, the system would quickly collapse.

This symbiotic relationship between entrepreneurial and public land-use planners is not without risk. The practice risks institutionalizing fleeting preferences of elites into law, or worse, drafting public planners into private attempts at antisocial objectives, such as racial or economic segregation (Weiss 1987; Glotzer 2020). Public planners should thus principally use entrepreneurial discovery to identify opportunities for *liberalizing* reform, focusing their efforts on traditional nuisances while ceding a large sphere of land-use planning to the co-production of private land-use governance and design (Ostrom 1990). To attempt to turn all private land-use innovation into law would be to mistake an ongoing process for a stable equilibrium, squelching opportunities for future discovery in land-use planning (Kirzner 1997).

The goal of this paper is to develop a market-process theory of the persistence of public land-use planning and its relationship to entrepreneurial discovery. While our present system of state near-monopolization of land-use planning is suboptimal, it survives by learning from and tolerating surviving pockets of decentralized land-use planning. This is not an argument for the *status quo*, nor is it an argument that public planners must slavishly follow market actors; on the contrary, by recognizing the extent to which state land-use planning depends on private land-use planning, we uncover an argument for refocusing the sphere of the former and expanding the sphere of the latter.

The following paper develops this thesis across five sections: A first section explains how land-use planning works today, with special attention paid to the dominant role of the state and mainstream critiques of this system. A second section maps out the Austrian critique of central planning, connecting this theoretical project to the questions raised by land-use planning. A third section explains how the persistence of this state system of land-use planning depends on entrepreneurial discovery within spheres of decentralized planning, in particular, through mechanisms such as zoning relief, deed restrictions, and town building on unincorporated land. A fourth section maps out the risks of public planners misunderstanding their relationship to private entrepreneurial discovery. A final section considers the implications of this theoretical discussion for planning practice.

CONTEMPORARY LAND-USE PLANNING
IN THE UNITED STATES

How should land be regulated? Few would doubt the need for sets of rules managing unwanted impacts or controlling the design of structures. While urban land markets naturally work to separate certain incompatible uses, and neighbors are always free to bargain their way to mutually agreeable externality management, these theoretical mechanisms are normally insufficient in a rapidly changing urban context (Coase 1960; Siegan 2020). The regulation of place is thus an important social project (Ben-Joseph and Szold 2005). Yet the optimal land-use ruleset for any given place or time is often a mystery. What should be allowed where? Under what restrictions on operation? In what built form? These are complex questions dependent on knowledge beyond the scope of a single mind, yet some form of coordination is necessary.

Contemporary land-use planning resolves this puzzle through extensive public regulation. By way of zoning and subdivision ordinances, local governments, in particular, can strictly control the distribution of permitted land uses, the allowable form that buildings may take, and the design of new subdivisions (Southworth and Ben-Joseph 1996; Hirt 2015). Such public forms of regulation give a complicated blend of civil servants, elected officials, and special interest groups the power to allow apartments here but not there, to set strict rules related to building heights and setbacks, and to force most new neighborhoods into the auto-oriented urban form that prevails across America today.

Zoning, a regulatory system that controls land use and density, lies at the center of this system (Fischel 2015). It can be broken out into two key components: a zoning ordinance, which defines the rules in any given zoning district, and a zoning map, which assigns every lot in a city to a particular zoning district. Each of these zoning districts sets out the permitted land uses in said district, which broadly fall within the categories of residential, commercial, or industrial. Each district also sets out the permitted intensity or density of allowed uses—for example, how tall buildings may be, how many parking spaces they must provide, or how far buildings must be set back from the street. From these seemingly innocuous rules, regulators are effectively able to determine what can or cannot be built on every single lot.

While zoning has received a great deal of academic and popular attention in recent years, it comprises only half of the typical local US land-use planning regime. The other half consists of subdivision regulations, which control the process of breaking large lots into smaller lots (Ben-Joseph 2003). Subdivisions are necessary for the creation of new neighborhoods and the extension of urban areas. Rules controlling the form this activity takes— including elements like street design, lot dimensions, open space requirements, and block dimensions—can effectively control urban form. These two forms of public land-use planning work hand-in-hand, supplemented by a web of related rules—from fire codes to building standards to environmental regulations—which also serve to shape land-use outcomes in subtle ways.

This system of public land-use planning has been heavily criticized on an as-applied basis. Many have argued that the form these rules take has had deleterious social outcomes (Gray 2022). There is now a consensus, for example, that the constraints imposed by zoning rules on new housing development, such as single-family zoning and minimum parking requirements, have played a key role in raising housing prices (Glaeser and Gyourko 2002; Shoup 2011; Manville et al. 2019). Such housing constraints in high-productivity regions have also sapped national economic growth by driving labor misallocation (Hsieh and Moretti 2017; Duranton and Puga 2019). Others have highlighted their role in perpetuating racial and class segregation (Silver 1991; Rothstein 2017; Trounstine 2019). And, in light of emerging concerns over climate change, the tendency of public land-use regulation to write carbon-intensive patterns of growth into law has also garnered heavy criticism (Levine 2005; Owen 2009).

THE AUSTRIAN CRITIQUE OF LAND-USE PLANNING

Beyond these as-applied critiques, a theoretical critique emerging from the Austrian tradition might call into question the very basis for contemporary public land-use planning (Gray 2019).[1] As Hayek (1948) observes, state economic planners face a knowledge problem: if all of the knowledge needed to produce a rational plan were given, plan development would be a simple matter of arithmetic. Instead, knowledge is distributed across society. Worse yet, this knowledge is often structured in a way that cannot be easily articulated and handed up to the state planner; it may be fleeting and temporal, or subjective, dependent on individual preferences (Polanyi 2015). The planner is thus forced to radically limit the scope of the problem to a handful of metrics that can be mapped or measured, stripping away important qualitative considerations and reducing allocation decisions to oversimplified technical questions, resulting in socially destructive plans (Scott 1998).

In her critique of urban planning, Jacobs (1961) notes similar issues concerning city planning: by its very nature, state land-use planning must reduce the scope of the problem to simple metrics that can be measured and mapped. To illustrate this point, Jacobs (1961, 6, 15) examines the case of a "tower-in-the-park" public housing development in New York City optimized around "air, light, sunshine, and landscaping." While the project succeeded along these superficial metrics, it ultimately failed to appreciate subjective and unmeasurable preferences for the integration of commercial uses and the maintenance of social networks. Bertaud (2018) notes a similar example of knowledge constraints forcing planners to reduce the question of building massings in China to hours of sunlight reaching each apartment window, a practice that yielded dull housing campuses that disrupted traditional patterns of living. The result, as both cases illustrate, are suboptimal massing standards that diminish the well-being of residents.

One way to escape the trap of the knowledge problem is to allow for a large sphere of decentralized planning. The question is not whether planning is necessary, but rather: Who should plan? As subsequent Austrian theorists have noted, the generation and application of the knowledge necessary to plan out an economy is constantly uncovered through a competitive process of entrepreneurial discovery (Kirzner 2013). By conducting small experiments in reallocating resources, entrepreneurs creatively test out new ways of organizing society (Schumpeter 2010). Some fail, some succeed; those that fail are scuttled, those that succeed are scaled up. In this way, entrepreneurs and the organizations they form act as islands of planning, surviving and thriving on their ability to discover and apply knowledge in a socially productive way (Coase 1937).

In a land-use context, the key entrepreneur is the developer: her job is to assemble capital, land, labor, and prospective consumers in remaking the urban landscape. Every given development might be conceptualized as a test of a hypothesis: What land uses are needed here? At what scale? And in what form? Where the public planner deals with such questions abstractly, at the scale of entire cities or neighborhoods, the developer deals with an individual lot, operating both on market feedback and conditions unique to the site. Where the public planner has little incentive to get these standards right—and may even face political pressures to facilitate socially harmful outcomes—the developer immediately feels the financial consequence of reordering society in a socially suboptimal way. The construction of a rational land-use order thus depends on the right of entrepreneurs to experimentally remake cities, within the context of emergent spontaneous orders, such as urban land markets.

Indeed, as Hayek (1948) observes, the result of this process is not necessarily chaos but spontaneous orders that serve to coordinate the actions of decentralized planners. Through the mechanism of land prices, developers have access to a singular numerical figure that represents both a signal and an incentive to allocate land to its highest and best use (Cowen and Tabarrok 2014). The outputs are so globally consistent as to seem planned, with densities rising around a central business district and gradually falling moving outward, with pockets of density around transit notes—that is to say, the rational density patterns that public planners are theoretically tasked with imposing (Alonso 1964; Muth 1969; Mills 1967; Brueckner 2011; Bertaud 2018). Land prices similarly serve to guide developers in separating incompatible uses—such as industrial and residential—and co-locating complementary uses—such as neighborhood commercial and residential (Siegan 2020).

The spontaneous orders that structure urban life do not always depend on price. On the contrary, the social coordination that Jacobs (1961) famously describes is often only tangentially related to economic activity, highlighting the capacity for cities to produce social order before top-down planning ever comes into the picture. Her work presages a half-century of social science to follow, calling our attention to the co-production of public safety via "eyes on the street," the value of polycentricity in urban governance, and the evolutionary nature of great streets and neighborhoods (Ostrom 1990; Brand 1995; Aligica and Tarko 2011). "Cities have the capability of providing something for everybody, only because, and only when, they are created by everybody" (Jacobs 1961, 238). The efforts of the public planner to impose order from the top down are not only often counterproductive—they may also be unnecessary.

HOW ENTREPRENEURIAL DISCOVERY INFORMS PUBLIC LAND-USE PLANNING

The salience of this critique then presents a puzzle: if public land-use planning is so dysfunctional—and in large part unnecessary to achieving rational land-use patterns—how does it persist? Why do zoning and subdivision ordinances remain in force in virtually every major US city? A compelling public choice story could no doubt be deployed to partly answer this question (Fischel 2005; Niskanen 2017).[2] The following paper will advance an Austrian hypothesis, namely that public land-use planning persists to the extent that it incorporates and tolerates those remaining spheres of entrepreneurial discovery that persist within land use. For all its ambitions of being consistent and comprehensive, US public land-use planning is both malleable and limited, retaining some scope for entrepreneurs to test out new ideas. The following subsections examine three such cases in which entrepreneurial discovery has remade and continues to remake public land-use planning policy.

Entrepreneurial Discovery through Regulatory Relief

Public land-use planning incorporates various avenues for regulatory relief. As typically set out, developers may request relief from the provisions of zoning or subdivision ordinances. This includes:

- Variances: minor relief from specific zoning provisions, typically in cases where massing compliance is prohibitively difficult owing to unique site conditions.
- Rezonings: a change to the zoning map; this action moves a lot from one zoning district to another.
- Text amendments: a change to the zoning text; this action revises standards in the ordinance applicable to all lots in a given district.
- Special permits: minor relief from specific zoning provisions, typically in cases where a land use may be allowed subject to certain strict conditions.
- Planned unit developments: a provision that allows developers to write their own rules, according to an agreement with public land-use planners; typically in exchange for substantial public benefits, such as open space or exactions.

These mechanisms give public land-use planners discretion in dealing with applications that do not comply with land-use ordinances. Indeed, a wide degree of discretion has become the norm (Ben-Joseph 2003). As Manville and Osman (2017) note, public planners often set strict rules with the *intention* of negotiating away relief in exchange for public benefits, a practice known as pretextual zoning.

To the extent that regulatory relief is forthcoming, public land-use planning retains some sphere of decentralized planning. Yet these regulatory relief functions also serve to communicate knowledge developed through entrepreneurial discovery to public planners. When a developer requests relief from parking requirements or requests the right to build an apartment building where previously only a single-family home has been allowed, she is communicating information about changed conditions to planning staff, which they can then use to bring state plans closer to reality—namely, by easing parking requirements or density restrictions. In many cases, public planners will simply issue case-specific relief to move on; but in some cases, they may use this information to optimize state plans.

Consider the case of minimum lot size reform in Houston, as detailed by Gray and Millsap (2020). In 1998, Houston reduced its residential minimum lot size down from 5,000 to 1,400 square feet. Public planners initiated this change on the stated basis of stimulating additional housing production, encouraging infill development, and raising densities. Yet the recognition that lower minimum lot sizes were appropriate did not originate with public planners. A study of permitting activity over the preceding decade indicates that the need for a new 1,400 square foot minimum lot size was *revealed* to public planners by private developers, who had successfully piloted a new townhouse concept in the early 1990s and were applying for relief from lot size provisions in droves by the mid-1990s. Public planners, to their credit, internalized these signals and made commensurate changes to Houston's land-use ordinances. In this indirect way, entrepreneurial discovery helped to optimize state planning.[3]

We might conceptualize the process like so: First, developers receive regulatory relief to try out a new form of development not permitted by state planning rules. In the Houston case, the new pattern of development was townhouses on 1,400 square foot lots. Second, if the experiment is success-ful in meeting an unmet need, many more developers replicate this original experiment, bombarding public planners with requests for relief. In the case of Houston, we see requests for minimum lot size relief skyrocketing in the lead up to 1998. Finally, planners interpret this flurry of relief requests as a signal of changed conditions and amend the plan to reflect this reality. In the case of Houston, public planners recognized the significant demand for sub-5,000 square foot lots near existing employment centers. In this way, regulatory relief provides an avenue for entrepreneurial discovery to reshape public planning efforts, producing state plans that better reflect local conditions.

Entrepreneurial Discovery Through Private Regulation

Since the 1960s, private forms of land-use regulation have rapidly spread across the US, principally within new residential developments on the sub-urban periphery (Nelson 2005). Through provisions such as deed restric-tions—or "covenants, conditions, and restrictions" (CC&Rs)—buyers must opt into a private set of rules governing land use as a condition of purchasing a property (McKenzie 1994). Deed restrictions are in effect for 60 percent of all new homes, a figure that rises to 80 percent for new homes in discrete subdivisions (Clarke and Freedman 2019). In communities with such rules, they either supplant or supplement state efforts at land-use planning; in either case, they serve as an important source of entrepreneurial discovery in the governance of urban land.

Why would a developer condition sales on such rules? And why would buyers opt into such agreements? If home value data is any indication, buyers value the added stability that deed restrictions offer. A survey of the literature finds a home value premium ranging from two to nine percent for deed-restricted properties (Speyrer 1989; Cannady 1994; Hughes and Turnbill 1996; Rogers 2006; Cheung and Meltzer 2013). A more comprehensive study by Clarke and Freedman (2019) puts the price premium for homes subject to private forms of land-use regulation at four percent. Unlike zoning, deed restrictions thus create a *market* for land-use regulation, in which developers have a clear profit incentive to experiment with new formulations and get the balance right. Set rules that are too strict or too liberal, and risk not selling the property; set the rules just right, and pocket additional profit at little additional cost.

Private land-use regulation can interact with state land-use planning in one of two ways: First, deed restrictions may supplant or supplement zoning. In many exurban contexts where zoning does not yet exist, deed restrictions are the operative set of rules governing land uses, density, and building design. In Houston, the singular major US city to have foregone zoning, deed restrictions are the principal form of land-use regulation, with state involvement limited to enforcement (Susman 1966; Siegan 2020). Alternatively, in urban contexts with zoning, deed restrictions may serve to supplement zoning, giving property owners a private form of conflict remediation or adding additional rules on top of the baseline of zoning, such as design or maintenance standards. In this sense, deed restrictions layer a "market for institutions" on top of state efforts at land-use planning (Rogers 2006).

Second, in the same way that regulatory relief may signal changing conditions to public planners, deed restrictions may help to signal preferences concerning land-use regulation. This was particularly true of zoning in its early stages, in which zoning ordinances were often explicitly modeled on local deed restrictions (Monchow 1928; Weiss 1987). In many suburban contexts, such as Country Club in Kansas City or Palos Verdes Estates in Southern California, deed restrictions were almost word-for-word converted into zoning codes (Worley 1990). Yet even today, we see elements of deed restrictions—such as strict architectural design rules—regularly incorporated into public land-use planning.[4] With most contemporary suburban developments subject to deed restrictions, we can likewise expect their eventual conversion into law, if and when zoning is adopted in those areas. In this way, entrepreneurial discovery within private land-use regulation heavily informs state land-use planning efforts.

Entrepreneurial Discovery Through
Private Town Building

If deed restrictions help to reveal changing preferences concerning land-use regulation—with important implications for zoning—the development of entire towns in unincorporated areas reveals changing preferences concerning urban design—with important implications for subdivision regulations. While subdivision regulations strictly define urban design parameters for elements like streets and blocks in incorporated areas, developers are often able to bypass these rules by building beyond the scope of local governments. Free from local subdivision regulations—and often on large consolidated greenfield lots exempt from whatever state standards may exist—developers can experiment with new ways of configuring cities.

Historically, these efforts were central to informing early subdivision standards. Beginning in the mid-to-late 1800s and early 1900s, a series of demonstration projects would challenge the historical norm of the short blocks and gridded streets (Jackson 1985). Developments like Llewellyn Park, New Jersey and Riverside, Illinois set out a new suburban design vision of long blocks and winding streets, heavily informing the substance of early urban design regulations, particularly in the post-war period (Ben-Joseph 2005). Subsequent subdivision innovations in unincorporated areas would drive the evolution of planning mechanisms like cluster zoning (Rosenthal 1960).

As Weiss (1987) notes, modern site planning standards were heavily shaped by early "community builders," or those developers who pioneered the subdivision of new neighborhoods in the early 1900s. Through professional networks, community builders set design and engineering standards for streets, sewer infrastructure, and lot sizes, giving us the winding streets, cul-de-sacs, and large lots that define modern American suburbia. Advocacy by professional groups like the National Association of Real Estate Boards and a revolving door between the development industry and the early city planning movement ultimately resulted in these rules being written into law, from local planning ordinances on up to Federal Housing Administration guidelines. To the extent that these standards survive a century later, contemporary zoning and subdivision rules represent the codified norms of ancient real estate markets.

This is not to say that entrepreneurial discovery in site planning has ended. On the contrary, these historical site planning standards have recently been challenged by a new generation of entrepreneurial developers operating in contexts with little or no land-use regulation. Since its inception in the 1980s, the New Urbanism movement has called into question many elements of these inherited standards, including strict land-use segregation, large winding streets, and long blocks (Talen 2013). Beyond theoretical critiques, the movement has proven the success of their ideas through new town demonstrations like Seaside and Celebration, new urbanist developments characterized by higher densities, greater use mixture, gridded streets, and short blocks to foster walkability (Katz 1996). Such developments could only have been developed in regulatory contexts beyond the reach of conventional zoning and subdivision ordinances.

The success of these developments has completely upended the discourse around suburban design. An aspiring public planner can now take parallel classes on new urbanist design and earn parallel new urbanist accreditations (Steuteville and Langdon 2009). This entrepreneurial experimentation with a parallel paradigm of land-use planning—helped along by the success of new urbanist land-use planning concepts in master-planned communities, as signaled by higher prices—has, in turn, reshaped state land-use planning. Many cities, including Miami and Denver, have replaced sections of their development ordinances with "form-based codes" along new urbanist design lines (Parolek et al. 2008). In many more cities, new urbanist ideas have remade public comprehensive planning and subdivision regulation, as cities attempt to replicate the success of privately developed new urbanist communities (Gray 2020). Of the three mechanisms discussed so far, entrepreneurial discovery through private town building has doubtless had the greatest influence on public land-use planning.

THE LIMITS OF THE ENTREPRENEUR-INFORMED PUBLIC PLANNING

To the extent that public land-use planning tolerates and responds to those spheres of private land-use planning that have survived the rise of zoning and subdivision regulations, it has been able to regularly reinvent itself. Yet we should be mindful of the limits of this framework. While the incorporation of elements of entrepreneurial discovery into public land-use planning has helped to keep the system from falling too far out of step with reality, certain fundamental issues remain. First, at a theoretical level, public land-use planning continues to mistake an ongoing process—the unending project of remaking cities—as an equilibrium that need only be tinkered with periodically. Second, the writing of successful design standards into law mistakes evolving subjective preferences for enduring objective standards and displaces future opportunities for entrepreneurial discovery. Finally, public adoption of private forms of land-use regulation risks drafting the state into antisocial efforts such as the private pursuit of segregation. Let us consider each of these concerns in turn.

The Unfinished Project of Land-Use Planning

A key insight of the Austrian School of social theory is that the market is a process, constantly equilibrating in light of changing conditions and new information (Kirzner 1992). Where standard economic theory assumes a market forever at or near equilibrium, Austrian theorists such as Kirzner (2013) understand the market to be in constant flux, forever *in pursuit* of a strictly theoretical equilibrium state. Within this framework, it is incumbent on entrepreneurs to constantly discover and leverage the knowledge needed to efficiently reallocate scarce resources. The dispersed, inarticulable, and constantly changing nature of this knowledge is one reason why the project of comprehensive economic planning has continually failed to achieve socially optimal outcomes (Lavoie 1986). Only by retaining a large sphere for decentralized economic planning can we collectively generate and act on the knowledge needed to maintain a modern economy.

As a spatial manifestation of markets, cities are subject to similar pressures. A city—like a market—is a forever unfinished social project, constantly evolving in response to changing preferences, needs, constraints, and challenges (Jacobs 1961). While standard planning aspires to uncover and enforce what we might call the "equilibrium city"—with planners carefully determining the form, scale, and location of every given land use at 10- to 50-year intervals—cities are far too dynamic to yield to this type of comprehensive control. Cities require constant retooling and experimentation by entrepreneurial developers to effectively function. While regulatory relief serves as a necessary safety valve, and the incorporation of entrepreneur-generated knowledge into plans has helped to keep planning somewhat responsive to changing conditions, these are minor tweaks to a system of planning that fundamentally misunderstands the nature of cities as spontaneous orders.

The Subjective Quality of Land-Use Planning

Another key insight of the Austrian School of social theory with implications for land-use planning is the subjective nature of value (Menger 1871). Value is not an inherent quality acquired by a good or service by any objective measure such as labor, but by the subjective needs and preferences of individuals at a particular time and place. Within the market process framework, prices are crucial to both revealing these values and reformulating them into a set of incentives. Using this information, which must be constantly rediscovered in real time, entrepreneurs can remake the social order to satisfy the changing preferences of consumers. Without prices or an ecosystem of entrepreneurs to act on them, economic calculation is impossible, with bureaucrats inevitably relying on heuristics, resulting in a suboptimal allocation (von Mises 1920).

As Bertaud (2018) notes, this dependence on arbitrary standards continues to characterize public land-use planning in the US. Questions that ultimately come down to subjective and context-specific preferences—such as the appropriate dimensions of a residential lot, or the acceptable mixture of uses along a given street—are recast as technical questions with objective answers. Efforts to incorporate standards that emerge from entrepreneurial discovery are at least tested by a market at some point and have helped to minimize the damage of this practice. Yet as Weiss (1987) observes, this prohibits all but the revealed standards of a particular time and place long after the conditions that inspired these standards have changed. Hence, our current frameworks for public land-use planning remain a reflection of the revealed preferences of the early 1900s when many zoning and subdivision ordinances were first drafted.

Institutionalizing Antisocial "Innovations"

A final risk with the incorporation of entrepreneurial discovery into public land-use planning is the fact that not all "successful" experiments deserve to be codified into law. Much of the history of private land-use planning in the US over the twentieth century has been a history of attempts at instituting racial segregation (Fogelson 2007; Rothstein 2017). While *Buchanan v. Warley* (1917) held any public attempts at institutionalizing formal racial segregation to be unconstitutional, public planners nonetheless spent much of the past century attempting to translate racial covenants—private deed restrictions which forbid the sale or habitation of a property by members of disfavored racial and ethnic groups—into law (Connerly 2005). Needless to say, this is not an appropriate objective of public land-use planning.

Even beyond explicit racial segregation, private land-use regulation is often concerned with enforcing the preferences of discrete groups of elites—including their preferences for economic segregation and exclusion—to the detriment of other segments of society. As Weiss (1987) and Fogelson (2007) observe, much of our modern framework for zoning and subdivision regulation was predicated on the revealed preferences of affluent Anglo-Americans at the turn of the twentieth century; hence, the preoccupation with class segregation, automobility, and a pastoral aesthetic. While we might tolerate private actors voluntarily opting into communities with such design considerations or private governance, it is inappropriate for the state to institutionalize and subsidize such preferences. Yet so long as public land-use planning is in the business of selecting and enforcing one universal set of standards, elite preferences will likely always receive undue deference.

IMPLICATIONS FOR PLANNING PRACTICE

The complicated role that entrepreneurial discovery continues to play in driving state land-use planning should inform public planning efforts in at least three ways: First, public planners should use the signals being sent by entrepreneurial efforts in land-use planning to identify liberalization priorities. As discussed above, there is now consensus that existing public land-use policies are potentially harmful. Yet public planners are often unclear as to which particular rules are distorting market outcomes in a harmful way, or which rules may have an existing constituency for reform. A bevy of regulatory requests, or observed non-compliance, or minimal legal compliance may identify those rules for which reform is both necessary and viable.

Consider again the issue of minimum lot size regulations. In some contexts, these are binding, forcing lot sizes to be larger than they might otherwise have been; in other contexts, this may not be the case. One way that public planners can uncover where public rules are binding is to track any number of quasi-market signals, such as whether developers are requesting lot size relief through variances, whether developers are repeatedly not complying with these provisions, or whether they are simply platting lots right at the legal limit. In one study of Texas, Gray and Furth (2019) observe lot sizes clustering right at the zoned minimum in three of four cities studied. This indicates that the current rules are binding, and public planners would do well to respond to these market signals by liberalizing lot size regulations.

Second, public planners should yield to a high degree of polycentricity in the production of land-use planning. Deed restrictions reveal the extent to which private entrepreneurs—whether of the social or economic variety—can discover and implement the optimal level of land-use regulations for a particular time and place. Such rules do not always need to be formalized into public regulations. Indeed, their voluntary nature is central to ensuring that private land-use regulations take a socially optimal form. As discussed above, this helps to facilitate a market for institutions in which residents can opt into the ruleset that matches their preferences, with prices signaling aggregate preferences for different sets of rules.

By writing the provisions of successful deed restrictions into law, public planners have heavily restricted this market. At best, zoning and subdivision regulations set a baseline of land-use regulation below which market actors may not go. Yet many communities may prefer more liberal land use or density rules, allowing uses such as corner groceries and accessory dwelling units, which are often prohibited by conventional zoning. Rather than writing any one set of private land-use regulations into law—no matter how successful—public planners should accept that land-use preferences vary spatially, temporarily, and across segments of the population, and embrace the emergent co-production of land-use planning.

Finally, public planners should expand the scope of entrepreneurial discovery within land-use planning. As argued above, decentralized planning is necessary for the generation and application of the knowledge necessary for optimal land-use arrangements. Even if public planners are unwilling to abolish zoning and subdivision regulations, they should still see value in expanding the scope of entrepreneurial land-use planning to the extent that it generates knowledge that might guide their efforts. Maintaining state land-use ordinances that do not reflect reality undermines the important work of planning for demographic changes and making necessary adjustments to public services, potentially undermining public willingness to fund planning agencies. Public planners should thus invite further entrepreneurial discovery in planning, even if it entails the cessation of power in limited respects.

So long as public planners are in the business of setting baseline land-use standards, their focus should be on those elements that are broadly knowable and consistent across time: traditional nuisances. While preferences concerning the appropriate mixture of uses or density of development may vary and change across time, public planners can assume with some certainty that impacts like noise and light pollution warrant remediation. Rather than attempting to dictate standards better managed by deed restrictions—such as use and density rules—or private developers—such as the design of neighborhoods—public planners should recognize where they can add the most value within a polycentric system of land-use planning and focus their efforts accordingly.

CONCLUSION

At the centennial of our national experiment with zoning, the persistence of a *dirigisme* approach to land-use planning in the US might puzzle Austrian social theorists. As mainstream scholars have pointed out, the system has manifestly failed to produce optimal outcomes, resulting in high housing costs, sluggish economic growth, racial and economic segregation, and environmentally harmful growth. What then explains the apparent staying power of this system? Perhaps the line between centralized and decentralized planning is not quite so clear as theory might assume. As this paper has argued, state land-use planning survives to the extent that it learns from the limited pockets of decentralized planning that are allowed to survive. Recognition of this should prompt planners to leverage the knowledge that decentralized planning produces to craft better land-use plans and expand its sphere.

Yet this paper has intentionally painted a complicated picture of the relationship between markets and public land-use planning. The periodic incorporation of the outputs of entrepreneurial discovery into public land-use planning efforts has helped to ease the damage, but it has not produced the level of efficiency that would be achieved by an unhindered urban land market. Rather than transforming private land-use planning innovations into law, public planners should use market signals to identify regulations in need of liberalization. More broadly, public planners should embrace the co-production of land-use planning through mechanisms like deed restrictions and seek to carve out a large space for private innovation in urban design. As with a market, a city is a process, an ever-unfinished social order constantly in the process of reinventing ourselves. Our approach to land-use planning should reflect this.

REFERENCES

Aligica, Paul D., and Vlad Tarko. 2011. "Polycentricity: From Polanyi to Ostrom, and Beyond." *Governance: An International Journal of Policy, Administration, and Institutions* 25 (2): 237–62.

Alonso, William. 1964. *Location and Land Use: Toward a General Theory of Land Rent.* Cambridge, MA: Harvard University Press.

Ben-Joseph, Eran. 2003. "Subdivision Regulations: Practices & Attitudes." *Lincoln Institute of Land Policy Working Paper.* http://web.mit.edu/ebj/www/LincolnWP.pdf.

Ben-Joseph, Eran, and Terry S. Szold. 2005. "Facing Subdivision Regulations."In *Regulating Place: Standards and the Shaping of Urban America,* edited by Eran Ben-Joseph and Terry S, Szold, 167–88. New York City, NY: Routledge.

Berke, Philip R., and David R. Godschalk. 2006. *Urban Land Use Planning.* 5th ed. Urbana, IL: University of Illinois Press.

Bertaud, Alain. 2018. *Order without Design: How Markets Shape Cities.* Cambridge, MA: The MIT Press.

Brand, Stewart. *1995. How Buildings Learn: What Happens after They're Built.* New York, NY: Penguin Books.

Brooks, Michael. 2002. *Planning Theory for Practitioners.* New York, NY: Routledge.

Brueckner, Jan. 2011. *Lectures on Urban Economics.* Cambridge, MA: The MIT Press.

Cannaday, Roger E. 1994. "Condominium Covenants: Cats, Yes; Dogs, No." *Journal of Urban Economics* 35 (1): 71–82.

Cheung, Ron, and Rachel Meltzer. 2013. "Homeowners Associations and the Demand for Land Use Regulation." *Journal of Regional Science* 53 (3): 511–34.

Clarke, Wyatt, and Matthew Freedman. 2019. "The Rise and Effects of Homeowners Associations." *Journal of Urban Economics* 112 (July): 1–15.

Coase, Ronald. 1937. "The Nature of the Firm." *Economica* 4 (16): 386–405.

————. 1960. "The Problem of Social Cost." *Journal of Law and Economics* 3: 1–44.

Connerly, Charles E. 2005. *"The Most Segregated City in America": City Planning and Civil Rights in Birmingham, 1920–1980.* Charlottesville, VA: University of Virginia Press.

Cowen, Tyler and Alexander Tabarrok. 2014. *Modern Principles of Economics.* 3rd ed. New York, NY: Worth Publishers Inc.

Duranton, Gilles, and Diego Puga. 2019. "Urban Growth and Its Aggregate Implications." *NBER Working Paper Series* 26591 (December): 1–55.

Fischel, William A. 2005. *The Homevoter Hypothesis: How Home Values Influence Local Government Taxation, School Finance, and Land-Use Policies.* Cambridge, MA: Harvard University Press.

————. 2015. *Zoning Rules!: The Economics of Land Use Regulation.* Cambridge, MA: Lincoln Institute of Land Policy.

Fogelson, Robert M. 2007. *Bourgeois Nightmares: Suburbia, 1870–1930.* New Haven, CT: Yale University Press.

Glaeser, Edward, and Joseph Gyourko. 2002. "The Impact of Zoning on Housing Affordability." *NBER Working Paper Series* 8835 (March): 1–35.

Glotzer, Paige. 2020. *How the Suburbs Were Segregated: Developers and the Business of Exclusionary Housing, 1890–1960.* New York, NY: Columbia University Press.

Gray, M. Nolan. 2019. "Who Plans? Jane Jacobs' Hayekian Critique of Urban Planning." In *Informing Public Policy: Analyzing Contemporary US and International Policy Issues through the Lens of Market Process Economics*, edited by Stefanie Haeffele, Abigail R. Hall, and Adam A. Millsap, 13–34. London, UK: Rowman & Littlefield.

————. 2020. "In a Land of Cul-De-Sacs, the Street Grid Stages a Comeback." *Bloomberg Citylab. Bloomberg*, October 21, 2020. https://www.bloomberg.com/news/articles/2020–10–21/scrap-that-cul-de-sac-suburbia-the-grid-is-back.

————. 2022. *Arbitrary Lines: How Zoning Broke the American City—and How We're Going to Fix It.* Washington, DC: Island Press.

Gray, M. Nolan and Salim Furth. 2019. "Do Minimum-Lot-Size Regulations Limit Housing Supply in Texas?" *Mercatus Research Paper* (May): 1–23.

Gray, M. Nolan, and Adam A. Millsap. 2020. "Subdividing the Unzoned City: An Analysis of the Causes and Effects of Houston's 1998 Subdivision Reform." *Journal of Planning Education and Research.* https://doi.org/10.1177/0739456x20935156.

Hayek, Friedrich A. 1948. *Individualism and Economic Order.* Chicago, IL: University of Chicago Press.

Hirt, Sonia. 2015. *Zoned in The USA: The Origins and Implications of American Land-Use Regulation.* Ithaca, NY: Cornell University Press.

Hsieh, Chang-Tai, and Enrico Moretti. 2017. "Housing Constraints and Spatial Misallocation." *NBER Working Paper Series* 21154 (May).

Hughes, Jr. William T., and Geoffrey K. Turnbull. 1996. "Uncertain Neighborhood Effects and Restrictive Covenants." *Journal of Urban Economics* 39 (2): 160–72.

Jackson, Kenneth T. 1985. *Crabgrass Frontier: The Suburbanization of America.* New York City, NY: Oxford University Press.

Jacobs, Jane. 1961. *The Death and Life of Great American Cities.* New York City, NY: Modern Library.

———. 1969. *The Economy of Cities.* New York, NY: Vintage Books, 1969.

Katz, Peter. 1996. *The New Urbanism: toward an Architecture of Community.* New York City, NY: McGraw-Hill.

Kirzner, Israel M. 1992. *The Meaning of the Market Process: Essays in the Development of Modern Austrian Economics.* London, UK: Routledge.

———. 1997. "Entrepreneurial Discovery and the Competitive Market Process: An Austrian Approach." *Journal of Economic Literature* 35 (1): 60–85.

———.2013. *Competition and Entrepreneurship.* Indianapolis, IN: Liberty Fund.

Lavoie, Don. 1986. "The Market as a Procedure for Discovery and Conveyance of Inarticulate Knowledge." *Comparative Economic Studies* 28 (1): 1–19.

Levine, Jonathan. 2005. *Zoned Out: Regulation, Markets, and Choices in Transportation and Metropolitan Land Use.* Washington, DC: Resources for the Future Press.

Manville, Michael, Paavo Monkkonen, and Michael Lens. 2019. "It's Time to End Single-Family Zoning." *Journal of the American Planning Association* 86 (1): 106–12.

Manville, Michael, and Taner Osman. 2017. "Motivations for Growth Revolts: Discretion and Pretext as Sources of Development Conflict." *City & Community* 16 (1): 66–85.

McKenzie, Evan. 1994, *Privatopia: Homeowner Associations and the Rise of Residential Private Government.* New Haven, CT: Yale University Press.

Meltzer, Rachel. 2013. "Do Homeowners Associations Affect Citywide Segregation? Evidence From Florida Municipalities." *Housing Policy Debate* 23 (4): 688–713.

Menger, Carl. 1871. *Principles of Economics.* Auburn, AL: Ludwig von Mises Institute.

Mills, Edwin S. 1967. "An Aggregative Model of Resource Allocation in a Metropolitan Area." *The American Economic Review* 57 (2): 197–210.

von Mises, Ludwig. 1920. "Die Wirtschaftsrechnung Im Sozialistischen Gemeinwesen." *Archiv für Sozialwissenschaften* 47: 86–121.

Monchow, Helen Corbin. 1928. *The Use of Deed Restrictions in Subdivision Development.* Chicago, IL: Institute for Research in Land Economics and Public Utilities.

Muth, Richard F. 1969. *Cities and Housing: The Spatial Pattern of Urban Residential Land Use.* Chicago, IL: The University of Chicago Press.

Nelson, Robert H. 2005. *Private Neighborhoods and the Transformation of Local Government.* Washington, DC: Urban Institute Press.

Niskanen, William A. 2017. *Bureaucracy and Representative Government.* New York City, NY: Routledge.

Ostrom, Elinor. 1990. *Governing the Commons: The Evolution of Institutions for Collective Action.* Cambridge, UK: Cambridge University Press.

Owen, David. 2009. *Green Metropolis: Why Living Smaller, Living Closer, and Driving Less Are the Keys to Sustainability.* New York City, NY: Riverhead Books.

Parolek, Daniel G., Karen Parolek, and Paul C. Crawford. 2008. *Form-Based Codes: A Guide for Planners, Urban Designers, Municipalities, and Developers.* Hoboken, NJ: John Wiley & Sons Inc.

Polanyi, Michael. 2015. *Personal Knowledge: Towards a Post-Critical Philosophy.* Chicago, IL: University of Chicago Press.

Rogers, W. H. 2006. "A Market for Institutions: Assessing the Impact of Restrictive Covenants on Housing." *Land Economics* 82 (4): 500–512.

Rothstein, Richard. 2017. *The Color of Law: A Forgotten History of How Our Government Segregated America.* New York City, NY: Liveright.

Rosenthal, Jon. 1960. *Cluster Subdivisions.* Information Report No. 135. Planning Advisory Service. Chicago, IL: American Society of Planning Officials.

Schumpeter, Joseph A. 2010. *Capitalism, Socialism and Democracy.* London, UK: Routledge.

Scott, James C. 1998. *Seeing Like a State: How Certain Schemes to Improve the Human Condition Have Failed.* New Haven, CT: Yale University Press.

Shkuda, Aaron. 2015. "The Artist as Developer and Advocate: Real Estate and Public Policy in SoHo, New York." *Journal of Urban History* 41 (6): 999–1016.

Shoup, Donald. 2011. *High Cost of Free Parking.* 2nd ed. New York City, NY: Routledge.

Siegan, Bernard H. 2020. *Land Use Without Zoning.* 2nd ed. London, UK: Rowman & Littlefield.

Silver, Christopher. 1991. "The Racial Origins of Zoning: Southern Cities from 1910–40." *Planning Perspectives* 6 (2): 189–205.

Southworth, Michael and Eran Ben-Joseph. 1996. *Streets and the Shaping of Towns and Cities.* Washington, DC: Island Press.

Speyrer, Janet Furman. 1989. "The Effect of Land-Use Restrictions on Market Values of Single-Family Homes in Houston." *The Journal of Real Estate Finance and Economics* 2 (2): 117–30.

Steuteville, Robert, and Philip Langdon. 2009. *New Urbanism: Best Practices Guide.* Ithaca, NY: New Urban News Publications.

Susman, Thomas M. 1966. "Municipal Enforcement of Private Restrictive Covenants: An Innovation in Land Use Control." *Texas Law Review* 44: 741–68.

Steiner, Frederick R., and Kent Butler. 2007. *Planning and Urban Design Standards.* Hoboken, NJ: Wiley.

Talen, Emily. 2012. *City Rules: How Regulations Affect Urban Form.* Washington, DC: Island Press.

———. 2013. *Charter of the New Urbanism: Congress for the New Urbanism.* New York City, NY: McGraw Hill Education.

Trounstine, Jessica. 2019. *Segregation by Design Local Politics and Inequality in American Cities.* Cambridge, MA: Cambridge University Press.

Weiss, Marc A. 1987. *The Rise of the Community Builders: The American Real Estate Industry and Urban Land Planning.* New York City, NY: Columbia University Press.

Worley, William S. 1990. *J. C. Nichols and the Shaping of Kansas City Innovation in Planned Residential Communities.* Columbia, MO: University of Missouri Press.

NOTES

1. This section is a partial reformulation of the argument advanced in Gray (2019).

2. For example, the persistence of harmful public land-use planning policies may reflect the desire of local bureaucrats and elected officials to maintain and enhance their power (Niskanen 2017). Alternatively, we might understand its persistence as a function of powerful local special interests, particularly homeowners concerned with enhancing their property values (Fischel 2005). These explanations should be understood as supplementing, rather than foreclosing, the Austrian hypothesis advanced in this paper.

3. In the Houston example, regulatory relief requests helped to reveal changed conditions to planners. Such knowledge may not always be communicated through a formal medium. The mere act of widespread non-compliance may serve a similar function. Consider the gradual conversion of SoHo from industrial to loft residential, a transition which occurred in defiance of the neighborhood's industrial zoning. Widespread non-compliance, combined with tenant advocacy, eventually forced public planners to accept the changed conditions reflected by the neighborhood-wide transition and adjust the underlying zoning to reflect this reality (Shkuda 2015).

4. For example, historic districts or design commissions give public entities extensive control over the architecture of new buildings—a power once deemed beyond the scope of public regulation.

Index

Page references for figures and tables are italicized.

About the Editors

Roberta Q. Herzberg is distinguished senior fellow in the F. A. Hayek Program for Advanced Study in Philosophy, Politics, and Economics in the Mercatus Center at George Mason University.

Gavin Roberts is associate professor of economics at Weber State University.

Brianne Wolf is assistant professor of political theory and constitutional democracy at James Madison College at Michigan State University.

About the Contributors

Emily Chamlee-Wright is president and CEO of the Institute for Humane Studies at George Mason University.

Mikołaj Firlej is a lecturer (assistant professor) at the University of Surrey and a research affiliate at the University of Oxford.

Olivia Gonzalez is a PhD student in economics at George Mason University.

M. Nolan Gray is a PhD student in urban planning at University of California, Los Angeles.

Ellen Hamlett is an MPP student at Georgetown University.

Alexander Köhler is an MA student in international affairs at Hertie School of Governance.

Carlos Noyola obtained his MSc in economics from the University of Bristol and is a PhD student in Iberian and Latin American studies at University of Notre Dame.

Emil Panzaru is a PhD student in political economy at King's College London.

Julie Thompson-Gomez is a program manager with the John Quincy Adams Society. She holds a master's degree in political science from the George Washington University and a master's degree in international affairs from the Bush School of Government and Public Service at Texas A&M University.

Arthur R. Wardle is a PhD student in agricultural and resource economics at University of California, Berkeley.

www.ingramcontent.com/pod-product-compliance
Lightning Source LLC
Chambersburg PA
CBHW031126270326
41929CB00011B/1516

"This is a book about five people who have made the world a better place, written by someone who knows both the world and the people he is writing about. The book documents how – by imagining the impossible and inspiring others around them – seemingly ordinary people can do extraordinary things. Today, more than ever, the world needs more leaders like Adolfo Figueroa, Ela Bhatt, Domingo Cavallo, Dzingai Mutumbuka, and Ngozi Okonjo-Iweala, and more writers like David de Ferranti to inspire thousands with their stories."–*Indermit Gill*, Chief Economist and Senior Vice President for Development Economics of the World Bank Group. Formerly at the Brookings Institution, Duke University, Georgetown University and the University of Chicago.

"There are thousands of books recommending development policies, but few on the policymakers implementing them. De Ferranti has written a wonderful book about five of them: people with vision and ambition, facing a complex political environment, taking risks, committing mistakes but, in the end, making a positive difference."–*Santiago Levy*, Brookings Institution. Former Chief Economist and Vice President for Sectors and Knowledge at the Inter-American Development Bank. Former Deputy Minister at the Ministry of Finance and Public Credit of Mexico. Former tenured Associate Professor of Economics at Boston University.

"David de Ferranti makes international development come alive through the captivating stories of five extraordinary global leaders, their personal journeys, struggles, and victories intertwined with global and regional development. This book captures what it means to be an agent of locally driven democratic change. The author sums up the features of strong leadership, including wisdom, integrity and courage. I would recommend this book to any student of the politics, political economy and political science of international development."–*Mariam Claeson*, Senior Advisor, Global Public Health, Karolinska Institute. Former Director of the Global Financing Facility for Women and Children, The World Bank.

"It is hard enough to convey the essence of one person's character but David de Ferranti manages to achieve this for five remarkable people. Their lives, the achievements and the disappointments, hold valuable lessons for anyone interested in understanding what constitutes leadership in challenging times."–*Masood Ahmed*, President of the Center for Global Development. Formerly a Director at the International Monetary Fund. Former Director General, Policy and International at the UK government's Department for International Development (DFID).

"Combining page-turner verve with painstaking research, this engrossing exploration of the true stories of five remarkable individuals will captivate anyone, whether they know a lot or nothing about its subject matter – global development and the ways that Africa, Asia, and Latin America will change the world in the decades ahead. The wake-up call in its messages will keep you riveted."–*Jean-Michel Severino*, Former CEO of AFD, France's government agency for international development. Former senior official of the World Bank. Currently CEO of Investisseurs et Partenaires (I&P), Member of the National Academy of Technologies of France (Académie des Technologies), and Senior Fellow at FERDI (Foundation for Studies and Research on International Development).

"In a book that profiles five remarkable leaders who have improved the lives and livelihoods of millions of people, David De Ferranti offers the gift of inspiration. The stories of these individuals sheds light on how each of us can rise to the challenges that confront us."–*Ruth Levine*, Vice President of Just Societies and Chief Learning Officer at the David and Lucile Packard Foundation. Formerly held senior roles within IDInsight, The Hewlett Foundation, USAID, and The Center for Global Development.

"Individuals make a difference and can help improve the wellbeing of whole communities. This is the central message of this book. With eloquence and empathy, David de Ferranti describes the lives of five extraordinary characters who changed international development for the better. A must-read that is also fun to read."–*Julio Frenk*, President of the University of Miami. Professor of public health science at the university's Leonard M. Miller School of Medicine, professor of health sector management at the university's Herbert Business School, and professor of sociology at its College of Arts of Sciences. Former Dean of the Harvard T.H. Chan School of Public Health at Harvard University. Former Secretary of Health in Mexico, the federal government cabinet post overseeing the country's health system and policies.